08 MAY 09

Bader's
TANGMERE
SPITFIRES

The untold story, 1941

Other books by the same author...

SPITFIRE SQUADRON
THE INVISIBLE THREAD: A SPITFIRE'S TALE
THROUGH PERIL TO THE STARS
ANGRIFF WESTLAND
A FEW OF THE MANY

As part of our ongoing market research, we are always pleased to receive comments about our books, suggestions for new titles, or requests for catalogues. Please write to: The Editorial Director, Patrick Stephens Limited, Sparkford, Near Yeovil, Somerset BA22 7JJ.

Bader's TANGMERE SPITFIRES
The untold story, 1941

Dilip Sarkar

Forewords by Sir Alan Smith CBE, DFC, DL
and Air Vice-Marshal 'Johnnie' Johnson CB, CBE, DSO**, DFC*

Patrick Stephens Limited

© Dilip Sarkar 1996

First published in 1996

British Library Cataloguing in Publication data
A catalogue record of this book is available
from the British Library.

ISBN 1 85260 563 4

Library of Congress catalog card no. 96-75822

Patrick Stephens Limited is an imprint of Haynes Publishing, Sparkford, Nr Yeovil,
Somerset BA22 7JJ

Designed by G&M, Raunds, Northamptonshire
Typeset by J. H. Haynes & Co. Ltd.
Printed in Great Britain by Biddles Limited, Guildford and King's Lynn.

Contents

Dedication

*B*ader's Tangmere Spitfires: The Untold Story, 1941, is dedicated to all of those anonymous servicemen and women who comprised the Tangmere Wing during the Non-stop Offensive, in particular:

Ron 'Cloudy' Rayner, a Sergeant pilot with 41 Squadron who was shot up over France on 31 August 1941, 20 years to the day before I was born. Fortunately Ron survived the experience to become my friend 50 years later, and very much an inspiration for this book.

'Buck' Casson and Bob Morton, both of 616 Squadron and captured in 1941, whose recollections inspired me enormously as an embryonic researcher.

Sergeant S.W.R. 'George' Mabbett of 616 Squadron, killed in action over France on 21 July 1941 and buried at St Omer with full military honours, and Brian Mabbett, who hero-worships his Spitfire pilot 'big brother' to this day.

Also to Squadron Leader Peter Brown, AFC RAF Retd, one of the Few, who very kindly gave us help when we needed it most; Dr Bernard-Marie Dupont and his family, without whose friendship 'Operation Dogsbody' would have been impossible; and especially to my wife, Anita, and our children, James and Hannah. I hope this book will prove an inspiration and example to all those born in peacetime.

Foreword

by

Sir Alan Smith CBE, DFC, DL

More than 50 years on and yet there remains the fascination of the Spitfire – even to the thousands not born during the war!

Previous books have been built around the personality of one particular fighter pilot or several well known figures from Fighter Command. 'Bader's Tangmere Spitfires' is different in one important respect, however: Dilip Sarkar not only deals with Bader's time as leader of the Tangmere Wing, but additionally much attention is paid to individual squadron wingmen, i.e. those pilots whose job it was to support and protect their particular leader.

Following the desperate shortage of pilots at the outbreak of war, 1940 saw the first surge of pilots from the RAF Volunteer Reserve. Most of them were week-end pilots, partially trained but very keen on flying. Throughout the year they graduated from Tiger Moths to Harvards, and then the ultimate – the Spitfire!

As the Spitfire was a single-seat fighter, obviously your first flight on the type was also a solo! A brief introduction to the controls, a clap on the back from an instructor and off you go. Almost certainly the most exhilarating moment of your life. A surge of power and before you know it you are a thousand feet up, and, if flying a Mk I, making an exhibition of yourself whilst hand pumping up the undercarriage!

With the urgent need for pilots in those early days you were more likely posted to a squadron with as little as 15 hours experience flying a Spitfire. Undoubtedly the longer you survived the more likely you were to live. Therefore the inexperienced pilot was either shot down fairly quickly or survived for quite some time.

War, like most things, is a question of leadership. Those of us in the Tangmere Wing were so fortunate to have an outstanding leader in Douglas Bader. A character in every sense of the word, a brilliant pilot and quite fearless.

If you cannot be a leader then be the best possible No 2, and that means several things. The protection of your leader is paramount. His job is to shoot down the enemy whilst you must protect his tail. Stick to him like glue. Be constantly alert for the 'Hun in the sun'. Early warning equates with longer life. The 'Finger Four' formation used by Bader was ideal for cross cover and a vast improvement on previous formations.

On August 9th, 1941, was Douglas Bader shot down or did he bale out following a collision? I doubt that we will ever know for certain. What I do know is that he left an indelible impression on each and every one of us who had the honour and privilege to fly in the Tangmere Wing with Douglas Bader our leader.

Foreword

by

Air Vice-Marshal J.E. 'Johnnie' Johnson, CB, CBE, DSO**, DFC*

High summer at Tangmere. I shall never forget those stirring days, when it seemed that the sky was always blue and the rays of the fierce sun hid the glinting Messerschmitts; or when there was a high layer of thin cirrus cloud (although this filtered the sun and lessened the glare, it was dangerous to climb through it, for your grey-green Spitfire stood out against the white backcloth); when the grass was burnt to a light brown colour and discoloured with dark oil stains where we parked our Spitfires, and when the waters of the Channel looked utterly serene and inviting as we raced out of France at ground level, hot and sweating in that tiny greenhouse of a cockpit.

High summer, and the air is heavy with the scent of white clover as we lounge in our deckchairs, watching a small tractor cut down the long clover and grass on our airfield. In some places it is almost a foot high, but it is not dangerous and we know that if we are skilful enough to stall our Spitfires just when the tips of the grasses caress the wheels then we shall pull off a perfect landing.

It is Sunday, and although it is not yet time for lunch we have already escorted some Stirlings to bomb an inland target. For some obscure reason the Luftwaffe seem to oppose our weekend penetrations with more than their usual ferocity, and now we are waiting for the second call which will surely come on this perfect day.

A car pulls up outside and our leader stumps into the dispersal hut, breezy and full of confidence. "They'll be about today, Billy. We'll run into them over the target, if not before. Our job is to see the Stirlings get clear and cover any stragglers. Stick together. Who's flying in my section?"

"Smith, Cocky and Johnnie, Sir," answers Billy Burton.

"Good," Bader grins at us. "Hang on and get back into the abreast formation when I straighten out. OK?"

"OK Sir," we chorus together.

My ground crew have been with the squadron since it was formed and have seen its changing fortunes and many pilots come and go. They know that for me these last few moments on the ground are full of tension, and as they strap me in the cockpit they maintain an even pressure of chatter. Vaguely I hear that the engine is perfect, the guns oiled and checked and the faulty radio set changed and tested since the last flight. The usual cockpit smell, that strange mixture of dope, fine mineral oil, and high-grade fuel, assails the nostrils and is somehow vaguely comforting. I tighten my helmet strap, swing the rudder with my feet on the pedals, watch the movement of the ailerons when I waggle the stick and look at the instruments without seeing them, for my mind is racing on to Lille and the 109s.

We slant into the clean sky. No movement in the cockpit except the slight trembling of the stick as though it is alive and not merely the focal point of a superb mechanical machine. Gone are the ugly tremors of apprehension which plagued us just before the take-off. Although we are sealed in our tiny cockpits and separated from each other, the static from our radios pours through the earphones of our tightly fitting helmets and fills our ears with reassuring crackles. When the leader speaks, his voice is warm and vital, and we know full well that once in the air like this we are bound together by a deeper intimacy than we can ever feel on the ground. Invisible threads of trust and comradeship hold us together and the mantle of Bader's leadership will sustain and protect us throughout the flight ahead. The Tangmere Wing is together.'

I wrote those words (about what my friend 'Laddie' Lucas called 'The Tangmere Wing of all the Talents') more than 40 years ago for *Wing Leader*, and they still ring true today because I was writing about the most exciting period of our lives, when we were privileged to fly with Douglas and from him learned something about the elusive qualities of leadership and how to conduct ourselves in battle. It is for these reasons that I highly commend Dilip Sarkar's most diligent and carefully researched account of how we fared with the master himself, who, we remain convinced, was brought down by a German fighter pilot.

Introduction

When contemplating this introduction to *Bader's Tangmere Spitfires: 1941, The Untold Story, 1941*, which is undoubtedly the most exciting project I have undertaken so far, I had to ask myself why the book came to be written. Was it because I was inspired by *Reach for the Sky*, Paul Brickhill's biography of the late Grp Capt Sir Douglas Bader, at the tender age of seven years, and I am now not only privileged to know personally many of those mentioned therein, but also to count them among my friends, or was it because my friend Ron Rayner was shot up in his Spitfire over France on 31 August 1941, subsequently making a forced landing at Manston 20 years to the day before I was born?

Equally, there might have been another unwitting catalyst. At the launch of my fifth book, *A Few of the Many*, a fellow young enthusiast, Larry McHale, kindly presented me with a framed copy of his poem *Tangmere: In Silent Tribute*, the moving script printed over an atmospheric monochrome photograph of Tangmere's now derelict control tower. Larry's poem would surely inspire any author.

> Tangmere sleeps, Her squadrons gone,
> Her pride intact, Her duty done.
> The Few no more like knights of old
> Their Merlins roar their courage bold
> They're with Her now as we stand and gaze,
> A ghostly link with distant days.
> Forever stay, oh ageless Few,
> For Tangmere stands to honour you.
> As years roll by 'neath Tangmere skies
> On spectral wings The Few still fly.
> Remember, too, in battles fought,
> Tangmere paid for freedom bought

Although Larry's poem ostensibly concerns the fabled Few, the sentiments expressed surely extend across the spectrum of wartime aviation. In 1941 Fighter Command's pilots awaited the possibility of a renewed Luftwaffe air offensive against England, with all of the ferocity of 1940's bloodstained summer. In the event this onslaught was not to be, for Hitler turned his territorial ambitions eastwards, and in that direction went many Luftwaffe units which had previously been stationed on the *Kanalfront*. Instead, it was the RAF which went on the offensive, albeit on a small scale compared with later in the war, but, considering the precarious situation of only a year before, this was a small miracle. Air Marshal Sir Denis Crowley-Milling puts the situation into context well: 'I think that the point for all of us was that we were now on the offensive, taking the battle to the Germans after the Battle of Britain'. Air Vice-Marshal 'Johnnie' Johnson adds: '... they were stirring times'. Statistics show, however, that Fighter Command actually lost the Non-stop Offensive of 1941. Many brave young men of both sides perished over the *Kanalfront* in 1941, but their sacrifices are often overlooked and the fighting is frequently overshadowed by the fascination of the Battle of Britain.

Furthermore, much of the existing literature on the subject is deficient in many respects, particularly regarding the 1941 Tangmere Wing, which consisted of three squadrons, Nos. 145, 610 and 616. One could be forgiven for thinking that the Wing's battles were fought solely by Wg Cdr Bader and 616 Squadron, at whose head he led the Wing. Despite the fact that Paul Brickhill did not write *Reach for the Sky* as an historical treatise of the subject, it remains the most widely quoted and cited work on Douglas Bader and his Wings. It was, I have to say, a brave step to undertake original research into what many would consider to be an already overexposed subject. The deeper my involvement progressed, however, the more surprised I was to discover not only new and extremely significant information, but how inaccurate Paul Brickhill's biography was in some respects. The 'facts' presented therein have hitherto been accepted by previous authors since 1954, and have been promulgated ever since in countless publications. It should be borne in mind, of course, that *Reach for the Sky* was written in a style typical of biographies of the 1940s and 1950s, and also that the authors of this period did not have access to the historical records that have since become available for public scrutiny. Moreover, Wg Cdr P.B. 'Laddie' Lucas, Bader's brother-in-law and one of several biographers, writing to me in February 1996, remarked:

> It doesn't surprise me that you are finding variations in the story which Paul Brickhill told. Douglas fed him the stuff, but dear old Douglas, bless his heart, didn't always get things quite right; indeed there were some instances where I am sure he deliberately twisted events for the sake of getting what *he* wanted – a nice twist to the story!
>
> A case in point was when he was going on at me about his father being in hospital in St Omer at the end of WW1: "... so the place, old boy, means much to me – my father was actually buried in the cemetery there". He wasn't at all! Six months or so after publication of my Bader biography *Flying Colours*, I received a letter from a War Graves Commissioner who confirmed that Major Frederick Bader had died in a nursing home in Brussels and was actually buried there! The hazards of a biographer, dear boy!

That Maj Bader was buried in Brussels also explains why Dr Bernard-Marie Dupont, Dr Dennis Williams, Nick Skinner of the *Daily Mail* and myself spent a fruitless hour searching St Omer cemetery for his grave. Paul Brickhill, with Douglas Bader's collaboration, did not write *Reach for the Sky* as an historical record; it was a yarn in the most gung-ho style. What is surprising, however, is how the book has become the standard reference on the subject of Douglas Bader.

Some of the pilots in Bader's Wings were to achieve great fame, and quite rightly they have published their autobiographies, Air Vice-Marshal 'Johnnie' Johnson's *Wing Leader* and the late Grp Capt Sir Hugh Dundas's *Flying Start* being outstanding amongst them (see Bibliography). However, no previous account has given a broad overview of the Tangmere Wing by relating the stories of those unsung heroes who have never before been given the opportunity to have their say. The accounts and opinions presented in this book therefore come from a wide and varied assortment of individuals, ranging from George Reid, an undercarriage and tyre inspector, to 'Johnnie' Johnson, the RAF's top-scoring Second World War fighter pilot. The end result is therefore an impartial appraisal of the subject matter. I believe this to be unique to date. Certainly this idea received great support from survivors. In 1941 Frank Twitchett was a sergeant pilot with 145 Squadron at Merston, a satellite of Tangmere, and in 1995 he confirmed my viewpoint:

It is true that so much has been written about Douglas Bader that the myth has grown that the Tangmere Wing consisted of him and sundry other pilots who are rarely referred to by name. Whilst in no way wishing to detract from Wing Commander Bader's efforts, I hope that something can perhaps be done to restore the balance.

Likewise, when first approached, AM Sir Denis Crowley-Milling, a flight commander with 610 Squadron and just plain 'Crow' in 1941, was adamant that the book should not focus upon the Wing's well-known pilots, but should tell the whole story:

> Your approach to "Bader's Bus Company" is interesting. Clearly you will be approaching all pilots still with us who flew with the Tangmere Wing, and of course many others of the supporting cast. I will certainly support the idea but only as one of the many pilots in the Wing. Our stories have been told, those of the supporting cast have not, and this recognition for the Red Twos and Threes is long overdue.

David Denchfield joined 610 Squadron as a Sergeant pilot on 7 October 1940, and with that squadron joined the Tangmere Wing on 15 December 1940, some three months before Douglas Bader was appointed Wing Commander (Flying). By that time David was already a prisoner of war. However, he also supported my idea:

> I certainly approve the principle of dealing with the "lesser lights" rather than the household names, as it is a sore point with me that almost every new book I pick up seems to regurgitate the same old details. So it is that regarding 610 Squadron, no-one ever hears of Squadron Leader John Ellis, Flight Lieutenants Stanley Norris and Joe Pegge, and Sergeant Ronnie Hamlyn. The latter's Spitfire was embellished at the time I joined 610 with a Walt Disney-type Pied Piper of Hamlyn being followed by 15 be-swastika'd rats. Sadly, however, this aircraft was crashed by a new pilot shortly afterwards. I seldom buy a new book regarding fighter pilots as such men are seldom mentioned. I know of at least one other Battle of Britain pilot who feels the same – there must be more.

I hope this book breathes life into long-forgotten dusty records and photographs, recreating through the first-hand accounts of survivors the tempo and atmosphere of this most famous of Spitfire Wings. Certainly Grp Capt Sir Hugh 'Cocky' Dundas appreciated the potential of my project: 'My first reaction is that it is a working idea. I certainly know from the letters I receive there are a great many people out there who have an abiding interest in this subject.' Sadly, however, Sir Hugh did not live to see this book published.

Although much has been written about the Luftwaffe in the Battle of Britain, on the Eastern Front and later during the defence of the Reich itself, comparatively little has been published regarding the Jagdwaffe reaction to the Non-stop Offensive. I believe that, for history's sake, a balanced view is essential, and so was delighted to hear from my German friend Ottomar Kruse, himself formerly an Fw 190 pilot with JG26: 'Our JG26 reunion was extremely successful, and I have found some survivors of 1941. I talked to them about you and your plans. They agreed to answer whatever questions you may have.' My fourth book, *Angriff Westland*, which told the action-packed stories of three Battle of Britain air raids, adopted a similar approach, providing essential background and first-hand accounts from both sides. Ottomar read this and remarked that it was a very 'fair and detailed description of the Luftwaffe and its operations during 1940'. I hope that German survivors will consider this book in the same vein, as it has been written without prejudice.

It is likely that this book will be read by many more participants in the 1941 air battles. If they have any information, memories or photographs to share, I hope they will not hesitate to get in touch via my publisher.

Time waits for no man, and I feel privileged indeed to have rubbed shoulders with the survivors of 'Bader's Bus Company' and their Teutonic adversaries, even if only in their twilight years.

In 1987 the Malvern Spitfire Team, a research society of which I am proud to be co-founder and chairman, recovered the remains of Spitfire R6644, the pilot of which, Plt Off Franek Surma, had baled out owing to an engine fire. The project attracted enormous interest, not least from the media, and culminated in my second book, *The Invisible Thread: A Spitfire's Tale*. In early 1995, as the Bader research project developed, it occurred to me that it would be a fascinating undertaking to try and locate the crash site of his Spitfire, W3185, in the Pas-de-Calais. The first complete and accurate account of progress with this exercise, which is still on-going, appears as an epilogue in this book.

Dilip Sarkar
Worcester,
March 1996.

Acknowledgements

Many people kindly helped me during the research for this book. Firstly, I would like to make specific mention of the Tangmere Wing's surviving pilots, in order of rank:
Air Marshal Sir Denis Crowley-Milling KCB CBE DSO DFC*
Air Vice-Marshal J.E. Johnson CBE DSO* DFC*
Air Commodore Sir Archie Winskill KCVO CBE DFC* AE
Air Commodore E.W. Merriman DFM MBE OBE CBE
The late Group Captain Sir Hugh Dundas KB DSO DFC* DL
Squadron Leader L.H. Casson DFC AFC
Squadron Leader F.A.O. Gaze DFC**
Squadron Leader R.A. Beardsley DFC
The late Squadron Leader W.J. Johnson DFC*
Flight Lieutenant Sir Alan Smith DFC
Flight Lieutenant R. Rayner DFC
Flight Lieutenant F. Twitchett AE
Flight Lieutenant P. Ward-Smith
Warrant Officer R.A. Morton.
Warrant Officer D. Denchfield.

Other pilots who helped were:
Air Vice-Marshal M.D. Lyne CB AFC
Wing Commander P.B. Lucas CBE DSO DFC
Wing Commander B.J. Jennings AFC DFM
The late Wing Commander P.I. Howard-Williams DFC
The late Wing Commander R.J.E. Boulding
The late Wing Commander F.N. Brinsden
Wing Commander G.C. Unwin DSO DFM
Wing Commander D.G.S.R. Cox DFC*
Squadron Leader G.H.E. Welford AE
The late Squadron Leader D.A. Adams
Squadron Leader J. Stokoe DFC
Squadron Leader M.P. Brown AFC
Flight Lieutenant W. Cunningham DFC
Flying Officer C. Hodgkinson
Warrant Officer P.H. Fox

Tangmere's supporting personnel:
Harry Jacks AE, Pat Goodenough, George Reid, Jack Younie, Dave Horne, Harold Clowes, Alan Baldwin, Arthur Berrowcliffe, 'Pop' Elvidge, Norman Jenkins and Douglas Roberts.

Mrs Jean Allom (widow of the late Wing Commander H.F. Burton DSO DFC), Mr

Martin Woodhall (son of the late Grp Capt A.B. Woodhall) and Mr Brian Mabbett (brother of the late Sergeant S.W.R. Mabbett) were especially kind. The 145 and 610 Squadron Associations were keen to help, as was Mrs Betty George MBE of the Blenheim Society. As ever, Wing Commander N.P.W. Hancock OBE DFC, Honorary Secretary of the Battle of Britain Fighter Association, helped with tracing the Few. Yet further debts are owed to the Keeper and staff of the Public Record Office, and the RAF Museum.

Regarding my specific research into Grp Capt Sir Douglas Bader, I am grateful to Lady Joan Bader, Dr Alfred Price, Air Cdre H.W. Mermagen CB CBE AFC, Wg Cdr P.B. 'Laddie' Lucas CBE DSO DFC, Kerry Taylor and C.J. Mckenzie of the *Sydney Telegraph Mirror*, and Grp Capt Ian Madelin of the Ministry of Defence Air Historical Branch.

On the German side I am indebted to Gerhard Schöpfel, Johannes Naumann, Ottomar Kruse and Josef Niesmark, all formerly of JG26, and Mr Frank Kamp. David and Alexander Kent, together with Mrs Erika Norton, helped with translation.

As ever, the wartime aviation historical movement rallied to the cause: Dr Alfred Price, Chris Shores, David Brocklehurst, Norman Franks, Larry McHale, Neil Sarkar, Michael Payne, Hugo Barwick, Colin Terry, Antony Whitehead, Gil Davies, Chris Goss, Graham Pitchfork, Andrew Long, Keith Delderfield of the Douglas Bader Foundation and Peter and Kay Arnold.

I must make mention of the extensive knowledge of two particular friends; John Foreman, the 'oracle' on losses and claims, whose support has been greatly appreciated over many years, and Don Caldwell of Texas, who was able to provide specialist information regarding all aspects of JG26.

In St Omer, we were made most welcome by Monsieur and Madame Jacques Fournier, and Madame Petit.

I must also thank Darryl Reach, Alison Roelich and Peter Nicholson at Haynes Publishing for instantly recognising the potential of my idea.

Dr Dennis Williams, my trusted friend and right-hand man, always only a telephone call away with advice and encouragement. Dennis also undertook all the photography work for this book.

Dr Bernard-Marie Dupont and his marvellous family, who welcomed us into their homes, and without whose friendship and kindness our French researches would have been impossible. We are also extremely grateful to all of those French eyewitnesses who welcomed us warmly and gave only their utmost co-operation, as did aviation archaeologists Laurent d'Hondt and Jean-Pierre Duriez.

Last, as is customary, but first in the true order of importance comes my wife, Anita, without whose interest and support the entire project would have remained just a dream.

If I have forgotten anybody, my apologies; it was unintentional.

CHAPTER ONE

Douglas Bader and the 'Big Wing'

Despite the best of intentions, it is impossible to write a book about the Tangmere Wing without its leader featuring prominently in the story. There is undoubtedly a particular and enduring fascination with the late Grp Capt Sir Douglas Bader CBE DSO DFC, the story of this legless fighter leader having been broadcast to an international and general audience in 1954 upon publication of the late Paul Brickhill's book *Reach for the Sky*. Bader's story continues to inspire successive generations. Ask any man in the street to name a Battle of Britain pilot, and his answer would most likely be 'Douglas Bader'. There are many biographies of Bader, so I have included here only what is necessary background to the man who took command of Tangmere in March 1941. Nevertheless, to understand the present book fully, some knowledge of Douglas Bader's 'Big Wing' is necessary; hence the following.

Born in St John's Wood, London, on 21 February 1910, Douglas Robert Steurt Bader spent his early years in India, where his father, Frederick, was a Civil Servant. In 1913

Squadron Leader Douglas Bader, Officer Commanding 242(F) Squadron, 1940. (Imperial War Museum)

the family returned home, Frederick Bader serving as a major in the Royal Engineers during the First World War. Having remained on the Continent to assist with rebuilding, Major Bader died prematurely in Brussels during 1922, succumbing to a head wound received in 1917. The Bader family then faced some financial pressure which forced Douglas Bader, a gifted sportsman but not an academic, to win a scholarship to St Edward's School, Oxford. Later the young Bader was inspired by his uncle, Flt Lt Cyril Burge, a Great War pilot, and in 1928 he won a prize cadetship to the RAF College, Cranwell.

Pilot Officer D.R.S. Bader passed out of Cranwell in July 1930, and a month later joined 23 Squadron at Kenley to fly the Gloster Gamecock biplane fighter. In 1931 23 Squadron won the pairs aerobatics competition at the annual RAF Display at Hendon, Plt Off Bader being a member of the victorious team. Now unquestionably a superb pilot, Bader continued his sporting activities with great zeal, playing both cricket and rugby for the RAF, and the latter also for the Harlequins, Surrey, and the Combined Services Team. Bader's place as fly-half in the England team seemed assured.

On 14 December 1931 Bader, in his Bristol Bulldog biplane, joined two other 23 Squadron aircraft on a flight to Woodley airfield near Reading. Not surprisingly Bader, the Hendon star, was the subject of much attention in the clubhouse, although he declined requests for an aerobatic display. Unfortunately, as the fighter pilots took their leave a civilian pilot suggested that Bader was 'windy'. This was akin to the proverbial 'red rag to a bull', and consequently Bader took off and began a series of very low rolls over the airfield. Suddenly his left wing brushed the ground, and within seconds the Bulldog was a bent and twisted mass of wreckage. Within the cockpit, Bader lay terribly injured. His right leg was consequently amputated above the knee, and the left below. A lesser man, without Douglas Bader's incredible toughness, resolve and indomitable spirit, would probably have died.

It is unthinkable that such a physically active young man as Douglas Bader should become an amputee, with no England rugby team place for him. Close to death, Bader was sustained by his irrepressible spirit, and defied the Reaper. To live was not enough, though; Bader wanted to compete with able-bodied men on equal terms. Although he returned to the RAF, having mastered mobility on 'tin' legs, the Service would not let him fly. On 30 April 1933 Fg Off D.R.S. Bader was retired 'on the grounds of ill health'. Benumbed at being forced to quit the Service he loved so much, Bader started work in the office of the Asiatic Petroleum Company's aviation department. With his salary and RAF pension his annual income was £399 10s. On the strength of this, at the age of 23, he married Thelma Edwards, a cousin of the Donaldson brothers who were all destined to achieve fame in the wartime RAF.

In 1938, if Neville Chamberlain thought he had preserved peace indefinitely, Douglas Bader was among those who disagreed. For many young men of his generation the Munich agreement brought the realisation that another war with Germany was inevitable. Realising that trained Service pilots would be in demand, and seeing this as his chance, Bader immediately wrote to the Air Ministry, asking for a refresher flying course. The negative response was tempered by the offer of a commission in the administrative branch, which he flatly refused. In April 1939, when Hitler's troops marched into the guaranteed portion of Czechoslovakia in contravention of Munich, he tried again. The Air Ministry's response was once more negative, but stated that in the event of war they would consider Bader's reinstatement to flying duties upon appropriate medical approval. While the world prayed that war would still be avoided, Bader saw the prospect of it as his salvation. On 1 September 1939 Hitler invaded Poland. Two days later Britain and France had declared war on Nazi Germany; the storm had finally broken.

Pilot Officer Michael Lyne. Shot down and wounded over Dunkirk, Lyne missed the Battle of Britain. He eventually retired from the RAF as an Air Vice-Marshal.

On 18 October 1939 Bader attended the Central Flying School at Upavon for a flying test, conducted by Sqn Ldr Rupert Leigh, a contemporary of Bader's from Cranwell days. Remarkably he passed, and on 16 November Fg Off Bader reported to Upavon for a refresher flying course. On 7 February 1940 Bader joined 19(F) Squadron at Duxford; he had not only argued his way back into the RAF, but also into the cockpit of a Supermarine Spitfire.

Number 19 Squadron became the first squadron to receive the Spitfire when Supermarine test pilot Jeffrey Quill delivered K9789 to Duxford on 4 August 1938. By the outbreak of war, just over a year later, the squadron was therefore the most experienced Spitfire squadron in the RAF. In January 1940 Sqn Ldr Cozens, who had done much to establish the Spitfire operationally, was promoted and left 19 Squadron for a staff appointment. His successor was another of Douglas Bader's Cranwell contemporaries and friends, Sqn Ldr Geoffrey Stephenson, who had formerly served as a chief flying instructor. On 7 February 1940 Fg Off Bader therefore reported to Sqn Ldr Stephenson for flying duties with 19 Squadron. Air Vice-Marshal Michael Lyne remembers those times when he was a Pilot Officer in 19 Squadron:

> By March 1940 the weather was better, but we now had Flying Officer Douglas Bader to contend with. He was very brave and determined but was having a hard time coming to grips with the Spitfire, a far more advanced machine than the biplanes he had flown when previously an RAF fighter pilot. He particularly experienced problems in cloud. More than once my friend Watson and I, lent to Bader as a formation by the CO, emerged from cloud faithfully following our leader only to find ourselves in a steep diving turn!

By the time of Bader's arrival at Duxford the Spitfire Mk I's original fixed-pitch

Bader's Cranwell contemporary, 'Tubby' Mermagen, pictured when he was a group captain and Officer Commanding RAF Cyprus, 1942.

propeller had been replaced by the de Havilland two-pitch airscrew. The pitch of a propeller blade is the angle at which it 'bites' into the air, and changing it from coarse to fine, as was now permitted by the new airscrew, is best likened to the effect of changing gear in a car. The biplanes flown by Bader before the war had fixed-pitch propellers similar to those of the original Spitfire. The new two-pitch propeller was to cause Fg Off Bader problems.

Throughout March 1940 19 Squadron continued to deploy three aircraft to Horsham daily. On 31 March Bader led his section to take off on a short run and slightly downwind. This would have saved precious time at only minimal risk, had he not forgotten to engage 'low gear' by selecting fine pitch. Halfway through take-off the other two pilots realised what had happened and opened their throttles wide, just in time to avoid the boundary hedge. Bader's Spitfire, however, cartwheeled across a ploughed field, clods of earth hurtling skywards. The aircraft was written off, as were its pilot's artificial legs.

Perhaps surprisingly, on the same day as the accident Douglas Bader was promoted to Flight Lieutenant and joined Sqn Ldr H.W. 'Tubby' Mermagen's 222 Squadron, also at Duxford, as a flight commander. It might be asked why Bader was chosen to be appointed a flight commander so soon after his return to the RAF, when perhaps other officers with more current experience were no doubt waiting for such promotion. In 1996 Air Cdre W.H. Mermagen CB CBE AFC recalled:

When I was commanding 222 Squadron at RAF Duxford during 1939/40, Douglas Bader, a personal friend from the early 1930s, was serving alongside us in 19 Squadron. However, he was finding it difficult to serve under Squadron Leader Geoffrey Stephenson, with whom he had once shared equal rank at Kenley before his accident. Bader therefore asked me if I would approach the AOC (Air Officer

Commanding), Leigh-Mallory, regarding the possibility of him being transferred to 222 as a flight commander. The AOC agreed. Bader was easy to keep in order, as it were, and he proved to be an excellent flight commander. He carried out several operational sorties under my command and displayed exceptional leadership qualities and was a fine Spitfire pilot.

Clearly many of Bader's pre-war contemporaries, such as Stephenson and Mermagen, had aspired to positions of command and responsibility. Undoubtedly, had Bader not been forced to leave the RAF following his accident, he too would have shared the same rank and status by 1940. As Air Cdre Mermagen's account testifies, however, Bader could rely upon the Cranwellian 'Old Boy' network to help him recover lost ground.

On 28 May 1940, just five days after Flt Lt Bader was posted to 222, the squadron arrived at Hornchurch to assist with air operations covering the Dunkirk evacuation; Operation *Dynamo*. The bulk of the air fighting to date had been borne by the Hawker Hurricane, which had been committed to the Battle of France while the Spitfire had sensibly been preserved for home defence. During the next few days the Spitfire would be properly blooded in combat over the French coast, and the German fighter pilots would at last meet an adversary equal to their superb Messerschmitt Me 109. Number 222 Squadron flew as part of a four-squadron Wing formation which also included 19, 41 and 616 Squadrons. On 1 June Bader scored his first victory when he destroyed an Me 109 over Dunkirk. Two days later, however, Operation *Dynamo* was complete, and the Allied forces remaining within the Dunkirk perimeter surrendered the following day.

In July 1940 Douglas Bader was promoted to Acting Squadron Leader, and took command of a Hurricane squadron, 242, at Coltishall in Norfolk. By this time he had been back in the RAF for just eight months, and so again there may have been other pre-war regular officers of greater experience awaiting their first command. Bader, on the other hand, had been a flight commander for just three months, and had just one enemy aircraft to his credit. He had led neither a squadron nor a Wing into action, and had yet to be recommended for any award. Again, it appears that Air Cdre Mermagen has the answer:

Soon after I left 222 Squadron, Douglas Bader was posted to command 242, a largely Canadian squadron suffering from bad morale. By this time Bader was known personally to the AOC who knew of his record and had particular respect for the way in which he had dealt with both the crash and amputations. I had spoken to Leigh-Mallory on several occasions, confirming that Bader was an "above average" Spitfire pilot, a most mature character and quite an outstanding personality in Fighter Command. I feel certain that my high opinion of Douglas Bader led to him achieving such rapid promotion which he rightly deserved and as proven by his later Service record.

The squadron had been formed from Canadian volunteers early in the war, and had seen action both during the Battle of France and over Dunkirk. It lost all of its aircraft and equipment in France, returning to England in a thoroughly dejected state. Many pilots had lost all documentation, and their pay was weeks in arrears. For its leader, 242 Squadron clearly required a man of deed and action; Sqn Ldr Bader rapidly restored morale, and the squadron was re-equipped and operational just one month after he took command.

Fighter Command's system of defending the United Kingdom included dividing

Pilots of 242 Squadron wait for action outside Duxford's dispersal in 1940: Plt Off W.L. McKnight, Flt Lt G.E. Ball, Sqn Ldr D.R.S. Bader, Plt Off N.N. Campbell and Plt Off Denis Crowley-Milling.

the defending forces into four separate groups. Each group had its own headquarters and commander, but was answerable to the Commander-in-Chief of Fighter Command, Air Chief Marshal Sir Hugh Dowding, at the Command's headquarters at Bentley Priory, near Stanmore in Middlesex. London and the south-east of England was defended by 11 Group, commanded by Air Vice-Marshal Keith Park, the south-west was protected by Air Vice-Marshal Sir Christopher Quintin Brand's 10 Group, and the Midlands and East Anglia by Air Vice-Marshal Trafford Leigh-Mallory's 12 Group. The north of England and Northern Ireland came under the umbrella of Air Vice-Marshal Richard Saul's 13 Group. During the 1930s Dowding himself had integrated Radio Direction Finding (RDF, later called radar) into this system of home defence, and in 1940 this tremendous farsightedness was to give the defenders a great advantage over the enemy.

As 11 Group covered the Channel coast, and as the Luftwaffe, now based in the Pas-de-Calais, was able to make its main thrust towards London and the south-east, Park's squadrons were more favourably located to intercept the enemy than Leigh-Mallory's Midland based 12 Group. Park's tactics were to break up the bombers before they could reach and inflict damage on their targets, and generally to shoot down as many enemy machines as possible. As the pressure of attacks on 11 Group's airfields increased, Park was forced to call upon Leigh-Mallory to protect the airfields while his fighter squadrons were in action. On 26 August 1940 11 Group called upon 12 Group for reinforcements, but before 12 Group arrived Debden airfield in Essex was severely damaged by German bombs. Park demanded to know why 12 Group was not in position when the Luftwaffe attacked. Leigh-Mallory's response was that his assistance had been requested too late.

On 30 August 1940 Sqn Ldr Douglas Bader waited impatiently for action at

Pilot Officer Peter Brown. Now Sqn Ldr M.P. Brown AFC, RAF Retd, this member of Churchill's Few has recently become an active researcher himself, and works closely with the author.

Coltishall. He was already deeply resentful that 242 Squadron had been forced to play a secondary role to the 11 Group units. This was surely understandable when the 11 Group squadrons were having such a tough time while 12 Group largely idled, awaiting a call to assist. On this day, however, Bader received orders for 242 Squadron to proceed from Coltishall to Duxford in Cambridgeshire, much closer to London. From Duxford the squadron was scrambled and intercepted a large formation of enemy raiders north of the capital. The Hurricane pilots subsequently claimed the destruction of 12 enemy aircraft and a further five probably destroyed. The squadron received a signal from Leigh-Mallory himself: 'Heartfelt congratulations on a first class show. Well done 242'. Further congratulatory messages were received from the Chief of the Air Staff (CAS) and the Under Secretary of State for Air. Bader subsequently spoke to his AOC, stating his belief that he could have inflicted far greater losses on the enemy had he been given a number of squadrons under his command, as opposed to a 'penny packet' force of just 12 aircraft, indeed as employed by 11 Group. Bader explained that, with several squadrons, all based at Duxford, a Wing could be scrambled, form up en route and arrive over the battle zone in strength to attack the enemy *en masse* and hopefully, therefore, on relatively equal terms. In Leigh-Mallory, Bader's suggested tactics found an important ally.

Much has been written concerning Bader's involvement in the Battle of Britain, particularly regarding the 'Big Wing' controversy, which has raged ever since. However, Sqn Ldr Peter Brown AFC is well qualified to remark on the Duxford Wing, for as a Pilot Officer during the Battle of Britain he flew Spitfires with 611 Squadron as a part of Bader's formation, and also with 41 Squadron in 11 Group. He says:

The major and most often voiced criticism of the Big Wing is that it took too long to form up. This is totally without foundation. Bader led the first Hurricane squadron out of Duxford, taking off into the prevailing south-west wind. His two other Hurricane squadrons then followed in correct order within minutes. After two or three minutes flying south-west, Bader executed a slow climbing turn to direct south – exactly where the Wing had been despatched, and enabling the following squadrons to cut the corner. The two Spitfire squadrons were based at Fowlmere, three miles to the west. We therefore took off parallel with the third Hurricane squadron which we could see, and on the flight south climbed up to 15,000 ft as top cover. The Wing was already in formation except for height which we achieved *en route*. When London was reached each squadron was in its prearranged position. There was no wasted time in formal forming up. (Of course there should be no confusion between the Duxford Big Wing of 1940 and the Wings used later in the sweeps over France...Their assembly procedures and functions were quite different.) London would certainly be in our sight within 15 min after take-off.

My main criticism of the five-squadron Wing was that it was not possible for the Wing Leader to control five squadrons effectively under Battle of Britain conditions when the enemy was met. There were too many of our own people milling about and too many attacking the same target, which is what led to the overclaiming problem. I would suggest that two or three squadron Wings would have been more effective, although not as prestigious of course, and would have shot down more aircraft. The two smaller Wings would have given controllers a double chance at interception. My view is that the most significant contribution of the five squadron Big Wing was on 15 September 1940, when by the grace of God, we intercepted both major raids of that day. For days previously the German aircrews had been told by the chiefs and general intelligence that RAF Fighter Command was finished, having just a few aircraft left. Imagine the psychological effect on those German aircrews over London to see 60, and probably looking like 100, RAF fighters diving out of the sun, fresh to the attack, the bombers themselves having been harried all the way in. The psychological effect was then doubled later in the day when the second major raid was similarly intercepted by our Wing of 60 aircraft. The Germans were not to know, of course, that this was the same Wing of 60 aircraft! I believe that, with the heavy losses inflicted by 11 Group and the two interceptions with the five-squadron Wing, it became obvious on 15 September to both the German aircrews and their commanders that the RAF was in fact far from finished and that there was no hope for a German aerial victory over England in 1940.

I believe that the Big Wing concept, which had a natural place later during the sweeps over France, was deliberately built up and publicised by 12 Group during the Battle of Britain as a means of trying to create 12 Group prestige and belittle the efforts of the squadrons in 11 Group. Keith Park of 11 Group did magnificently, however. If Dowding had given him a further five squadrons under his own direct sector control he would have had the reserves he desperately needed. That would have been the correct tactical decision.

In conclusion I would say that the Battle was fought in the south of England and over London. Tactically that is where all our best squadrons, well rested, and the best aircraft should have been. Our forces should not have been split by an out of date black line on the Group plotting table.

The Battle of Britain was one of the most important battles in history, fought over England in 1940 and won against superior odds. During the Battle, the serious problems caused by jealousy and ambitions at Air rank level should have been resolved resolutely and instantly. When the Battle ended in victory, one would have expected that both the Commander-in-Chief and the 11 Group commander would have automatically received high honours, not only for themselves but as a reflection

Sir Trafford Leigh-Mallory (right).

of the sacrifice of the many young pilots of Fighter Command. Instead both were, however, removed from office without any major recognition. Air Vice-Marshal Park was replaced by Air Vice-Marshal Leigh-Mallory who had battled against him and had helped create the myth of the Big Wing. The pilots who fought the Battle of Britain never forgave the RAF and felt that the treatment of their leaders was just another sign of the political jockeying at high level which took place away from the dangers of the Battle.

It is probably fair to say that history has proven that, given their geographical areas of responsibility, both Park and Leigh-Mallory were right in the use of their respective tactics. I wish to emphasise, however, that the information provided here is really intended as basic background reading only. In fact, as a direct result of writing this book I have become so absorbed by the air fighting, personalities, and politics pertaining to the Big Wing that I am now researching a detailed account dedicated to this subject and for future publication: *Bader's Duxford Fighters: The Big Wing, 1940.*

After the Battle of Britain, Sqn Ldr Bader and 242 Squadron remained at Coltishall, on the Norfolk coast. Owing to its daylight defeat during the summer of 1940, the Luftwaffe had begun the night blitz of English cities, the raiders being guided to their targets by the blind-bombing aids *Knickebein* and *X-Verfahren*, which used intersecting beams, and the very accurate *Y-Verfahren*, which used a beam plus a ranging system. As nightfighter defences were in their infancy, the nocturnal raiders were able to operate over the British Isles in comparative safety. Desperate again was the hour, and to assist the Boulton Paul Defiant and Bristol Blenheim nightfighters, single-engined day fighters were pressed into service after darkness. Largely because of the two rows of glowing exhaust stubs, either side of the engine and situated in front of the pilot,

The tomfoolery evident in this picture, taken at Coltishall in 1940 and captioned 'Poses by 242 Pursuit Squadron' in Sir Denis Crowley-Milling's photograph album, is indicative of the squadron's restored morale! Squadron Leader Bader at extreme left.

ruining his night vision, both the Spitfire and Hurricane were far from ideal for this role. Successes were few, and the fighter pilots became increasingly frustrated with the inadequacy of their equipment in the light of the terrible destruction being wrought by the raiders. Many cities were aflame, and civilian casualties high. London, Coventry, Birmingham, Plymouth, Liverpool, Swansea and many others were subjected to sustained attack in that awful winter of death.

Bader's 242 Squadron was among the Fighter Command day units desperately attempting to stem the tide, with little or no success. One can imagine, however, the deep frustration experienced by Bader and Flt Lts Turner and Ball when patrolling over Coventry on the night of 14/15 November 1940. The German bomber streams destroyed not only the heart of the ancient city but also much of the outlying industrial and residential areas. The 242 Squadron pilots, while witnessing the enormous conflagration below them, saw not one bomber. In fact, only a single raider was brought down that terrible night, a Dornier Do 17 destroyed by AA fire. Ultimately, however, Germany would reap more than the whirlwind for this *Nachtangriff*.

During daylight, Bader's Hurricane pilots flew countless hours shepherding convoys down the east coast of England, occasionally driving off a raider. These convoy patrols were rather repetitive chores for the pilots, however. For example, between 27 December 1940 and 28 February 1941 Plt Off Franek Surma, an experienced Polish fighter pilot freshly posted to 242 Squadron, flew 17 such sorties. Although the opposing fighters continued to clash over south-east England and the Channel well into 1941, with the onset of winter any chance of significant action during daylight in 12 Group was slim.

Sir Denis Crowley-Milling captioned this photograph: 'That's where he went'. Bader and his pilots are examining a map, although why their headgear is so arranged remains unclear!

After Dowding and Park were replaced, towards the end of 1940, Air Chief Marshal William Sholto Douglas became C-in-C of Fighter Command, while the prestigious 11 Group went to the ambitious Air Vice-Marshal Sir Trafford Leigh-Mallory. Thus the 'Big Wing' passed into history, but the lessons learned in 1940 very much helped to set the scene for the new offensive policy of 1941. Soon it would be Fighter Command's turn to 'dish some out'.

CHAPTER TWO

Leaning into France: the Early Days

During the winter months following the Battle of Britain, Fighter Command was able to regroup. Many of its deficiencies in equipment and personnel were rectified. The Command had ended 1940 with a total of 1,243 pilots, and by early 1941 that figure had increased to 1,655. Lord Beaverbrook, the Minister of Aircraft Production, had swiftly organised the manufacture and supply of fighters, in particular Spitfires at Vickers Armstrongs' huge Castle Bromwich shadow factory near Birmingham. The RAF's Operational Training Units (OTUs) were also able to expand upon the meagre facilities provided during 1940. Help continued to come from abroad as an increasing number of pilots who had escaped the occupied territories started to fly and fight with the RAF. American volunteers also swelled Fighter Command's ranks with their 'Eagle Squadrons'.

Although there was no reason to expect anything other than a renewed aerial offensive against England during the summer of 1941, Fighter Command itself sought an offensive initiative as early as the autumn of 1940. Between 21 October and 20 December 1940 a new policy was formulated of 'Leaning into France', which was enthusiastically supported by Fighter Command's new C-in-C, Air Chief Marshal William Sholto Douglas. This newly-found offensive spirit was later summed up by Air Vice-Marshal Leigh-Mallory: 'We have stopped licking our wounds. We are now going over to the offensive. Last year the fighting was desperate. Now we're entitled to be cocky.'

At that preliminary stage, proposed offensive fighter operations were referred to merely as 'Rhubarbs', and were to consist primarily of patrols over enemy territory by single fighters or formations of up to flight strength (six aircraft), using cloud cover. Clearly, such sorties were flyable only if the cloudbase was at 2,000 ft or less. The purpose of these sorties was to 'attack and destroy enemy aircraft, or, if impractical, suitable ground military objectives'. The first Rhubarb was flown on 20 December 1940 by Flt Lt Christie and Plt Off Bodie of 66 Squadron. The Spitfire pilots subsequently reported having successfully attacked an enemy airfield at either Berck or Le Touquet on the French coast.

Five days before Christie and Bodie made military aviation history by flying the first Rhubarb, the Spitfires of 610 'County of Chester' Squadron of the Royal Auxiliary Air Force (RAuxAF) touched down at Westhampnett to begin a long period of service with the Tangmere Wing. Among those pilots was Sgt David Denchfield, who had joined the squadron on 7 October 1940, while it was resting at Acklington, Northumberland. In 1995 David Denchfield recalled the following regarding the start of the Non-stop Offensive:

> We of 610 Squadron were proudly a part of the Tangmere Wing some time before Douglas Bader came on the scene; also involved were 65, 145 and 302 (Polish) Squadrons. In early January 1941 all of the Wing's pilots attended a meeting at which future policy was explained to us. We learned that:
> Rhubarb raids would be carried out whenever possible. We had known of these

Flight Lieutenant Ron Rayner DFC. As 41 Squadron made good its Battle of Britain losses and prepared for the Non-Stop Offensive of 1941, Ron joined the squadron as a replacement NCO pilot. He consequently flew Spitfires throughout the war, and won a well-earned DFC while serving in Italy.

since mid-December 1940, back then known as "Mosquito" raids. The name was actually changed to Rhubarb roundabout the time we received information regarding a new RAF twin-engined type which we were to leave alone. Later we discovered this to be the de Havilland Mosquito!

All Spitfire pilots were also to be night operational and take part in the "Layer" system of night-fighting over specified areas which were to be protected; in our case Portsmouth and Southampton. This system predated the Luftwaffe's *Wilde Sau* by two years or so. After notching up just an hour's nightflying, we were declared "night operational"!

We were also to escort bombers to France in an attempt to tempt the Me 109s up to be dealt with by the heavy escort. At this, Sergeant Ronnie Hamlyn DFM, secure in his reputation, interjected: "Why do this, Sir, they're no trouble if left on the ground!". Of course we all hooted, but reading now of the great disparity of losses I wonder if Ham was nearer the bull than we thought.

As the tempo of the first Rhubarbs increased, however, it was discovered that the intruding RAF fighters actually failed to incite the Luftwaffe to join battle. In consequence, Fighter Command only retained Rhubarbs for opportunist 'seek and destroy' missions.

Flight Lieutenant Ron Rayner DFC was a sergeant pilot with 41 Squadron at Merston, a part of the Tangmere Wing, when the offensive got under way. In 1995 he recalled Rhubarbs:

Rhubarbs were eventually used only when the weather was unsuitable for fighter sweeps. It was just so that, regardless, we could continue with some offensive activity. Two Spitfires used to cross the Channel to France, shoot up a target of opportunity and return. I wouldn't say that we achieved a great deal, these attacks were more of nuisance value. We would try and find a train or German troops, sometimes shooting up a "staff car", although I have wondered since whether on occasions these were perhaps French civilian vehicles. My log book records that on one occasion I flew a Rhubarb and "shot up Le Havre". That was a long flight, 160 miles across the sea. Navigational aids were somewhat rudimentary, and so on the return flight we received no assistance from the ground until we had reached the English coast. That was one of the reasons why these sorties were so unpopular with pilots, the fact that they were flown in poor weather compounding the problem.

Such low-level sorties over Europe meant that single-engine fighters were always at the mercy of the weather. Without any sophisticated navigational equipment, the pilots often had to overcome such problems as mist, rainstorms, and high winds. If the weather became marginal, pilots could just disappear, their names being added to the ever-growing list of those reported 'Missing'. In these early days the Air Sea Rescue (ASR) service was in its infancy. During the Battle of Britain, just a few months previously, pilots down in the Channel generally had to hope for a passing ship, or, if within sight of land, assistance from a local lifeboat. By early 1941 most fighter pilots had yet to be issued with inflatable dinghies, and relied chiefly on their 'Mae West' lifejackets for buoyancy. Spitfires were frequently lost due to a lucky shot fired from the ground, as many RAF pilots were to discover. Rhubarbs required little planning and could be virtually opportunist, although fairly hazardous. When offset against the damage, or 'nuisance', achieved, such sorties were clearly not cost-effective. Many pilots were to end up 'in the bag', or even as statistics in the casualty lists, as a result of Rhubarbs.

On 9 January 1941 a more complex type of operation took place when five RAF fighter squadrons swept across France and thus opened the Non-stop Offensive, although their presence was ignored by the Luftwaffe. The previous use of Wing formations, however, was not actually peculiar to 12 Group in 1940. During Operation *Dynamo* Spitfire squadrons had operated in Wing formations over the French coast, although, as with the Duxford Wing, this was also in a defensive context. For example, on 28 May 1940 19, 54 and 65 Squadrons operated as a Wing over the Channel and French coast, and on 1 June a four-squadron Wing comprising 19, 41, 222 and 616 Squadrons was led into action by the 19 Squadron's Flt Lt Brian Lane (see the author's *Spitfire Squadron*). During the Battle of Britain the German *Freie Jagd* intrusions over south-east England had been made in numbers; frequently in Gruppe strength (three squadrons) and occasionally even at Geschwader level (12 squadrons). That Fighter Command's sweeps in 1941 should be undertaken by Wings, as opposed to individual squadrons, made complete sense in the offensive context. These offensive Wings were not to experience the frustration of the Duxford Wing at being scrambled too late when being used defensively. Conversely, an offensive Wing actually held the initiative.

That the Luftwaffe ignored the presence of 60 enemy fighters over their territory on 9 January 1941 is perhaps worth explaining. A fighter, unlike a bomber, can inflict only marginal damage to ground targets, and so is really only a danger to intercepting fighters. The most sensible thing for a controller to do was to ignore these excursions, thus preserving his own forces, as indeed Fighter Command had discovered during 1940.

In late 1940, when Fighter Command was considering its tactics for the forthcoming offensive, it was in a position to benefit from the Luftwaffe's experiences and mistakes. Therefore, while Fighter Command was not to get it all right straight away, it did not use single-engined fighters as fighter-bombers in an effort to incite reaction from the German fighters. Certainly the Allied fighter-bomber proved its worth later and in many theatres of war, but these operations were largely conducted

A Bristol Blenheim bomber as supplied by 2 Group, Bomber Command, for many Circus operations in 1941. This particular aircraft was the camera ship for the 1940s film 'The First of the Few', which told the morale boosting story of the Spitfire's designer, R.J. Mitchell. It was snapped 'on location' at Ibsley by Peter Howard-Williams.

in close support of the army or in conditions leaning towards Allied aerial supremacy. However, accepting that bombers were a prerequisite to enticing the Germans to join battle, it was decided to add a small force of light bombers to the offensive formation, usually the Bristol Blenheims of 2 Group, Bomber Command. These raids were to be mounted against specific targets of both strategic and military importance in northern France, such as enemy airfields, power stations and railway marshalling yards. Whilst the Blenheims were clearly unable to cause extensive damage owing to their limited bomb loads, their presence could not be ignored. Such operations were codenamed 'Circuses', and were complex undertakings involving hundreds of aircraft. The basic idea was that the German controllers could not ignore bombers in the 'Beehive' and would scramble fighters to intercept. The bombers would be heavily escorted so that the ensuing battle would take place under optimum conditions for the RAF pilots, who should therefore control height and numbers. At the time, Wg Cdr David Cox DFC and Bar was a recently promoted Pilot Officer with 19 Squadron. He recalls:

1941 saw the start of Fighter Command's offensive operations over the Continent. It was mainly over France for the first part of the year, then Belgium and later Holland. At first it was just a Wing of Spitfires and Hurricanes, either two or three squadrons. When only fighters appeared the Luftwaffe was content to stay on the ground and let Fighter Command waste fuel. To provoke the enemy, Blenheim bombers joined in the offensive, and later even four-engined Stirlings. This resulted in quite a sharp reaction from the German fighters. I remember that on one operation we escorted one Stirling bomber to St Omer – quite a sight looking at ONE Stirling surrounded by about 200 Spitfires!

In a way, Circus operations were similar to the raids mounted against England during the Battle of Britain, when short-range German fighters had escorted medium bombers across the Channel to targets in England. However, although the Luftwaffe

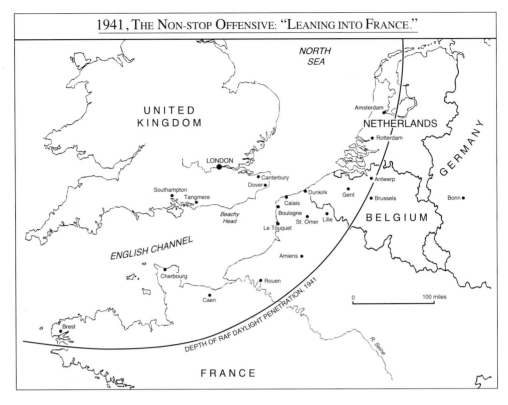

was a tactical air force, not designed for use in the strategic bombing role, in this onslaught against England it found itself employed in a quasi-strategic role for which it was not equipped. This was a mistake, however, that the RAF did not make in 1941, its bombers being used essentially as bait for the enemy fighters, and therefore in a tactical context. The two respective offensive undertakings were entirely different.

Circus operations were to become complex affairs requiring much planning and co-ordination. Whereas a flight commander could initiate a Rhubarb, a Circus required planning at Fighter Command level, as fighters from 10, 11 and 12 Group would often participate. Each squadron would be allocated a certain job:

Close Escort: Surrounding and remaining with the bombers at all time.

Escort Cover: Protecting the Close Escort fighters.

High Cover: Preventing enemy fighters getting between the Close and Escort Wings.

Top Cover: Restricted to the bomber route, but having a roving commission to sweep the sky immediately in front of the 'Beehive'.

Target Support: Independently routed fighters flying directly to and covering the target area.

Withdrawal Cover: Fighters supporting the return flight, by which time escorting fighters would be running short of both fuel and ammunition.

Fighter Diversion: A Wing, or even Wings eventually, creating a diversionary sweep to keep hostile aircraft from the target area during 'Ramrod' operations, the Ramrod being similar to a Circus but entailing the destruction of a specific target, not just amounting to an elaborate nuisance raid.

On 10 January 1941 Circus No. 1 was dispatched against ammunition supplies hidden in the Forêt de Guines. Six Blenheims of 114 Squadron were closely escorted

Pilot Officer Bob Beardsley in his 41 Squadron Spitfire at Catterick before the Non-stop Offensive of 1941. 'Eileen' is Mrs Beardsley. Bob retired from the RAF as a Squadron Leader with a DFC to his credit.

by the Hurricanes of 56 Squadron (11 Group), forward support being provided by 242 (12 Group) and 249 (11 Group) Squadrons flying the same type. Target support was given by 302 Squadron's Hurricanes and 610 Squadron's Spitfires (11 Group). Nos. 41, 64 and 611 Squadrons (11 Group) contributed top cover, while Spitfires of 66, 74 and 92 Squadrons (11 Group) flew rear cover. Interestingly, the only 12 Group squadron involved was Sqn Ldr Bader's 242, perhaps another indication of his continued standing with Leigh-Mallory, now commanding 11 Group and a principal architect of the Non-stop Offensive. However, it is fair to say that, as Bader was then the most experienced exponent of the Wing principle, it was only natural that he, too, should play an important part in these early offensive operations.

Circus No. 1 was significant. For the first time since the Blitzkrieg of spring 1940, an escorted RAF bomber force intruded into German-held airspace and continued the role-reversal begun by the previous day's fighter sweep. Both I and II/JG53 reacted to the RAF presence, and the RAF fighters were engaged. As the forward support squadrons crossed the French coast at Calais, Oberleutnant (Oblt) Michalek bounced 249 Squadron and shot down a Hurricane. Despite accurate flak, the bombers successfully attacked the target. As the Blenheims withdrew and recrossed the French coastline, the rear cover Spitfires arrived, only to be attacked by a strong force of Me 109s. Over Wissant, 41 Squadron was bounced by five Me 109s and Sgt Bob Beardsley's Spitfire was badly hit. In 1995 Sqn Ldr Bob Beardsley DFC remembered:

I was flying with another experienced sergeant pilot as "Arse-end Charlie". We were in the coastal area, heading outbound, when I saw six Me 109s in my rear-view mirror. Before I could give a warning I received the "full dose" from their leader. This attack damaged my aileron control and my radio would not transmit. However, by chance the EAs (enemy aircraft) did not follow me down as I dived frantically to catch up with the squadron. My other "rearguard" had not seen anything happen to me, and as I was unable to contact the squadron I tagged on behind, at the same time discovering that I had neither guns nor flaps. Obviously the pneumatic system had been damaged. I let the squadron land at Hornchurch and flew a large circuit; with no ailerons it must have been clear that I was in trouble! Thank heavens that the engine was undamaged. I blew down the undercarriage using the emergency bottle and landed safely on flat tyres! I was met by the fire engine and driven back to dispersal to be greeted by the flight commander with: "Where the hell have you been, and where is your aircraft?", most definitely not the "How are you old chap?" that I thought the situation merited! When he finally realised the situation and condition of my Spitfire (Category 3! (written off)) he was somewhat mollified. I was rather hacked off about all this as the Spitfire concerned was mine!

During this first Circus the RAF fighters had come off second best. Two had been lost, and despite several claims not a single Me 109 had been hit. Fortunately Plt Off McConnell, Oblt Michalek's victim, had baled out into the Channel, swiftly being picked up by ASR. The Channel, 22 miles across at its narrowest point, was to cause many problems for the fighter pilots of both sides during those first years of war. In the Battle of Britain it was the Me 109 pilots who had to make two crossings, their return flights always plagued by the spectre of low fuel states and the possibility of having to nurse damaged aircraft across the forbidding water. This situation was now faced by Fighter Command. One must remember, of course, that neither the Me 109 nor the Spitfire was designed as an offensive fighter. The endurances of both were fairly short, the Spitfire's maximum range taking it to Lille in northern France, near the Belgian border, a return flight of about an hour and a half.

This is a fitting point at which to examine the Spitfires in use at the time, for it is with this type that the Non-stop Offensive became largely concerned as Supermarine designer Reginald J. Mitchell's fighter gradually replaced Sydney Camm's Hurricane. During the Battle of Britain, Fighter Command's Spitfire squadrons had largely flown the Mk IA, equipped with eight 0.303 in Browning machine-guns. The Me 109E, however, was equipped with two light machine-guns and two 20mm cannon, the later providing tremendous destructive power. It was clear that the Spitfire required heavier armament to counter this threat, so the Mk IB was produced as an experimental expedient and issued to 19 Squadron. This Spitfire was armed with just two 20mm Hispano Suiza cannon mounted on their sides, rather than upright as intended by the manufacturer. This caused countless problems with rounds jamming, and 19 Squadron's pilots became understandably frustrated.

On 11 August 1940 X4231 was returned to 19 Squadron fitted with one cannon and two machine-guns in each wing. The unit's CO, Sqn Ldr Phillip Pinkham AFC, recorded in his log book that the Spitfire flew quite normally and was 'obviously the right combination'. Although the squadron Operations Record Book (ORB) agreed, stating that this Spitfire was 'a step in the right direction', it adds that 'possibly another step in the same direction would be re-equipping with the old eight-gun machines'. On 3 September 1940 the Mk IB was replaced by the Mk IA, but trials continued.

On 5 October 1940 Plt Off Arthur Vokes returned to 19 Squadron with Spitfire R6889, allocated for thorough evaluation. The cannon's feed mechanism had a booster coil fitted which helped to push in each new round as the spring within the magazine ran down, and the feed chute had a wider sweep and went through one of the wing struts. Over the next few days Vokes tested R6889 on the range at Sutton Bridge, suffering one stoppage due to 'g', but after his next sortie recording in his log book: 'No stoppages, target bounced up in the air!' On 5 November 1940 19 Squadron met elements of II and III/JG26 undertaking a *Freie Jagd* over south-east England. Sergeant Charnock hit an Me 109 with cannon fire, and later reported that 'it literally fell to pieces'. Arthur Vokes wrote in his log book: 'Charnock got a cert., and Lawson blew another to bits with the cannon, its first success since July'. These entries certainly indicate the terrific destructive power of the 20mm cannon, and the importance of the Spitfire being so armed cannot be over-emphasised. Eventually the cannon problem was resolved by adding faired blisters to the wing's upper and lower surfaces to accommodate the ammunition drum, thus enabling the weapon to be mounted upright. The situation was therefore rectified in time for the Non-stop Offensive.

Spitfires were originally built in Supermarine's busy factory on the banks of the River Itchen near Southampton, but wartime demands soon indicated that production would have to increase beyond the capacity of Supermarine itself. The new site chosen for a 'Shadow Factory' was at Castle Bromwich, near Birmingham. The theory was that the mass-production methods of the automobile industry could be adapted to construct Spitfires. Lord Nuffield himself, pioneer of the inexpensive and mass produced motor car, was chosen to oversee the project.

The Castle Bromwich Aircraft Factory (CBAF) commenced production of the first Spitfire Mk IIs in June 1940, and these began reaching the squadrons in July. Unlike the early Spitfire Mk Is, all production Mk IIs incorporated an engine-driven hydraulic system for undercarriage operation and constant-speed airscrews. This type of airscrew, manufactured by Rotol or de Havilland, was powered by an improved Rolls-Royce Merlin, the XII, which gave the Spitfire Mk II an extra 2,000 ft ceiling. This was also the first Merlin-powered Spitfire to run on 100-octane petrol, previous engines having used 85 octane, and it was fitted with a Coffman cartridge starter. All 921 Mk IIs produced were built at the CBAF. The CBAF undoubtedly had a pronounced effect on Spitfire production even during those early days. In 1940 the production total was 1,246, and in 1941 it reached 2,518. By late 1940 all squadrons in the front line of 11 Group had been re-equipped with the type. The Mk II was also designated 'A' or 'B', the former being armed with the standard eight machine-guns and the latter having a combination of two cannon and four machine-guns. By early 1941, therefore, the squadrons were equipped with a mixture of Mks IIA and IIB, although these were soon to be replaced by the Mk V.

There was a constant requirement for the Spitfire to have more height, speed and range, together with heavier armament. However, the improvement offered by the Spitfire Mk II was not nearly enough. The extra weight imposed by the cannon required a more powerful engine, so the Mk IBs formerly operated by 19 Squadron, which were languishing in Maintenance Units, were re-engined with the Merlin 45. The take-off weight of this new Spitfire was 6,622 lb, and its top speed 359 mph at 25,000 ft, an altitude it could attain in 8½ min. In just under 15 min it could climb to 35,000 ft. This new Spitfire, designated Mk V, first equipped 92 Squadron at Biggin Hill, but began reaching the squadrons in numbers by May 1941.

Although the Spitfire was undoubtedly a superb aircraft in its day, it is incomparable to the fast jets of today's RAF, the 'fly-by-wire' technology of which is truly amazing. This should be borne in mind when reading of great wartime air battles. Ron Rayner recalls a little of Spitfire flying in 1941:

> I suppose it was noisy, but with the flying helmet strapped tight, the ears were almost sealed by the ear pieces' rubber rings, which helped. Anyway, after a combat started from then on until back at Merston the R/T was chattering away constantly. Of course these Spitfires had no cockpit heating at all, and so we had to take steps to protect against the cold. My mother knitted me some woollen stockings which I used to pull up over my legs at high altitude. Flying a Spitfire was also a very physical business, especially when in formation, which required constant jiggling about of the control column. Regarding range, this depended on the use of throttle, and of course combat used up more petrol; when attacked you would automatically go into a steep climbing turn, pushing the throttle forward for maximum boost as you did so. After an operational flight I suppose we were tired, but we were fit and just glad not to be in the infantry! Crossing the water with one engine was always a concern, and of course we monitored our fuel gauges very carefully.

Squadron Leader Jack Stokoe DFC was a Pilot Officer with 54 Squadron, also flying

Jack Stokoe as a Sergeant pilot during the Battle of Britain, while flying Spitfires with 603 Squadron at Hornchurch. He was later commissioned and awarded the DFC.

Spitfires in 1941. Jack recalls that: 'the offensive operations of 1941 were actually just as vital as the Battle of Britain, and certainly more nerve-racking as we were operating at range over enemy occupied territory'. On 20 April 1941 Jack Stokoe discovered just how 'nerve-racking' such operations could be:

I have some difficulty remembering the exact sequence of events before and after I was shot down; not entirely surprising as when admitted to hospital I was suffering from shock, concussion, exhaustion and hypothermia, all aided and abetted by a generous helping of Navy rum, for which at the time I was extremely grateful!

So far as I can remember, we were patrolling about 10–20 miles out in the North Sea off Clacton, probably vectored there by Control reporting "bandits" in that area. Suddenly we were in a combat situation and I was firing at an enemy aircraft. Then – a blank! I was still in the air, but minus a Spitfire which had disappeared entirely, probably as the result of one or more direct hits from cannon shells behind the armour-plated seat.

I had not opened the hood, nor disconnected my oxygen supply or intercom, or unstrapped the seat harness, but I seemed not to be surprised or unduly worried that I was apparently flying without any visible means of support. Nor did I have any sensation of falling! My helmet was missing, as were my gloves and one of my flying boots. When I got round to looking, my parachute appeared somewhat the worse for wear. However, I pulled the ripcord, the 'chute opened, and I landed in a very cold and somewhat wild sea.

My hands did not seem to be functioning properly, and so I was unable to free myself from the parachute. I slowly recollected that I ought to have an inflatable dinghy, and after another struggle managed to inflate it, only for it to burst. Whether it was damaged, or whether I inflated it too quickly we will never know, but I certainly reached a new low in the survival stakes. However, I managed to hang on grimly to a certain amount of air in an undamaged corner of the otherwise deflated dinghy, and struggled feebly to remain afloat. When I had just about given up hope, I heard voices, a ship was near me and ropes were thrown. I grabbed one and was hauled aboard.

I remember little else, but I was told the rest of the story by a couple of the crew members when they visited me in Harwich Hospital and presented me with a photograph you now have a copy of.

Apparently they had wrapped me in blankets, giving me an unspecified hot drink, and laid me to rest in a bunk. Apparently an RAF Air Sea Rescue launch arrived and

Pilot Officer Jack Stokoe being rescued from the North Sea on 20 April 1941.

wanted to take me back, but fortunately the Skipper said I was comfortably resting on board and he was returning to port anyway, so I remained where I was. I say fortunately because I was told that the launch actually overturned in rough sea outside the harbour – I was in no state to face another struggle.

The crew also reported seeing an enemy aircraft crash into the sea before fishing me out. I was in hospital for seven days and then had a week's leave, but strangely enough I have no recollection now as to whether I went home or not, although it is likely that I did. I returned to duty with 54 Squadron at Hornchurch and was back in action on 6 May 1941.

On that day, 54 Squadron had taken off from Hornchurch at 16:25 hrs to patrol Barrow Deep. Upon arrival at their destination a Staffel of Me 109s was sighted above. One of the enemy fighters made a head-on attack, passing above the Spitfires before turning to engage 'A' Flight from astern. The squadron scattered, but Plt Off Stokoe was shot down. The unit was also missing Plt Off Colebrook, although another pilot reported having seen a Spitfire going down into the sea streaming glycol. One claim was made by Oblt Winfried Balfanz of Stab/JG51 for a Spitfire destroyed. It is likely that his victim was Plt Off Colebrook. The Royal Navy also claimed the destruction of two Me 109s in this engagement, but in fact the Germans again suffered no casualties. It is possible therefore, that Jack Stokoe was actually a victim of the Naval gunners in an incident which would now be called 'Friendly Fire'.

In 1941 Bob Morton was a sergeant pilot with 616 Squadron and a part of the Tangmere Wing. He has some interesting observations of the fighting at that time:

Although we maintained strict radio silence on the way across, the enemy fighters generally got wind of our approach and were waiting near their ceiling by the time we crossed the coast. This meant that they could gain speed far in excess of ours in a long dive, come up rapidly behind us, get in one long burst, and break away. To avoid this, one Spitfire pilot in each section had to fly with his chin on his shoulder, watching his tail. This naturally did not make for good formation flying; the four-aircraft sections quickly split into two pairs when action began, but almost every pilot found himself unaccompanied after a time. At this point the Me 109s which had split up the Spitfire formation would begin climbing to engage "loners". In the subsequent scraps we were disadvantaged in several ways. In the matter of claims, for example. To claim an aircraft destroyed, one had to have seen one of three events:

1. The aircraft concerned striking the ground.
2. The pilot baling out.
3. The aircraft bursting into flames.

The first was almost impossible; most of our fighting would be carried out above 10,000 ft, and no-one would be fool enough to keep his eyes on an aircraft he had shot at, or follow it down. The second took time to occur, and other aircraft were likely to be shooting at the attacker as the Germans always worked in pairs. As for the third, although in the film "The Battle of Britain", every machine shot at immediately burst into flames and exploded after a few seconds, I never saw either of these events take place. Finally, of course, to lose any battle meant that we would spend the rest of the war incarcerated in Germany.

In these circumstances we could not help but envy the Few, who appear to have been credited with most machines they shot down, and if met with the same fate merely had to make their way back to base where another aircraft would be waiting for them. If by any chance they were wounded, these pilots had a wonderful time in hospital worshipped by all the nurses (I speak from their own reports)!

On 5 February 1941 Circus No. 3 was flown to St Omer/Wizernes. Among the participating RAF fighter squadrons was 610, of the Tangmere Wing. This squadron flew as top cover with 65 and 302 Squadrons. The enemy airfield was successfully bombed before any interception, although 610 Squadron had reported Me 109s stalking the RAF formation in the target area. When the Beehive was between St Omer and the French coast during the return flight, Me 109Es of I/JG3 attacked 610 Squadron from above. In the ensuing action 610 Squadron lost Spitfire N3249, flown by Sgt H.D. Denchfield. In 1995 Dave Denchfield recalled the incident and gave his impressions of being a fighter pilot in 1941:

I cannot recall any special feelings regarding 5 February 1941, other than thinking that the trips over France were going to be a little more fraught than those over here. The Channel may well protect this "sceptred isle", but for us, at the very least, it was going to be just another bloody hazard! I had marked my half-a-million map with the extent of sea rescue or otherwise between Dover and Weymouth, and tried to forget the red lines which ran for most of that distance and meant "Don't ditch here!" Apart from that I was only concerned to ensure that my ground staff topped up the tanks after engine runs, as I was "B" Flight's weaver and would therefore fly further than the rest. No adverse thoughts, though, it was, after all what we had joined for.

On Circus No. 3, it was about 1 p.m. and I was weaving at about 15,000 ft. Without warning we were bounced by Me 109s. I saw sparks on my wingtip and saw pieces flying off, and felt the aircraft shudder. I attempted to turn sharply to starboard and to gain height but my rudder pedals did not respond. My glycol tank was hit and the cockpit stank of petrol which was beginning to swill around my feet. I lost height swiftly and baled out, minus one boot, at about 5,000 ft, somersaulting until my parachute opened at about 1,000 ft. I landed unharmed and saw my plane crash about a mile away.

I was picked up almost immediately, although not before I hid various belongings and papers in a nearby thicket (the ground was covered in about two inches of snow). A local French boy asked me how old I was; I could not gather my thoughts sufficiently to respond in French and so I signalled "21" by holding up my fingers. Two Germans took me to the nearby aerodrome at Longuenesse.

I was astonished by the civility of my reception at the pilots' dispersal area. The pilots there saluted and all said they were glad I had got to earth safely. Shortly, the pilot who had actually shot me down arrived, and Oberleutnant Walter Oesau who shook my hand and through an interpreter reiterated the sentiments of his colleagues. I was entertained to afternoon tea and Oesau insisted that I sign my name in pencil on the inside of his silver cigarette case which could then be engraved over. There were seven other signatures in that case. I learnt that I had been Oesau's 40th kill and so the following day he received the coveted Oak Leaves to his existing Knight's Cross which he had received for 20 victories. He went on to record over 100 claims but was himself shot down and killed over Germany by Mustangs in 1945.

To conclude, I've often said, after apologising for any scandalous feeling I may give the listener, that from my viewpoint, until the day I was shot down out of it, the war was an exciting affair which I would not have missed for all the tea in China. It had released me from a humdrum office job and realised my ambition to fly HM combat fighters, and paid me to do it! It sounds outrageous and naive, but many of we pre-war VR (Volunteer Reserve) types felt the same. We seldom spoke, or even thought, of the downside. We had certainly read enough about First World War air fighting to know that the occupation held not much of an "after the war is over" future, but we were young and unimaginative enough to think "it won't be me". We all, I think, had a feeling of apprehension before take-off, but usually concentration pushed it aside. Mark you, as I took a very inauspicious part in the proceedings it is quite possible that had I carried on for some months or flown in a bomber, my thoughts might have been a little different. I could say that I grew up in four years of POW camps, a real character builder. All in all I have no regrets whatsoever. Nowadays I do a bit with the local aviation archaeological groups and went to France when a "buff" over there excavated my Spitfire. I am also a member of the East Anglian branch of the POW Association but don't bother with the Battle of

Sergeant David Denchfield of 610 Squadron at Longuenesse airfield after being shot down over St Omer by Oberleutnant Walter Oesau and captured on 5 February 1941.

Luftwaffe personnel examine the wreckage of Sgt Denchfield's Spitfire.

Britain reunions. In 1990 I was invited to the 50th anniversary at Buckingham Palace but declined. There were so many more deserving blokes than me, and anyway I can't stand the London traffic!

Back in 1941, although the squadrons were operating as Wings, there was as yet no such thing as a Wing Leader. The situation largely involved three independent squadrons operating in one formation, although squadron commanders often worked out between themselves who would actually be designated overall leader in the air, this usually being the most senior amongst them. Such complex cross-Channel operations required great fine-tuning and overall control, especially of the fighters in the air. Consequently Leigh-Mallory created a new post at each of the main Sector Stations, that of 'Wing Commander (Flying)', which, as its name suggests, was an operational as opposed to administrative job. A shortlist of suitably experienced officers was actually drawn up on 7 December 1940 by Leigh-Mallory when he was still AOC 12 Group.

In early March 1941 Sqn Ldr D.R.S. Bader DSO DFC was summoned by Leigh-Mallory. The AOC offered Bader the job of Wing Commander (Flying) at either Biggin Hill or Tangmere. Considering Biggin Hill too close to the distractions of London for his pilots, whom he wanted fresh for the fight across the Channel, Douglas Bader chose Tangmere, on the south coast of Sussex.

On 18 March 1941 Bader took leave of 242 Squadron and wrote in his log book: 'Handed over command of 242 (Canadian) Squadron. Reported to Tangmere as Wing Commander.' Sir Denis Crowley-Milling recalls Bader's departure from 242 Squadron:

We were all very disappointed to see him go. He had really put the squadron through its paces and built up a splendid fighting unit from a bunch of mainly Canadians, and a Bolshie lot they were to begin with!

A new era however was about to begin.

CHAPTER THREE

The Tangmere Wing: 'Bader's Bus Company'

On 18 March 1941 Wg Cdr Douglas Bader reported to RAF Tangmere's Station Commander, Grp Capt J.A. Boret OBE MC AFC, and took up his new appointment as one of the RAF's first Wing Leaders. Under his command were 145 Squadron, commanded by Sqn Ldr W.J. Leather, DFC; 610 Squadron, commanded by Sqn Ldr J. Ellis, DFC; and 616 Squadron, commanded by Sqn Ldr H.F. Burton, DFC. The following day he flew a 616 Squadron Spitfire Mk IIA coded QJ-A for 50 min to gain 'experience on type'. That same day, never one to waste time, Bader flew QJ-B on a 'Wing Channel Sweep'. On 21 March he again flew with 616 Squadron. Over half a century later Sir Alan Smith remembers that day vividly:

> Sitting in readiness at dispersal I heard the roar of a Spitfire as it dived low, climbed, did a half-roll and lowered its undercarriage whilst inverted, rolled out, side-slipped and made a perfect landing. Out of the cockpit climbed Wing Commander Douglas Bader and he walked with his distinctive gait into dispersal.

Left: *Wing Commander D.R.S. Bader DSO, DFC, Tangmere Wing Leader.*

Right: *Bader models the fighter pilot's headgear, circa 1941.*

Above: *The motto on Sgt Smith's sports car, 'Fear Not', was appropriate. Sir Alan recalls that the car 'died of old age and 100 octane fuel'.*

Left: *Sergeant (now Sir) Alan Smith.*

The Wing Commander announced himself, said he would be leading the Tangmere Wing, and explained that he would do so with 616 Squadron. He obviously knew Flying Officer "Cocky" Dundas and Pilot Officer "Johnnie" Johnson, and said: "You'll be Red 3, Cocky, and you Johnnie will be Red 4". Looking around he caught my eye and said: "Who are you?"

"Sergeant Smith, Sir", I replied.

"Right, you fly as my Red 2 and God help you if you don't watch my tail!"

I couldn't believe my ears, it was like God asking me to keep an eye on heaven for him! Flying with Douglas, "Cocky" and "Johnnie" was to become the greatest experience of my life and I considered myself quite the most fortunate Sergeant pilot in the RAF.

Why did Bader choose to lead the Wing with one particular squadron? During the Battle of Britain he had always led the Duxford Wing at the head of his own 242 Squadron, and no doubt he therefore assumed it was sound practice always to lead his new Spitfire Wing with the same squadron. In any case, 616 was a squadron he knew from 1940, as it had flown with the Duxford Wing during the latter part of the Battle of Britain. Previously the squadron had been virtually annihilated while flying from Kenley. Between that time and joining Bader at Duxford, 616 received a new CO, Sqn Ldr Howard Frizelle 'Billy' Burton. At Tangmere Burton was to become Bader's right-hand man.

Burton was born on 21 June 1916 at Letchworth, Hertfordshire, the third son of Maj Louis Burton, Royal Artillery, and Mrs Burton of Norwich. Sadly his father was killed in France while on active service during 1917. Educated at Bedford from 1930 to 1934, Burton gained a King's Cadetship to RAF Cranwell with outstandingly high marks. When he passed out in December 1936, Billy was awarded the coveted Cranwell Sword of Honour; the blade is the only one inscribed 'Edward VIII'. From Cranwell,

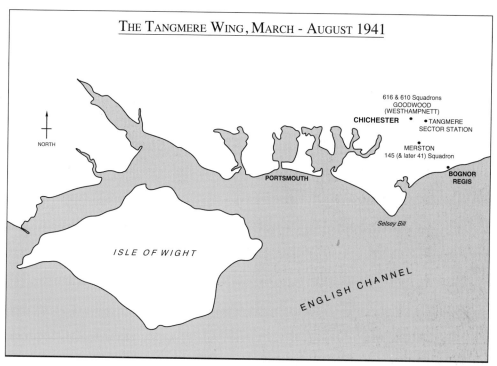

THE TANGMERE WING, MARCH - AUGUST 1941

616 & 610 Squadrons
GOODWOOD
(WESTHAMPNETT)

CHICHESTER ● ● TANGMERE
SECTOR STATION

MERSTON
145 (& later 41) Squadron

NORTH

PORTSMOUTH

BOGNOR
REGIS

Selsey Bill

ISLE OF WIGHT

ENGLISH CHANNEL

Squadron Leader H.F. 'Billy' Burton, CO of 616 Squadron. Note the Squadron Leader's pennant and pilot's black pre-war flying suit.

'Billy' Burton with a Tommy gun. On the left is Flt Lt Gibbs, who evaded and made a 'home run' after being shot down over France.

Plt Off Burton started his operational career with Gloster Gauntlet equipped 46(F) Squadron at Kenley. In November 1937 the squadron moved to Digby in Lincolnshire. There, 46 Squadron's CO, Sqn Ldr Barwell, assessed Burton's ability as follows:

> As a fighter pilot: 'Above the average'.
> As a Pilot-Navigator: 'Above the average'.
> In Air Gunnery: 'Exceptional'.

In June 1938 Billy was promoted to Flying Officer, and the following year he maintained an identical high standard of assessment. In March 1939 he became an Acting Flight Lieutenant, and in June was posted to 12 Group HQ at Hucknall, Nottinghamshire, on Operations Staff Duties. Four days after the declaration of war, however, Flt Lt Burton was posted to Duxford's second Spitfire squadron, No. 66, where he took over 'B' Flight. During the Battle of France Burton shared a Heinkel He 111 on 12 May 1940, and destroyed a Heinkel over Dunkirk on 2 June. On 19 June he shared a Ju 88 over the Channel. The same month he married Jean, only daughter of Air Cdre E.D.M. Robertson CB DFC and Mrs Robertson of Ashtead, Surrey. Exactly one year after war was declared, Burton was promoted to Acting Squadron Leader and took command of 616 Squadron, which was licking its wounds at Coltishall. On 9 September the squadron moved to Kirton as a 'C' unit, but nevertheless provided experienced pilots to fly with the Duxford Wing, led, of course, by Douglas Bader.

Whilst at Kirton, 616 Squadron had, as a 'C' unit, been used as an extension of the OTU process, receiving new pilots direct therefrom and offering further training flights before their postings to fighter squadrons in 11 Group. However, some of these pilots remained with the squadron as part of its front-line strength when it moved to Tangmere, including young men such as 'Johnnie' Johnson, a police inspector's son from Loughborough, Leicestershire, and a graduate in civil engineering; George Mabbett, a farmer's son from Cheltenham, Gloucester; and Philip 'Nip' Hepple, the son of a Royal Flying Corps pilot. These men had been greeted at Kirton by the 'old hands', men like Fg Off Hugh 'Cocky' Dundas, a veteran at 21, and Fg Off 'Buck' Casson, 26. Both had been among the squadron's original pre-war Auxiliary members and had survived the Battle of Britain. On 22 August 1940, however, Dundas was shot down over Dover, probably by JG51's Kommodore, Maj Werner Mölders, narrowly escaping with his life. Wounded, Dundas did not return to the squadron until 13 September, by which time 616 was at Kirton. Before his death in 1995, Grp Capt Sir Hugh Dundas CBE DSO DFC DL RAF Ret'd agreed that this enforced break from operations 'probably saved my life'. 'Buck' Casson was more experienced, having also flown Hurricanes during the Battle of France with 79 Squadron.

Squadron Leader L.H. Casson DFC AFC RAF Ret'd remembers Wg Cdr Bader during the spring of 1941:

> I had first met him at Coltishall on 3 September 1940, when he tried to tick some of us off for having our top buttons undone in true fighter pilot's style. I came to know him briefly during early 1941, when we occasionally joined up with 242 Squadron as a 12 Group Wing flying from either Duxford or Wittering. Of course I came to know him much better at Tangmere from March 1941 onwards. We enjoyed playing golf with Douglas at Goodwood, and at the house where he was billeted with his wife,

A 616 Squadron line-up at Kirton-in-Lindsey. The squadron re-formed there after the Battle of Britain, and many of these young pilots were to fight with Bader's Tangmere Wing. Left to right, back row: n/k, Morton, n/k, n/k, Holden, Heppell, Burton (CO), MacFie, Mabbett, Le Cheminant, n/k, Pietrascovich. Front row: Sellars, n/k, Brewster, Casson, McCairns, Proctor and Jenks.

Above: *Off duty: Colin MacFie, Ken Holden, 'Buck' Casson and 'Cocky' Dundas.*

Left: *Sergeant Bob Morton: 'My mother asked me to have a photograph taken for her, so I did!'*

Thelma, the "Bay House" (known by the pilots as the "Bag House") near Bognor, we carried him to the pool where he swam extremely well. He always wanted company so we often went to his digs for a drink and a chat.

At Tangmere, 616 Squadron's two flight commanders were Flt Lts Ken Holden ('A' Flight) and Colin Macfie ('B' Flight). A solid Yorkshireman, Holden was also an original 616 Squadron Auxiliary who had seen action during Operation *Dynamo* and the Battle of Britain. Also one of the Few, Colin Macfie was just 20 during the spring of 1941.

Sergeant Bob 'Butch' Morton was among the replacement pilots to join 616 Squadron before it arrived at Tangmere; he now remembers:

When we flew south and relieved 65 Squadron at Tangmere, we exchanged our tired old Spitfire Mk IAs for their newer Mk IIAs. Shortly after our arrival, Flight Lieutenant Macfie took "B" Flight for a "recce" over the surrounding countryside to pick out a few landmarks which we could make use of later. After about half an hour, we were crossing the coast when I saw Macfie looking worried as he compared the map in his hand with the ground below. We were heading east. Suddenly my seven months at ITW (Initial Training Wing) paid off. "That's Hastings," I shouted, "We're 50 miles east of base." Macfie looked somewhat relieved and said: "Take us home, Butch", which I did.

At Tangmere we were joined by Wing Commander Bader, who was already something of a legend. My first sight of him was sitting on the radiator of Billy Burton's car holding a shotgun, whilst the CO drove him erratically across the field in pursuit of rabbits!

A few days later, Wing Commander Bader, who always used the radio callsign "Dogsbody", took the whole squadron on a patrol from which we returned rather short of fuel. I was one of the last to make my approach, by which time it was dark. Our petrol gauges were never reliable, and it was no surprise that when I turned crosswind I found that, on blipping the throttle, the engine was dead. Fortunately my circuit, for once, was impeccable, and my glide landed me exactly beside the Chance light, whereupon my propeller, which had previously been windmilling, just stopped dead. I trundled happily down the flarepath and turned off just before I lost my way. Walking back to dispersal, I said casually to the ground-mechanics: "Sorry chaps, you'll have to bring it in yourselves this time!"

At this time I had a coat of arms painted on my Mae West: argent, on a pale azure, three crowns for Hull, on a chief of the second the tail of a Spitfire diving into a cloud; the motto was "Spotto, Squirto, Scrammo", or "I spot, I squirt, I remove myself". It was highly commended by Wing Commander Bader!

Outside "A" Flight's hut appeared a notice:

BADER'S BUS COMPANY
Daily trips to the Continent
RETURN TICKETS ONLY!

The "trip" turned out to be, usually, twice daily, although my season pass was to expire in July 1941.

Throughout this time, Sgt Alan Smith flew regularly in 'Dogsbody' Section as Bader's Red Two. Sir Alan Smith recalls:

Whenever we flew over France on fighter sweeps or escorting bombers, we were always the last to return to base. Mission completed and everyone else going home, Douglas would hang around looking for a Hun to engage so long as we had ammunition and enough fuel to get us back to base.

As soon as we crossed over the English coast, Douglas would slide back his cockpit cover, and out would come his pipe which he lit and puffed away upon contentedly. I could not help reflecting that he was virtually sitting on his petrol tank!

'Johnnie' Johnson, too, remembered Bader smoking while piloting a volatile combination of fuel and ammunition: 'Oh yes, he used to light a match in the cockpit,

"Swan Vestas"; he'd be there puffing away, couldn't see him for smoke sometimes!' Smoking aboard His Majesty's aircraft was not only strictly forbidden, it was also extremely dangerous, but in Bader's case this only served to enhance the growing myth that he was indestructible. Even his wife, Thelma, living at the Bay House with her sister, Jill, came to believe wholeheartedly that the Germans would never get Douglas. When he returned from a sortie over France, Spitfire DB would swoop low overhead. At night, however, Bader slept at Tangmere in the Officers' Mess, 'just to keep in touch'.

As Dave Denchfield has previously observed regarding 610 Squadron, 616 was also serviced by an excellent, largely pre-war-trained groundcrew, most of whom had been with the squadron for some time. Among them was Pat Goodenough:

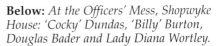
Left: *Sergeant Alan Smith, left, with 616 Squadron's Intelligence Officer, Fg Off 'Spy' Gibbs.*

Below: *At the Officers' Mess, Shopwyke House: 'Cocky' Dundas, 'Billy' Burton, Douglas Bader and Lady Diana Wortley.*

As a young man in the 1930s I was very interested in speed. Whilst (I was) still a schoolboy we used to walk to the main road on a Sunday afternoon to watch a particular chap speed past in an Austin Swallow – 45 mph, always the talking point of the week!

I later became an apprentice at the Doncaster Plant Works, and to see "Gresley Locomotives" travelling through there at 60 mph was really something. Malcolm Campbell was chasing both the land and water speed records at the time, so that was

Above: *At dispersal, Westhampnett: Sqn Ldr Burton, Plt Off Johnson, Fg Off Dundas, Wg Cdr Bader and Sgt Alan Smith. With the exception of Burton, these pilots largely comprised 'Dogsbody' Section throughout the summer of 1941.*

Right: *Pat Goodenough, one of 616 Squadron's stalwart groundcrew.*

followed with great interest. We also used to go and watch Sir Alan Cobham's Flying Circus; the biplanes landed so sedately.

When I joined 616 Squadron we had (Hawker) Hinds and then Gloster Gauntlets. I went to RAF St Athan to be trained on Rolls-Royce engines, and when I returned the squadron had received Spitfires. These landed at 90 mph plus, it was hard to believe that they were possessed of such speed and power. Most of the new airfields appeared to have been built on swamps, as if the aircraft taxied off the concrete runways they just sank in the mud. Then several airmen would drape themselves over the rear fuselage whilst the pilot opened up the throttle, the Spitfire then travelling back to the runway on its tailwheel. Pilots were often in a hurry and sometimes did not stop to let us off. Many an airman had bruises to show for it!

During dogfights which we could see from the ground, we often cheered when we saw aircraft shot down, only to learn later that the casualty was actually one of our own. The Spitfires were constantly modified, it seemed, with such frequency that before we got information about one modification another had already taken its place. Of course we were bombed, and ground staff had to perform such duties as fire pickets, and dawn and dusk security patrols of the airfields, this of course being before formation of the RAF Regiment. All in all they were exciting times, but we only lived from day to day. We lost Spitfires, too, but we received replacements very quickly. I think it was the morale of the pilots which counted most.

An interesting little story concerns the 616 Squadron Intelligence Officer, Flying Officer Gibbs. He had once lived on the continent and every now and again took his bicycle off in the Lysander and disappeared. I said that he must have dropped the bike out over France as he always returned with it wrecked, and I had to help repair it! As a result of this favour, Gibbs gave me an early chit to start my leave. When I was away there was another big raid on Tangmere, 16 were killed and 15 injured. Block Five suffered a direct hit and when I returned I had to salvage my kit and slept on the stairs at Shopwyke House.

Ken Holden and Hugh Dundas examine bomb damage at Tangmere, March 1941.

In April I left 616 Squadron to start a fitter's course at RAF Halton, but I was no hero and played only a very minor role.

George Reid served with 145 Squadron's groundcrew at Tangmere during the Battle of Britain, but soon afterwards joined 616 Squadron:

After 145 Squadron received its Spitfires, I was given the job of spraying on the code letters. Whilst the aircraft were standing on the flight line they were in constant use, so this work often had to be carried out immediately after they returned from a sortie. I was sent off on a Fitter's course, but when I returned 145 Squadron had been sent north for a rest so I joined 616 as this squadron was short of my type of groundcrew. The squadron had only recently moved to Westhampnett and so we slept at Goodwood racecourse until something more permanent could be found. 616 then sent me on a course to Fort Dunlop in Erdington, Birmingham, to study tyres and mixings. I came back a "boffin" on oleo legs and tyres, so my time with 616 Squadron was as a form of undercarriage and tyre inspector. I was not very popular for I wandered around the Flights and aircraft and had the authority to make a Spitfire u/s (unserviceable). All the chaps had to do then was taxi the aircraft over to the blister hangar and the fault would be put right.

When Wing Commander Bader arrived at Tangmere, he was already a legend, there being quite a myth building up around him. Whilst with 616 Squadron I came into direct contact with him and learned to both fear and dislike the fellow. He had a filthy mouth and lacked patience. He was a show-off and the most pompous chap I had ever met. My last recollection of Wing Commander Bader was when his Spitfire's wheels would not lock up correctly. There was a sweep to be flown at 3 p.m. and by this time it was already 2 of the clock. He came over in his car, stomped up to the Chiefy Sergeant and myself and raged, turning on high powered filth from the mouth, and thumped his car bonnet with a stick. I actually thought that he would strike Chiefy with that cane. I dived back under the Spitfire and fortunately off he went! In the end he settled for a new Spitfire just delivered by a female ATA (Air Transport Auxiliary) ferry pilot.

Flying Officer Gibbs and pushbike. Could this have been the cycle repaired by Pat Goodenough?

616 Squadron Dispersal, Westhampnett. Left to right: Sqn Ldr Burton, Wg Cdr Bader, Flt Lt Dundas, Plt Off Heppell.

Perhaps Sgt Harold Clowes, Tangmere's Link Instructor, overheard the same incident: 'I never actually met Wing Commander Bader, but once I heard him cursing the groundcrew in a nearby hangar'.

Squadron Leader Burton's 21-year-old wife, Jean, was a 'camp follower', and in 1995, now Mrs Jean Allom, revived her own indelible memories of 1941:

> Now, looking back over half a century, I realise that there is always the temptation to view the events of that summer through rose-tinted spectacles, but even allowing for this and the undisputed effect of time on one's memory, I cannot reflect upon the summer of 1941 as anything but a succession of beautiful English sunny days, such as one would long for in peacetime.
>
> However, in the wartime, from an RAF wife's point of view, it would prove to be the reverse. After the gallant defensive fighting of the previous summer, 1941 was to be the start of Fighter Command taking the war to the enemy, and these sweeps over France and the occupied territories were mostly conducted from airfields in southern England, amongst them Tangmere. Thus nearly every day the wonderful weather presented yet another chance of risk to life or limb for my husband, so for me bad weather with a day without flying was something to be thankful for.
>
> 616 was one of three Spitfire squadrons comprising the Tangmere Wing, led by Douglas Bader, and was also the squadron with which he chose to fly. Douglas and Billy were great friends despite the gap in age and seniority, but no doubt their mutual Cranwell background played a part in this. On 9 May 1941 616 moved to Westhampnett. I had spent a very cold and snowy winter up at Kirton and so was delighted to be back in warmer climes and to find lodgings in a large country house in Lavant; from the bottom of the garden I had a ringside seat of the squadron taking off and landing. I could thus approximately gauge the time 616 would return from a

sweep and station myself in the garden anxiously and hopefully to await the return of Billy's Spitfire, 'QJ-K'. Although this was to prove a somewhat stressful occupation, the relief when I saw the familiar aircraft letters landing was more than worth it.

Most of 616 Squadron's pilots were young bachelors, and as it was a South Yorkshire Auxiliary squadron very few of those who were married had brought their wives down south with them. It was a strange feeling at the tender age of 21 to be the CO's wife, as before the war officers were rarely allowed to marry or be eligible for a Marriage Allowance either before the age of 30 or attaining the rank of Squadron Leader. However, during that summer, hardly any of the normal duties of a CO's wife fell on my youthful shoulders. The sole occasion was when one of the older 616 Squadron pilots did not return from operations. His wife was one of the few at Tangmere and so, feeling extremely nervous, I was despatched by Billy to offer such support and words of comfort as I was able. All I can recall is that the wife in question was naturally very upset and overwrought, and I fear that I was probably not of much help. I was very pleased to discover later, however, that her husband had actually safely landed in France and cleverly evaded capture, making his way back to England via the escape route through Spain.

I was, of course, liable to be called up for war work, but as luck would have it I was invited to drive a mobile canteen in the Goodwood area. The canteen not only catered for the needs of the many army units in the area, largely ack-ack posts, but also to Westhampnett airfield, which of course meant visiting 616 Squadron which I would otherwise have been unable to do!

I had already met Douglas Bader and his wife, Thelma, the previous summer in Norfolk, but during the summer of 1941 got to know them really well, largely due to their generous open-house entertaining at the Bay House, Aldwick, in the evenings to which Billy and I, together with other members of the Wing, were often invited. It was a friendship which lasted until the Baders' deaths and one which I valued greatly.

Owing to the demanding routine of operational flying day after day, organised social events were a rarity. Only one such evening stands out in my memory, a dance held at Shopwyke House, the Officers' Mess, when hospitality was of a pre-war standard. I recall thinking as the band played: "We'll gather Lilacs" that the atmosphere was reminiscent of the famous ball in Brussels on the eve of Waterloo; behind all the glitter, the reality of war was uncomfortably close as the Wing would soon be in action again.

The rest of the summer passed swiftly by, Billy with little respite from Ops; my driving the mobile canteen and snatching what little time we could together.

In 1995 Air Vice-Marshal 'Johnnie' Johnson CB CBE DSO** DFC*, who in the spring of 1941 was a recently commissioned Pilot Officer in 616 Squadron and with just a shared damaged Do 17 to his credit, recalled his impressions of Douglas Bader:

I suppose it was fairly awe-inspiring really, we were Pilot Officers and so on and he was older, Wing Commander DSO DFC, legendary, but he treated us all as equals; he was a great leader. Of course we faced that summer with the prospect of a renewed Battle of Britain-type bombardment, but Douglas would rub his hands together and say: "Let the buggers come across, we've got the Wing and the cannon now, bloody good show old boy, and if they don't come then we'll go over there, won't we?" To say that he was enthusiastic was an understatement. He'd come stumping into dispersal and say to Billy Burton: "What are we doing today then, Billy?", and Billy might respond: "Well the Form 'D' (Operational Order) has come

Above: *Pilot Officer 'Johnnie' Johnson, a genuine hero straight out of the* Boy's Own Paper!

Left: *Squadron Leader 'Billy' Burton and Wg Cdr Douglas Bader at Westhampnett in 1941.*

through, Sir, but we're not on it. The other Wings are but not us." Bader would say: "Right, we'll see about that, I'll have a bloody word with L-M!". And then he would ring the AOC and, lo and behold, we would be on Ops!

The Spitfires which Bader flew himself were on charge with 616 Squadron. His first seven flights as Wing Leader, between 19 and 25 March 1941, were in 'QJ-A', 'QJ-B',

Squadron Leader Burton, Flt Lt Dundas, Flt Lt MacFie, Wg Cdr Bader and Plt Off Johnson. Note the trousers worn by Dundas and Johnson, the first issue of 'Battledress'.

Bader's first Tangmere Spitfire, Mk IIA P7666.

'QJ-D', and 'QJ-J'. However, on 27 March he soared aloft in Spitfire Mk IIA P7966, practising aerobatics. This Spitfire had been presented to the Air Ministry under the auspices of Lord Beaverbrook's 'Spitfire Fund', enthusiasm for which gripped the nation, particularly during 1940 and 1941. Called *Manxman*, it was coded 'DB', the

Engineers install the new Kodak colour cine-gun camera into Bader's Spitfire Mk IIA, P7666. Note the caricature of Hitler being kicked in the backside by a flying boot, identical to the nose art which adorned Bader's Hurricane in 1940.

Left: *The Kodak camera installed.*

Right: *Another photograph indicating the nose art on Bader's Spitfire Mk IIA. From left: Sgt Jeff West (NZ), Sgt Brewer, Sgt Mabbett, and Plt Off Heppell. Brewer and Mabbett were killed in action during 1941; Heppell died in the late 1980s.*

Wing Leaders having adopted the practice of carrying their initials on their aircraft for ease of identification in the air. Additionally the aircraft proudly bore the Wing Commander's rank pennant, painted on the fuselage slightly in front of and below the windscreen on both sides. The Spitfire was finished in the standard green and brown camouflage on the upper surfaces and had 'sky' undersurfaces, the day-fighter band around the rear fuselage being added in April 1941. The spinner was also sky.

In the summer of 1995, however, I made an intriguing discovery regarding Wg Cdr Bader's Spitfire when I visited Norman Jenkins. Before the war, Norman had been in the 16 mm film-making business, and was then commissioned into the RAF as a Photographic Officer. In July 1941 Flt Lt Jenkins was tasked with modifying a Kodak cine-gun camera, the first to carry colour film. At some time that month he visited Westhampnett and oversaw the fitting of that camera to Bader's Spitfire, and this activity he photographed. When I first saw those snapshots I was astonished, as there, on the port engine cowling below the exhaust stubs, was painted a caricature of Hitler being kicked in the backside by a flying boot. An identical motif had adorned Bader's 242 Squadron Hurricane during the Battle of Britain, and many well-known photographs show it on that aircraft. That Wg Cdr Bader's Spitfire carried such 'nose art' was a revelation, as every painting, line illustration and model hitherto produced has omitted it. Norman's photograph, published for the first time here, was apparently unique, but 'Johnnie' Johnson's personal photograph album revealed more snapshots of the artwork. He recalled: 'It was a pretty awful thing really, just painted by an erk!' Sir Alan Smith and 'Buck' Casson were able to confirm that the marking was not applied to all 616 Squadron Spitfires and was definitely only on Bader's aircraft.

In July and August 1941 the Wing's squadrons exchanged their Spitfire Mk IIAs and Bs for the Mk VB, with its new engine, two 20 mm cannon and four 0.303 in Brownings. Bader, however, believed that the powerful cannon would encourage pilots to shoot from too far away. He was wrong on this point, but typically he would not be swayed. It has been said that Douglas Bader would not tolerate opposition to his own ideas, so it was just as well that most of his ideas were sound.

The first squadron to receive the new Mk VB was 145 Squadron, as it flew as top cover between 24,000 ft and 30,000 ft, usually up-sun but just below the condensation-trail level so that any aircraft above would immediately betray their presence. Next to receive the new Spitfire was 610 Squadron, flying medium cover, behind and to the left at 22,000 ft, and finally it re-equipped 616 Squadron, the lowest of the Wing's squadrons in its battle formation, at 20,000 ft.

Bader still refused to fly the new cannon-armed Spitfire Mk VB, insisting instead upon flying Mk VA W3185, which enjoyed the benefits of the new Merlin engine but retained the original eight machine-guns. This particular Spitfire was taken on charge by 145 Squadron on 30 June 1941, its Form 78 (aircraft movement record) indicating a move on 28 July to 41 Squadron and thence to 616 Squadron on the same day. This aircraft was to become Bader's personal mount, also bearing the code 'DB', but whether or not it carried the Hitler motif is unknown. The only known photographs of 'DB' coded Spitfires fail to show the aircraft serial numbers, so it is impossible to identify whether they depict P7966 or W3185, there being no external features to distinguish the Mk IIA from the Mk VA. The problem of trying to differentiate between P7966 and W3185 is further confounded by the fact that Norman's photographs were taken on an unspecified date in July 1941, the same month that

A unique snapshot encapsulating the spirit of youthful optimism prevalent in Fighter Command during 1941. Left to right: Flt Lt Denys Gillam (visiting 616 Squadron, with whom he had served in 1940), Sgt McCairns, Plt Off Heppell, Sgt West, Sgt Brewer, Squadron clerk, Plt Off Johnson. With pipes: Sqn Ldr Burton and Wg Cdr Bader.

Flight Lieutenant Colin MacFie, Flt Lt Hugh 'Cocky' Dundas, Plt Off Phillip 'Nip' Heppell, and Plt Off 'Johnnie' Johnson. Again, note that Johnson wears Battledress and Dundas a black pre-war flying suit.

The 1st XI? 'A' Flight of 616 Squadron. Back row, left to right: Plt Off Johnson, Sgt Mabbett, Sgt Scott, Sgt McCairns. Front: Flt Lt Dundas, Plt Off Heppell, and Sgt Smith.

Bader changed his Spitfire. However, he was only to fly the latter aircraft for two weeks, and on balance I suspect that the photographs depict P7966.

It is also worth mentioning the confusion concerning 616 Squadron's code letters at this time. Upon the outbreak of war a secret instruction was issued ordering all squadrons to change their code letters. A number failed to comply, however, among them 616, which had used 'QJ' since April 1939. Although 92 Squadron had been allocated the letters 'GR', through an oversight these letters were also given to 301 (Polish) Squadron, and 92 Squadron was therefore instructed to adopt 'QJ'. This was another oversight, as someone had obviously overlooked the fact that this code was already in use by 616. Therefore, throughout the Battle of Britain and well into 1941, these two Spitfire squadrons used the same code letters. This has caused enormous confusion for latter-day students of the period, photographs of 'QJ'-coded Spitfires only being positively identified through checking the aircraft's serial number against the relevant Form 78. Unfortunately few researchers have gone to such lengths, so a multitude of incorrectly captioned photographs have been published over the years. On 25 June 1941, however, the Air Ministry resolved the matter by allocating 616 Squadron the letters 'YQ'.

When 616 Squadron arrived at Tangmere, 610 'County of Chester' Squadron had been in residence at Tangmere satellite Westhampnett since 15 December 1940. Sir Denis Crowley-Milling remembers:

> Douglas Bader found 610 Squadron at Westhampnett in poor shape and low morale. He ... promoted Ken Holden, from 616, to command, and both Flight Lieutenant Lee-Knight and myself from 242 to be his flight commanders. He had already taken Stan Turner from 242 to command 145 at Tangmere. From then on one never looked back: sweeps over Northern France daily, very often twice daily in fact, escorting a few bombers, often Stirlings, to ensure a German reaction. I felt rather sorry for the

Sergeant Peter Ward-Smith of 610 Squadron at 'readiness', Westhampnett, 1941.

Above: *Bullseye! To occupy them at dispersal, the Tangmere Wing pilots were issued with bows and arrows. Ron Rayner recalled that when they were produced the groundcrews made themselves scarce! Here 610 Squadron pilots assess their results; Sgt Peter Ward-Smith at extreme right.*

Pilots of 610 Squadron at 'readiness'.

'A' Flight of 610 Squadron. Ronnie Hamlyn is standing, centre, and Peter Ward-Smith is kneeling at extreme right.

Stirlings operating in daylight, a dramatic change from night ops, attracting all the flak! As usual, Douglas Bader maintained a running commentary from the time we approached the French coast to the time we left on return. Also coming over the ether as we saw the French coast approaching was the voice of Stan Turner: "Okay, chaps, put your corks in!", or in other words, "Now is the time to look out for German fighters but don't be scared!" The Germans listening on the ground to this radio chatter must have thought it an order to activate some special equipment! After the war, in fact, I learned from one of our pilots who had been shot down that during his interrogation the German asked: "What does 'put your corks in' mean?" Needless to say, we both had a good laugh!

There were, of course, numerous encounters with Me 109s, mainly from Galland's JG26 based around St Omer. Although it now appears that the losses were not actually in our favour, for us it was the first time we had taken the fight to the Germans in a big way, so we were very inspired by it all and our morale was very high.

Flight Lieutenant Peter Ward-Smith also recalls 610 Squadron, with which he flew as a Sergeant pilot:

When Wing Commander Bader took over at Tangmere we realised that something was in the offing, but never this air offensive on the Big Wing scale.

Our take-off point for one of the first attacks was the small airfield behind Beachy Head. We stooged around waiting for other squadrons to join up, then the whole mass headed for France covering Blenheim bombers detailed to knock hell out of the shipping in Brest, although of their success no-one would say.

At first there was little reaction from our enemy, or so we thought, but on this and subsequent sweeps one or even two of the squadron would fail to return. We put this down to high-flying Me 109s diving through the formation and picking of the odd aircraft as they went.

On one occasion we flew through intense flak which rocked my Spitfire. I remember looking back and seeing the whole sky filled with dirty brown puffs. I remember thinking: "Christ, have we really just flown through that lot!" Another time I saw a 109 formating alongside me. I got behind him but realised that to open fire would spatter my pals. When the 109 broke away I followed him down, against strict instructions of course, but could not catch up and lost him near the ground. I met intense flak and not finding any other suitable target I high-tailed it north and eventually hit the Channel in great danger of running out of fuel. Unable to reach an airfield, I landed on the Dymchurch Marshes. It was deemed impossible to take-off, so I had to make my way back to base by train.

Sergeant Edward William Merriman, who has, however, 'known no other name than Peter,' joined 610 Squadron at Westhampnett in April 1941. Air Commodore E.W. Merriman DFM MBE OBE CBE now recalls:

We NCO pilots frequented the "Unicorn" pub in Chichester, and returned from some of our sorties thereto with various road signs which then littered the garden of "Fishers Cottage" (our billet) until retrieved by the police, when the whole thing would just repeat itself. I remember that one day Tony Gaze produced a shotgun with which he blasted huge holes in the metal stovepipes attached to some outdoor boilers. On seeing this, Joe Doley asked if the shot would penetrate his steel helmet, to which Gaze replied: "I don't know, put it on and we'll see!" He did, and a huge dent appeared on the helmet, beneath which was a very stunned Joe Doley! There was also a troop of light tanks based on the airfield, commanded by a Lieutenant,

Sergeant E.W. 'Peter' Merriman of 610 Squadron.

which we used to drive with great enthusiasm. I remember also that we used to take the cordite from 0.303 in and 20 mm rounds to make bombs and rockets, albeit without much success. Finally, I recall that often upon returning from a sortie we would land at Beachy Head, where there was a sort of NAAFI hut where we could buy oranges.

Among the 610 Squadron ground crew was LAC Cliff Airey, a Flight Mechanic (Engines). In 1995 Mr C.F. Airey recalled:

My role was a lesser one, but I am nevertheless proud of my association with 610 Squadron. I felt that I had to respond to your appeal for help as your advertisement revived proud memories of having been personally involved with so many heroes.

Left: *Sergeants Doley and Horner inspect badly damaged 610 Squadron Spitfire R6599, which suffered a flying accident while based at Acklington.*

Right: *Sergeant Merriman and his groundcrew at the Sergeants' Mess, 'Fishers Cottage'.*

One thing I seem to recall about Wing Commander Bader is that he said polished buttons glinted far too brightly. As a result orders came round that there was to be no more button cleaning. Eventually our battledresses were fitted with black plastic buttons, an unimportant point but perhaps of interest.

I found it such a thrill when you replied to my letter and stirred my memory by mentioning names like "Johnnie" Johnson and "Crow" Milling. It reminded me of those dispersal days on readiness, awaiting the scramble call, having the parachutes hanging on the wing for the pilot to run into, starting up and generally helping to ensure that your aircraft got away okay in the shortest time possible. Usually they went off in a line of three across the grass. Then the waiting, the hoping and relief when "your" Spitfire returned. The inspections and checks I well recall, giving particular attention to see if the throttle had broken the locking wire to go "through the gate", if so resulting in further work on the Rolls-Royce Merlin 45 engine before the aircraft could be returned to service.

All of my rambling thoughts at the age of 74 are insignificant when compared to the pilots' exploits, but having failed to obtain my pilot's course on entry into the RAF, I nevertheless was, and still am, very proud to have been a part of 610 Squadron at Westhampnett and Tangmere.

Harry Jacks served with 610 Squadron as an Administration Clerk. He particularly recalled Bader:

Whilst 610 Squadron operated out of Westhampnett, there were a couple of events which caused Wing Commander Bader to blow his "stack" and use very strong language to senior officers at Group HQ. On one occasion a signal was received ordering the Wing Commander to exchange his Vauxhall staff car for a smaller 8 hp model, and, second, another signal arrived ordering him to return to Group inventory one of his two aircraft, either his black-painted night-flying Hurricane or his Spitfire. It is my recollection that neither instruction was acted upon by the time of Wing Commander Bader's capture!

The longest-serving fighter squadron in the Tangmere Sector at this time was 145 Squadron, which, as we have seen, had already flown with distinction from Westhampnett during the Battle of Britain. After resting as a 'C' unit in Scotland since 31 August 1940, on 9 October the squadron returned to Tangmere. Sergeant Frank Twitchett joined the squadron in December; in 1995, Flt Lt F.J. Twitchett recalled:

I arrived at Tangmere in December 1940, having been posted from 229 Squadron

Sergeant W.J. 'Johnny' Johnson and Sgt Frank Twitchett, both of 145 Squadron, at Merston.

where I had commenced my operational period of service three months previously. The squadron at that time was commanded by Squadron Leader J.R.A. Peel DFC and was flying Hurricanes. In January 1941 Squadron Leader Peel was posted (he became Wing Leader at Kenley in March 1941), and was replaced by Squadron Leader W.J. "Jack" Leather DFC who oversaw our conversion to Spitfires, he having flown this type with 611 Squadron during the Battle of Britain.

Between December 1940 and February 1941 our role remained almost entirely defensive, and soon after receiving Spitfire Mk Is we converted again to the Spitfire Mk II. In March 1941, having fully converted to the Spitfire by that time, we had our first success when a section of aircraft, of which I was a member, intercepted and destroyed a Ju 88 off Selsey Bill. We also began to do Channel sweeps, although these were largely ineffective as they were purely fighter operations and the Luftwaffe very sensibly remained on the ground, not intercepting aircraft which posed no threat unless engaged. Wing Commander Bader arrived in March 1941, however, and by April things were really starting to happen. Shortly after Wing Commander Bader arrived, Squadron Leader Leather was posted and in April our new CO was the Canadian, Squadron Leader P.S. "Stan" Turner DFC, who had been a flight commander in Bader's 242 Squadron during the Battle of Britain. We carried out our first bomber escort, to Cherbourg, on 17 April, and at around the same time received a new flight commander, Flight Lieutenant C.I.R. Arthur, another Canadian and also of Bader's former 242 Squadron.

Throughout May 1941 we undertook several sorties up and down the Channel, attempting to flush out some opposition. In June 1941, with the Wing in position and with 145 Squadron now established at Merston, whilst both 616 and 610 were based at Westhampnett, the sweeps started in earnest and we often swept to Dunkirk, Calais, Boulogne, usually taking Blenheims. On one occasion, 18 June, we even took three Stirlings. Later, the Forêt de Licques was bombed and on this occasion we lost Sergeants Turnbull and Palmer. The average per pilot was two sweeps daily, and this, you can appreciate, became a little wearing on the nerves. We flew to such targets as Lille, Hazebrouck, Béthune, Le Touquet, St Omer, and even one to Knocke on the Belgian coast. That was particularly worrying as we escorted six Blenheims to bomb an oil tanker which had anchored just off the coast and was covered by six flak ships. Four of the six Blenheims were lost and two squadrons of Me 109s attacked us. The whole operation and dogfight took place about 500 ft above the sea!

Merston was a landing ground with no runways or living accommodation, so we were billeted in a farmhouse on the far corner of the airfield. Two years ago I tried to find this building, only to discover that it had been demolished and a new, rather nice four-bedroom house had been built in its place. Going back to our old farmhouse, we had one airman who was a general potter-around, keep the place clean type of chap, and a cook to feed us. His job was to feed the 11 or 12 NCO pilots whom we normally had on the squadron strength. The conditions were such that, bearing in mind that this was a private house with fairly small rooms, we lived about four to a room, so your accommodation consisted of just a bed and a very narrow steel wardrobe in which you could put some clothes. Mostly the beds were unmade, you fell out of them in the morning then got back into them at night! The general state of living was pretty squalid, but we coped all right. We used a local pub right on the corner of the airfield itself called the "Walnut Tree"; this became a great favourite with all the squadron, irrespective of rank, and we tended to congregate there after getting released at night. Assuming, of course, that the pub was open and had supplies of beer, the landlord did a brisk trade.

Time off was erratic; it could be given at short notice if the weather deteriorated, but to think in terms of a day off in a week's time was just impossible. The idea was

Pilots of 145 Squadron at 'readiness; left to right: Grant, Johnson, Scott and Sabourin.

that when you were on the airfield you were available for duty at any time. Quite often you would be called to go on a sweep in the morning, only to find that although you were not required for the rest of the day, you were still expected to remain on the airfield and not clear off into Chichester or any of the surrounding towns. Days were generally very long, in June of course we were on the longest days, compounded by Double Summer Time, so that it was not uncommon to come on to readiness at 4 a.m., and still be on the airfield until perhaps 10 p.m. You could be warned for a sweep in the morning, as I have said, or in the morning find that you were not required for sweeping until later in the afternoon. All this hanging about, most of which was spent half asleep in chairs or even on the old camp beds which we had in the dispersal hut, was a bit wearing on the nerves to say the least. Another problem was that you could often be strapped in the cockpit and ready to go on a sweep only for the sortie to be put back for one hour, or even two, and the instructions usually were to remain in the cockpit until a further signal told us to start our engines and begin taxiing. You can appreciate that this also caused a lot of wear and tear on the nerves, particularly as in the summertime you could be sitting there in full flying kit, out in the hot sun on the middle of the airfield.

We could apply for leave, if we were due days off, and under those circumstances we could usually expect for it to be granted. Even that was not completely secure, however, there were occasions when people were told to delay their leave by a few days, for example if we were working in conditions like a limited number of pilots, but by and large leave was granted when requested. Days off, however, again as I have said, were a different matter, largely dependent upon weather conditions preventing flying and very precious indeed.

We had a first-class CO in Stan Turner, who was a craggy Canadian who stood no nonsense from anybody but treated all his pilots, regardless of rank, with absolute fairness. I, for one, had much admiration for him. The feeling that we were going on to the offensive ourselves gave everyone a great fillip in the sense that we had finished having our backs to the wall and were finally going to deal out some of the punishment which we felt Jerry richly deserved. Perhaps if we had looked forward

Left: *Squadron Leader Stan Turner DFC, 145 Squadron's CO, photographed in the Middle East in 1942.*

Right: *Dave Horne, right, and Harry Patenal, both members of 145 Squadron's groundcrew, at Merston in 1941.*

to the enormous efforts of the couple of years following 1941, we might have seen life a little differently. A very good friend of mine once summed up the Non-stop Offensive by saying that at that point in time we were sure that we would win the war, but were not sure how; sooner or later we would prevail and emerge victorious. Fortunately for us his prophecy came true.

Such, then, was life at Tangmere from March 1941 onwards, when Bader became Wing Commander (Flying). The three Spitfire squadrons, 145, 610 and 616, were to

Drew and Pattison, the crew of Frank Twitchett's Spitfire, 'SO-J'.

Frank Twitchett's 'War Horse', P7990.

Above: *Flight Lieutenant Newlin's 145 Squadron Spitfire. This pilot was killed in action on 6 July 1941, in another aircraft (see Appendix).*

Below: *A rare air-to-air snapshot taken by Frank Twitchett, depicting 145 Squadron's Sgt Johnson aloft from Merston in 1941.*

Tangmere's popular station commander during the Bader era: Group Captain A.B. Woodhall, who had already controlled Bader's Duxford Wing in 1940, became the fighter controller par excellence of the war. Previous authors have stated that 'Woody' was a Great War RFC pilot but in fact this is not so; he made his first flight with the FAA in 1925!

remain together until 28 July 1941, when 41 Squadron relieved 145 at Merston (the arrival of 41 Squadron will be examined in the War Diary chapter of this book).

Possibly the most interesting thing arising from an overall Wing viewpoint is how Bader quickly began gathering 'his' men about him, with Ken Holden being promoted to command 610 Squadron and Stan Turner being brought in from 242 to lead 145. In addition, both Charles Bush and Denis Crowley-Milling, who had also flown with Bader's 242 Squadron, became flight commanders with 610 Squadron; Flt Lt Charles Arthur, another Canadian who had joined 242 during the winter of 1940, became a flight commander with 145 Squadron. Nevertheless, it is not unreasonable for any captain to choose his own lieutenants, and clearly Douglas Bader wished to impress his own personality and style of leadership upon his pilots straight away.

During the Battle of Britain, Duxford's Station Commander and Chief Controller was Wg Cdr A.B. Woodhall. Bader and 'Woody' had developed quite a rapport during 1940, and the latter, not only supported his subordinate's Big Wing theory but also that of allowing the leader in the air to make many of his own decisions, as opposed to being inflexibly tied to instructions from the ground. 'Woody' established a special bond of understanding between himself on the ground and those in the air, as not all controllers were able to do. In April 1941 this partnership was to resume when Grp Capt A.B. Woodhall OBE became Station Commander of RAF Tangmere, a posting and promotion no doubt engineered by Leigh-Mallory, who wanted his old team back together. For Bader's Spitfire pilots the monocled 'Woody' was to become a popular figure. Over France his steady, unruffled voice in the pilots' headphones would inspire confidence and assurance, giving encouragement and advice when required. He would constantly monitor changing weather conditions which could hamper the Wing's withdrawal, such as headwinds or approaching low cloud which might shroud the British airfields. When the Spitfires landed the Group Captain was always waiting at Westhampnett to discuss the action with Bader and his squadron commanders, but nonetheless had a friendly word for the new boys. In the Mess, Woodhall was often at the centre of boisterous parties, playing an accordion or saxophone with some talent. He was to become the most outstanding fighter controller of the Second World War.

Clearly, by the spring of 1941, the Tangmere Wing was already taking on a new identity with which to play as the 'away team' during the forthcoming 'season'.

The Tangmere Wing's radio callsign became 'Greenline Bus', from which the unofficial 'Bader's Bus Company' was derived. Tangmere Control became 'Beetle'. Bader was to operate his squadrons in a fashion similar to that of Duxford days; there was no forming up over the airfield, squadrons would slot into their allocated positions as the Wing progressed outbound. The usual practice would then be for the

Wing to rendezvous with bombers over Beachy Head, codenamed 'Diamond'. Ron Rayner remembers: 'There would be this mass of Spitfires orbiting Beachy Head, going round and round in circles over the English coast until everyone was together. Then Bader would say: "Okay, we're going", and the Beehive would then proceed across the Channel to France.'

The position of the sun was critical, as indeed it had been for the Germans during the Battle of Britain, and this dictated the direction and route of attacks. During the morning the Beehive would try to cross the French coast, both in and outward bound, in the north-east, near Gravelines, but in the afternoon it would cross further to the south-west, near Boulogne or Le Touquet, the latter codenamed 'Golf Course' after the upmarket resort's famous course. Between 11:00 and 14:00 hrs, however, the sun was high and therefore favoured the Germans, flying from such bases as St Omer, the 'Big Wood'. The French coast was a dangerous flak belt, the excellent German 88mm guns banging away at the RAF formations passing inland. As with the 1940 Big Wing operations, when combat started the Wing was split up. Standing Orders were issued, however, that, if separated and alone over France, a pilot should head for home immediately and attempt to join up with other friendly aircraft, there being safety in numbers.

In the Tangmere Operations Room were the WAAF plotters, the 'Beauty Chorus', who pushed counters representing the squadrons across a map of southern England and northern France. A Tannoy system enabled them to share the action when battle was joined. However, on occasions Grp Capt Woodhall felt obliged to turn off the sound! Among the offenders was Wg Cdr Bader, as 'Johnnie' Johnson recalls: 'Well Douglas was very "salty", you know, always "effing and blinding". Woodhall would shout up and say: "Come on, Douglas, I've got WAAFs down here," and Bader would just reply: "Oh, it's all right, I'll come and see 'em and apologise!"'

Bader appears to have been a swashbuckling, buccaneer-like character, on occasions semi-humorous but perhaps with a somewhat bloodthirsty outlook. In fairness, however, such qualities were exactly what were required in war, and morale in the Westhampnett-based Spitfire squadrons soared. At Merston, however, this was not necessarily the case. Frank Twitchett makes an interesting observation from Merston's viewpoint:

We had a first-class CO in Stan Turner, but I cannot say the same for Wing Commander Bader. Obviously we admired the man tremendously, but he did create problems through persistently basing himself at Westhampnett and flying solely with 616 Squadron. We very rarely saw him at all. In fact, despite having been with 145 for its entire tour at Tangmere in 1941, I can only recall having seen him twice.

Ron Rayner, who arrived at Tangmere when 41 Squadron relieved 145 in July 1941, agrees:

At Merston we rarely saw Wing Commander Bader. He used to come stomping into dispersal to give us a pep-talk, saying: "Don't go off on your own, do what I say and you'll be all right". I can still see him now, pipe in mouth, gently rocking from side to side so as to retain his balance. He would definitely have created more team spirit if he had not led solely with 616. For us, the most important thing was the squadron, and our own squadron CO, not the Wing or its leader.

'Johnnie' Johnson also observed:

Because Douglas Bader always flew at the head of 616 Squadron, our CO, Billy

Sergeant Ron Rayner of 41 Squadron at Merston in 1941. His newspaper headline appropriately reads: 'Bombs on a Nazi Aerodrome'.

Burton, was unhappy as he never got to lead his own squadron. I do not think it was necessary for Douglas to do this. Later in the war, when I was a Wing Leader, I flew with all of my squadrons by rotation, although I liked to keep the same No. 2 in each one. It would definitely have been better for the Tangmere Wing generally if Douglas had done this too.

Sir Denis Crowley-Milling says:

Squadron Leader Burton was certainly fed up on occasions as he was never given the opportunity to lead his own squadron, Douglas Bader always led it and he always wanted Dundas and Johnson with him. I can understand both sides – Bader wanted pilots with him with whom he was thoroughly familiar in combat, and they with him, whilst Billy Burton, a Squadron Leader, never had the status of that rank. You could say that he tried "desperately" to persuade D.B. to lead each of the three squadrons in turn, i.e. with different pilots round him on each operation, but Burton failed for obvious reasons and it must have got him down. You must know the pilots you lead and depend on, both on the ground and in the air. Having said all that, at no time was there any air of mutiny as suggested by Air Chief Marshal "Bing" Cross in his book.

The foregoing accounts provide a view of life in the Tangmere Sector, and of Douglas Bader as the Wing Leader. We now have some idea of how the Wing operated and the conditions under which its personnel lived and worked. Next, to understand the air battles of 1941 fully, we must look at the enemy. Across the Channel waited young Germans who loved flying equally; the Luftwaffe, too, had its heroes.

CHAPTER FOUR

Der Kanaljäger

Numerous books have been published about the 1939–45 air war, but most concentrate on one side or the other. I consider it essential that a balanced overview of events should be provided, and believe that to gain a full understanding of any military situation the combatant or student must have a sound knowledge of the enemy. Having said that, it is surprising how little the RAF pilots actually knew about their German adversaries, whom they certainly respected. For example, above the fireplace in Wg Cdr David Cox DFC's home is not a painting of a Spitfire, which one might expect this member of Churchill's Few to display, but one of Adolf Galland's Me 109F. As David said: 'Why not? They were damned good.' Many Fighter Command survivors are now keen to learn more about their erstwhile enemies, whom they often greet today as fellow enthusiasts at various aviation events. At a recent branch meeting of the Aircrew Association I was invited to give a presentation; the subject, at the members' request, was the Luftwaffe! This chapter, therefore, provides background information on the Luftwaffe day-fighter force with whom the Tangmere Wing clashed on frequent occasions over France during 1941, facilitating a better understanding of both the War Diary and Conclusion of this book.

In the wake of the First World War, the victorious Allies determined that Germany would never again rise to military prominence. Consequently the Treaty of Versailles, signed by Germany in 1919, significantly reduced the sizes of both its army and navy, in addition to prohibiting the manufacture and possession of submarines, and banned the air corps completely. Restrictions were even placed on the engine size and weight of German civil aircraft. Despite this, however, the German aviation industry later produced many designs which, though ostensibly civil, revealed many military characteristics to the knowledgeable observer. While such machines became the backbone of the new Luftwaffe, the training of personnel without arousing the suspicions of watchful nations presented considerable difficulties. In 1923 the Reichswehr-Ministerium, or Defence Ministry, made a secret agreement with the Soviet Government which provided training facilities for German air and ground crews in Russia.

Hitler revealed the new Luftwaffe to a disbelieving world in 1935. Just one year later the German Wehrmacht fought for the first time since 1918, on the side of the fascist General Franco in the Spanish Civil War. By early 1937 a complete German expeditionary force, the Condor Legion, had been assembled to fight in Spain. Commanded by Gen Hugo Sperrle, it included a fully integrated tactical air force with fighter, bomber, and ground-attack units supported by transport, army liaison and reconnaissance units. The Legion's fighter complement was Jagdgruppe 88, comprising four Staffeln (each equivalent to an RAF squadron) of Heinkel biplanes. J88's pilots were successful in the Madrid area, but later, when operating over the northern front, they encountered fierce opposition from the Loyalists, flying Soviet supplied machines. In April 1937 the 2nd Staffel of J88 was the first to receive the new Messerschmitt Me 109B-2 monoplane fighter. This new machine swiftly dominated

Spitfires of 610 Squadron flying close formation aerobatics; a photograph which perfectly illustrates the useless Fighter Command 'vic' formation.

the Spanish sky and began escorting Heinkel bombers on high-altitude raids, the biplane fighters being relegated to ground-attack in support of the army.

To distribute as much combat experience as possible throughout the Luftwaffe, units and personnel were frequently rotated. Thus, on 24 May 1937, Oblt Werner Mölders replaced Oblt Adolf Galland as Staffelkapitän of 3/J88. These two officers were to become synonymous with the excellence of German air fighting. By July the whole of J88 was equipped with the new Me 109B. Mölders quickly realised that fighter tactics in 1938 were geared towards slow biplanes, and therefore largely inapplicable to the new, fast monoplanes. The basic combat formation used by virtually every air force was V shaped, with the leader at the apex, and known to the RAF as a 'vic' and to the Luftwaffe as a 'Kette'. One reason for this formation was that, prior to air-to-air radio communications, pilots had to formate closely on their leader to receive visual hand signals. With four such vics operating as a squadron, it was found that pilots were forced to spend too much time concentrating on formation flying and not nearly enough in searching for the enemy. In tight formations travelling at over 300 mph collisions could occur quickly, so an alternative formation had to be found.

Mölders replaced the Kette with the 'Rotte', a new concept consisting of leader and wingman. The leader was the primary attacker, the wingman, or 'Rottenflieger', being responsible for protecting his leader's tail. Assured that his rear was covered, the leader could concentrate on attacking the enemy. The aircraft flew about 200 yds apart, a distance which allowed the opportunity to manoeuvre safely and search the sky without fear of collision. Expanding upon this principle, two Rotte formed the 'Schwärm' of four aircraft. The Schwärm flew either in line abreast or in the positions of the four fingertips of an outstretched hand; hence the expression 'Finger Four'. When combat was joined, the Schwärm broke into two fighting pairs. It is a great tribute to Werner 'Vatti' Mölders that this new combat formation was eventually adopted by every air force in the world, and even today forms the basis of fighter-to-fighter combat.

In addition to the revolution in fighter tactics, in Spain the Wehrmacht developed the 'Blitzkrieg' tactics that were later to shock western Europe. Fast-moving tanks and motorised infantry were supported by flying artillery, medium bombers and dive-bombers which pounded the ground ahead of the advancing army. The Condor Legion's outstanding and unprecedented success with these shock tactics, however, made the Luftwaffe think only in terms of a tactical, and not a balanced, air force. This was to have profound consequences for Germany during the Second World War.

On 1 September 1939 Germany unleashed Blitzkrieg against Poland. Within three weeks it was all over, although the Polish Air Force had fought stubbornly with its antiquated biplanes, shooting down 285 German aircraft. On 3 September Britain and

Major Werner Mölders, the 'Father of German Air Fighting', responsible for implementing the tactically brilliant Schwärme combat formation. (Chris Goss)

France declared war on Germany. Both sides began air operations tentatively, however, and aerial activity was largely restricted to reconnaissance flights and attacks on shipping. Throughout the rest of 1939 unescorted RAF bomber formations frequently made daylight attacks on German naval bases. However, the unprotected British bombers suffered very heavy losses when intercepted by Me 109s and consequently such raids were sensibly abandoned.

On 9 April 1940 the Wehrmacht launched Operation *Weserübung* and invaded Norway. Again the Luftwaffe flew in support of ground forces, which had made an amphibious landing, and by 1 May Germany was again victorious. Once more, however, the Me 109s had encountered obsolete biplanes, but the German fighter pilots (Jagdflieger) remained confident that when the time came they would master the RAF's Spitfires and Hurricanes.

On 10 May 1940 Blitzkrieg struck in the west when the Wehrmacht invaded Belgium, Holland, Luxembourg, and France, starting a lightning advance to the Channel ports. Two days later Liege fell and Panzers crashed across the Meuse at Dinant and Sedan; the following day Rotterdam surrendered and the Dutch army capitulated. Luftwaffe successes rose to a crescendo on 14 May 'Tag der Jagdflieger' (Fighter Pilots' Day). That day, 814 fighter sorties over Sedan resulted in more than 90 victories. By 20 May the legions of field grey had reached Laon, Cambrai, Arras, Amiens, and Abbeville. Over France the Me 109s had met the Hawker Hurricane for the first time, but, although it proved a more daunting adversary than anything previously encountered, the Germans still had the edge. By 26 May, with some

300,000 Allied troops awaiting evacuation from the port of Dunkirk, the Spitfire, hitherto reserved for home defence, was at last committed to battle during Operation *Dynamo*, the air operation to cover the evacuation. The Me 109 at last met its match. No longer would the Jagdflieger have everything their own way.

As it had vanquished all previous opponents, however, the Luftwaffe's supreme confidence in its ability to defeat RAF Fighter Command is easily understood. Reichsmarschall Hermann Göring, Air Minister and Commander-in-Chief of the Luftwaffe, was among Hitler's closest confidants, and indeed was his designated successor. During the first year of the Second World War the Luftwaffe's triumphs in Poland and the West had enormously increased both his prestige and his lust for power, and by the time of the Battle of Britain Göring, too, was at his zenith. The Reichsmarschall believed that the RAF could be defeated within a month of launching a major aerial assault as a prelude to a seaborne invasion of England; Operation *Seelöwe*.

In preparation for the air assault against England, the Luftwaffe in France organised itself into two Luftflotten (Air Fleets), each virtually a self-contained air force. Luftflotte 2 covered north-eastern France and the Low Countries, and was commanded by Generalfeldmarschall Albrecht Kesselring, whose headquarters were at Brussels. Luftflotte 3 embraced north-western France and was commanded by Generalfeldmarschall Hugo Sperrle, formerly commander of the Condor Legion and in 1940 probably the most experienced officer in the entire Luftwaffe. His headquarters were at the fabulous Palais du Luxembourg, where he enjoyed a lavish lifestyle which, some said, matched that of the Reichsmarschall himself. The two Luftflotten commanders took their orders directly from Göring.

Each Luftflotte exercised responsibility for both offensive operations over a specific area of the United Kingdom and the defence of its part of the occupied territories. The specialist elements within each Luftflotte were controlled by a Fliegerkorps HQ. In 1940 the new post of Jagdfliegerführer (Jafu), or fighter leader, was created to centralise control of the fighters under one man answerable to the Luftflotte commander. In reality, however, the bomber Fliegerkorps HQ, responsible for many more men, always outweighed the Jafu in policy arguments. Thus the Jafu became little more than a liaison officer, informing the fighters what the bomber crews expected of them. During the Battle of Britain this was to be another serious negative implication.

At operational level the Luftflotten fighters, heavy fighters (destroyers) and bombers were organised into Geschwader: Jagd, Zerstörer, and Kampfgeschwader. It is with the Jagdgeschwader that this book is concerned, and all remarks relate to such fighter units unless otherwise indicated.

Irrespective of denomination, each Jagdgeschwader consisted of some 100 aircraft commanded by the Geschwaderkommodore, usually a Major. Each Geschwader had its own staff flight, the Geschwaderstabschwärm, led by the Kommodore and including such pilots as the Adjutant, Technical and Operations Officers. The Geschwader was divided into three Gruppen (Groups), I, II and III, each commanded by a Gruppenkommandeur, a Hauptmann. Again, each Gruppe had its own Gruppenstabschwärm. An Operations Headquarters existed at both Geschwader and Gruppe level; Geschwadergefechsstand and Gruppengefechsstand. Each Gruppe was then further divided into three Staffeln, each being the equivalent of an RAF squadron and commanded by a Staffelkapitän, usually an Oberleutnant and an office directly comparable to that of an RAF Squadron Leader. Geschwader's 12 Staffeln were numbered 1–12. Thus 4/JG26 refers to the II Gruppe's 4th Staffel of Jagdgeschwader 26. Every Geschwader also had its own Ergänzungsstaffel, in effect an extra squadron which provided operational training to new pilots fresh from flying school before they joined the Geschwader proper.

The Knight's Cross with Oak Leaves, Swords and Diamonds, an award to which only the select few aspired.

Each Staffel was subdivided into three Schwärme, these being further subdivided into the pairs, or Rotte. Individual aircraft within each Staffel were marked with numbers from 1 onwards, painted or outlined in the Staffel colour forward of the national cross on the fuselage. The marking aft of the cross indicated the aircraft's Gruppe: no marking indicated I Gruppe, a horizontal or vertical bar II Gruppe, and a wavy line III Gruppe. Both the Geschwaderstab and Gruppenstabschwärm used a system of black-and-white chevron, horizontal bar and circular symbols to indicate to which officer each aircraft belonged. Each Geschwader usually had its own emblem painted on all of its fighters, which may also have borne further badges peculiar to both particular Gruppe and Staffel. After 28 August 1940 engine cowlings, rudders and wingtips were also painted yellow or white to ease identification in the air. Contrary to the situation in the RAF, air-to-air and air-to-ground communications were a problem for the Luftwaffe, particularly in 1940. For example, fighter pilots could talk to each other in the air, but neither to the ground nor, in the case of the Battle of Britain, to the bombers they escorted. Therefore the system of colour coding to identify a particular Geschwader, Gruppe, Staffel and individual aircraft became of paramount importance in the air. White indicated the first Staffel in each Gruppe, red the second, and yellow the third. Subsequently many RAF fighter pilots reported combats with yellow-nosed Me 109s which were universally believed to be from some élite unit.

Many authors have, in fact, wrongly compared an RAF fighter Wing to a Jagdgeschwader, and therefore equated the status of the Geschwaderkommodore to a Wing Commander (Flying). From the foregoing, however, it can be seen that this was not so. While an RAF Wing Leader commanded three squadrons, the Kommodore commanded 12, and in effect had three Gruppenkommandeure under him, each commanding three Staffeln. A Geschwader, therefore, represented the equivalent of an RAF Bomber Group, not a mere three-squadron fighter wing. An RAF fighter Wing Leader, in terms of the men and aircraft he controlled, actually compared to a Gruppenkommandeur. What the Wing Commander (Flying) and Kommodore did have in common was that both were operational, as opposed to administrative, posts, and they also shared a similar tactical responsibility and authority.

During mid-August 1940, when Göring's disillusionment with the Battle of Britain set in, he claimed that the older men or 'Alte Adler' who commanded Jagdgeschwader were not aggressive enough. He wanted his Kommodore to be young, high-scoring combat aces who would lead the Jagdwaffe into battle and provide a shining example for their pilots to follow. Consequently these men were replaced by the most promising young Gruppenkommandeure. Heralding this change, Mölders had already succeeded Osterkamp as Kommodore of JG51 on 27 July. In August Adolf Galland replaced Gotthardt Handrick in JG26 and Johannes Trautloft took over from Mettig in JG54. Satisfied with this decision, Göring continued this trend during September and October.

Although the Jagdverbände (fighter formations), fought hard to achieve superiority, the Me 109 was not designed as an escort fighter. With precious little fuel available for combat over England as it was, the fighters were tied so inflexibly to escorting the slower bombers that the Jagdflieger were constantly adjusting their throttle levers to keep pace with their slower charges, thus burning more fuel and exacerbating the situation. On their return flights across the Channel the Me 109 pilots constantly monitored their fuel gauges. Oberleutnant von Hahn of I/JG3 reported: 'There are only a few of us left who have not yet had to ditch in the Channel with either a shot-up aircraft or a stationary airscrew'. On 9 September 1940 some 18 Me 109s failed to reach their bases after action over England, either ditching in the 'Kanal' (English Channel) or making forced landings along the French coast.

Numerically the opposing fighter forces were fairly evenly matched, although when interrogated a captured Me 110 pilot was forced to concede that the RAF pilots were fighting with 'Kolossalen Verbissenheit' (tremendous determination). Leutnant Helmut Ostermann of III/JG54 wrote: 'Utter exhaustion from the English operations has set in. For the first time one hears pilots talking of a posting to a quieter sector.' More recently, a survivor, Oblt Ulrich Steinhilper of 3/JG52, has written of 'Kanalkrankheit' (Channel sickness), the symptoms of which included the feigning of mechanical failure so as not to risk combat over England. It should be remembered that while Fighter Command was hard-pressed to defend its nation alone, the German aircrews in the west had been under virtually constant pressure since May 1940. By the end of August JG54 'Grünherz' was daily flying almost constant escort sorties or 'Freie Jagd' (literally 'free fighting') across the Channel as far as London. Among those Me 109 pilots was Lt Ostermann, who had so far fought throughout the western campaign:

At once I flung my machine around and went down after them. Now I was about 200 yds behind the Tommy. Steady does it, wait. The range was much too far. I crept slowly nearer until I was only a hundred yards away when the Spit's wings filled my reflector gunsight. Suddenly the Tommy opened fire and the Me 109 in front of him went into a dive. I too had pressed the firing button after having taken careful aim. I was only in a gentle turn as I did so. The Spit caught fire at once and, streaming a long grey plume of smoke, dived down vertically into the sea.

The Jagdflieger had certainly learned to respect the Spitfire during the Battle of Britain. Early in 1941 Lt Heinz Knocke of 1/JG52 wrote:

The Supermarine Spitfire, because of its manoeuvrability and technical performance, has given the German formations plenty of trouble. "Achtung – Spitfire!" – German pilots have learned to pay particular attention when they hear this warning shouted in their earphones. We consider shooting down a Spitfire to be an outstanding achievement, which it most certainly is.

At the start of the Battle of Britain a force of some 700 Me 109s had gathered on the

Channel coast, but this was inadequate for the double role of engaging RAF fighters and providing close escort for bombers. Because the Me 109's range was limited to London, the German bombers were largely restricted to targets in the south-east of England. On 28 August 1940 the Jagdgeschwader concentrated in the Pas-de-Calais for the next few weeks of intensive air assault against England. The Jagdflieger, however, were to become increasingly frustrated by Göring's insistence that they remain inflexibly tied to the bomber escort role. The fighter was in essence a hunter, and the Jagdwaffe certainly enjoyed great success when operating Freie Jagd sweeps over England. The final straw came when Göring issued orders that one Staffel from each Jagdgeschwader should become fighter-bombers (see Chapter Two). On 20 September 1940, however, the first day such hit-and-run tactics were employed, Fighter Command received a salutary reminder of just how dangerous the Me 109E could be. The Jabos were preceded by a large-scale Freie Jagd over Kent, and consequently Fighter Command lost four pilots killed in addition to several wounded. Only one Me 109 was lost.

While the RAF in 1940 comprised regular officers and servicemen, Auxiliaries and Volunteer Reservists, the Luftwaffe was a totally professional air force. Arguably, the cream of this force was lost over England in 1940, either killed in action or captured, a factor which was undoubtedly to affect the battles ahead. Of course, Luftwaffe aircrew who survived being shot down over England were always captured. When the situation was reversed a year later, one advantage that Fighter Command pilots had when at large on French soil was the possibility of being helped down the 'Line' to freedom via the Underground network. Many RAF pilots made 'home runs' in 1941. There is no doubt that, during 1940, the German aircrews fought with bravery, skill, and determination, but they were badly let down by Göring, who had personally assumed control of the attacks on England but repeatedly jumped from one objective to another. This split the available forces instead of concentrating them long enough on one focal point. Owing to such heavy losses in daylight, after 30 September the attack became mainly nocturnal in an attempt to break the will of the British people. Even the heaviest raids, however, such as those on London and Coventry, failed in this objective, achieving instead the opposite effect and strengthening the civilian population's resolve.

This Me 109 'Emil' of an unknown Geschwader's IIIrd Gruppe appears to have suffered a landing accident, probably at a base in Germany early in the war. The photograph was taken from a German house as a souvenir by a British soldier in 1945.

In short, Göring had tried to defeat Fighter Command with a tactical air force, one superbly equipped for supporting the army, the role for which it had been created, but not for a prolonged strategic air offensive. The Luftwaffe's bombers were of medium capacity only, the Kampfgeschwader lacking a heavy, long-range bomber. For example, the He 111's maximum bomb load was 4,400 lb, whereas the Avro Lancaster was to carry 22,000 lb. Before the war, however, Gen Walter Wever, the Luftwaffe Chief of Staff, had recognised both the need for a balanced air force and a heavy bomber, the latter being known as the 'Ural Bomber' after Russia's Ural mountains, which he considered a prime strategic target in the event of war against the Soviets. Wever was killed in a flying accident at Dresden during 1936, and with him perished the Ural Bomber concept. Ottomar Kruse, himself a former Jagdflieger, remarks:

> Had the Luftwaffe a fighter in 1940 with twice the range of the Me 109, and likewise a four-engined heavy bomber, the outcome of the Battle of Britain might have been very different. In fact, contrary to the B-17s and other American "heavies" which I attacked during the defence of Germany later in the war, I consider the He 111s, Do 17s and Ju 88s operating over England in daylight during 1940 to have been "sitting ducks".

As late as 1938 Hitler still believed that there would be no war against England. His principal territorial ambitions, therefore, always lay eastwards, and his decision to invade Russia was made just as the Battle of Britain began. German historians argue, therefore, that from then on the war in the west no longer had priority in the eyes of the German High Command. As far as the British are concerned, the Battle of Britain officially ended on 31 October 1940, though Hitler had actually postponed Operation *Seelöwe* indefinitely on 12 October. The *Nachtangriff* against British cities continued until May 1941, however, and the day fighters continued to clash fiercely over both the Channel and south-east England throughout late 1940 and into early 1941. German historians argue that it is the attacker who dictates the dates of battle, and therefore, so far as they are concerned, the Battle of Britain did not end until May 1941. On 21 May Sperrle became sole air commander in the west, Luftflotte 2 having been completely withdrawn in preparation for the attack on Russia.

By 4 June 1941 just two Jagdgeschwader, Oblt Adolf Galland's JG26 'Schlageter' and Maj Wilhelm Balthasar's JG2 'Richthofen', remained on the Kanalfront as the Luftwaffe's strength withdrew eastwards for Operation *Barbarossa*, the blitzkrieg to be unleashed against Russia on 22 June 1941. Between them, Galland and Balthasar were responsible for defending the western European coast from the Netherlands to the Bay of Biscay. The Kanalfront Jafu, however, Gen Theo Osterkamp, an ace in both world wars, briefed the two 'Kanalgeschwadern Kommodore' that they were to inflict maximum losses upon the enemy but ensure preservation of their own limited forces in the process.

Having been the first to receive the Me 109, JG2, named after the 'Red Baron', Rittmeister Manfred Freiherr von Richthofen, considered itself the Luftwaffe's senior fighter unit. Its pilots wore a prestigious honour title bearing his name on their left sleeves. Throughout much of the Battle of Britain JG2 operated from bases within Luftflotte 3's area of north-west France, such as the huge cornfields around Beaumont-le-Roger and the airfield at Le Havre. In late August 1940, along with the other Jagdwaffe units gathering in the Pas-de-Calais for the assault on London, JG2 moved to Théville, Mardyck, and Oye Plage. After the failure of the daylight campaign against 'Loge' (the codename for London, inspired by the Teutonic mythological god of fire), JG2 returned to Luftflotte 3 and, in addition to escorting such bomber units as KG51 and KG55 to targets along the south coast of England including Portsmouth and Southampton, its pilots also operated over the West

Walter Oesau in his staff car when he was Kommodore of JG2 'Richthofen' on the Kanalfront. (Michael Payne)

JG2's Kommandbunker at Beaumont-le-Roger, 1941. (Michael Payne)

Me 109Fs of JG2s Stabsstaffel, Beaumont-le-Roger, 1941. (Michael Payne)

Country, flying escort to raids mounted against the Westland Aircraft factory at Yeovil in Somerset on both 30 September and 7 October 1940. On the former raid Unteroffizier (Uffz) Alois Dollinger of 5/JG2 was shot down and killed by Fg Off Tadeuz Nowierski of 609 Squadron, crashing at Sydling St Nicholas, Dorset, and thus becoming the most westerly Me 109 casualty.

All of JG2's Me 109s bore the Geschwader's emblem, a white or silver shield bearing the letter 'R' in red. The aircraft of 1/JG2 sported a 'Bonzo Dog' badge, and those of 3/JG2 carried a blue pennant bearing a dagger and the word 'Horrido', the hunters' victory cry. This also became the personal marking of Hptm Helmut Wick, Kommandeur of I/JG2 from 9 September 1940. At 22 years of age Wick was the Jagdwaffe's leading *Experte*. On 25 August he had received the Ritterkreuz (Knight's Cross) for achieving 20 victories, and on 6 October, with 41 kills, he became only the fourth Experte to receive the coveted Eichenlaub (Oak Leaves) to add to his Ritterkreuz. On 20 October Wick replaced Max Schellman as JG2's Kommodore and located his HQ at the luxurious chateau at Beaumont-le-Roger, home of the Duchesse de Magenta, whose husband spied on JG2's activities. With his score at 56, however, Maj Wick lost his life on 28 November 1940 when he was shot down over the Solent. Seconds later the Spitfire pilot responsible, Flt Lt John Dundas DFC of 609 Squadron (the brother of Hugh 'Cocky' Dundas), was himself shot down by the Kommodore's No. 2, Oblt Rudi Pflanz. Neither Wick nor Dundas has ever been found.

After Wick's death, Hptm Karl-Heinz Greisert became the acting Kommodore of JG2 until 16 February 1941, when Wilhelm Balthasar was permanently appointed to the command. Like many other leading Experten, Balthasar had flown in Spain, scoring his first victory, a Russian-built I-16 Rata, with III/J88 on 20 January 1938. Six months later, while serving at home with JG2, Balthasar received international acclaim when he flew a twin-engined Siebel 104 on a 40,000 km journey around Africa. During the Battle of France Hptm Balthasar was Kapitän of 7/JG27, and on 6 June 1940 he destroyed nine aircraft in one day. On 14 June he became only the second Luftwaffe serviceman to receive the Knight's Cross. At the end of the French campaign Balthasar was the most successful Experte, with 23 victories. During the Battle of Britain he was Kommandeur of III/JG3, but on 4 September 1940 he was badly wounded over England when his Me 109 was damaged by 222 Squadron Spitfires. Returning to operational duties as JG2's Kommodore, Maj Balthasar again added to his score on 5 May 1941. On 27 June he achieved both his 39th and 40th victories, and was awarded the Eichenlaub (Oak Leaves). On 3 July, however, whilst test-flying a new Me 109F, the Kommodore was attacked and shot down by Spitfires near Hazebrouck, and crashed at Aire. The 26-year-old was buried near Abbeville, next to the father he never knew, who had been killed in France during the First World War.

Balthasar's successor was another notable Experte, Maj Walter 'Gulle' Oesau, who had become an ace in Spain, destroying eight aircraft. During the Battle of Britain Oesau was Kommandeur of III/JG51 and received his Ritterkreuz on 20 August 1940. His 40th kill, on 2 February 1941, brought him the Eichenlaub. In June Oesau became Kommandeur of III/JG3 in preparation for *Barbarossa*. During just one month's fighting over Russia he destroyed a staggering 44 Soviet machines, adding the Schwerten (Swords) to his Ritterkreuz mit Eichenlaub on 15 July 1941. That same month he was recalled to the Kanalfront to lead JG2. On 26 October, when he claimed his 100th victory, Maj Oseau became only the third Experte to score a century.

In fact, JG2 boasted a number of Experten amongst its pilots, including Oblt Erich Leie, who served as Geschwader Adjutant under Wick, Balthasar and Oesau. As a Stabsoffizier at Geschwader level, Leie flew in the Kommodore's Stabschwärm. Leie's Ritterkreuz was awarded on 1 August 1941, when his score stood at 21. Egon Mayer had joined JG2 in December 1939, achieving his first victory during the French war. By July 1943 he was Kommodore of the 'Richthofen' Geschwader, and the following year he became the first Experte to achieve 100 victories all on the Kanalfront. Kurt Buhligen began his service as a mechanic in KG4 'General Wever', an He 111 unit, but Hptm Hermann Kell, Staffelkapitän of 3/KG4, recommended that he be sent to train as a Jagdflieger. By July 1940 Uffz Buhligen was flying Me 109s with JG2, scoring his first victory over England on 4 September 1940. By the war's end Buhligen was Kommodore of JG2 and had a total of 112 victories, all scored in the west. Not surprisingly, he was also a Träger des Eichenlaubs mit Schwerten zum Ritterkreuz des Eisernen Kreuzes (holder of the Knight's Cross with Oak Leaves and Swords). This truly remarkable Experte survived the war. Another popular Jagdwaffe personality, Hans 'Assi' Hahn, was also a member of JG2. His Ritterkreuz was awarded on 24 September 1940, at which time he was elevated from Kapitän of 4/JG2 to Kommandeur of III/JG2. On 14 August 1941 he recorded his 41st kill and added the Oak Leaves to his Knight's Cross. Before being posted to Russia as Kommandeur of II/JG54 in November 1942, Hahn had destroyed no fewer than 68 RAF aircraft.

Considering that the officially recognised top-scoring British pilot of the Second World War, 'Johnnie' Johnson, scored a total of 34 and seven shared destroyed, it is easy to understand why the German scores have often been questioned. However, there are several reasons for their comparatively huge tallies. Firstly, RAF fighter pilots flew tours of operational duty, upon conclusion of which they would be rested, often as flying instructors. In the Luftwaffe, however, the Jagdfliegern were not rested, but instead were constantly in action unless incapacitated by wounds or killed, thus giving them more time in which to accumulate large scores. Secondly, and quite simply, after 1940 they had more targets at which to shoot. Moreover, those who flew on the Eastern Front, particularly during the early part of the Russian campaign, were again pitched against an inferior foe. The really huge scores were achieved over Russia, the frequency being indicated by Oesau's 44 kills in just one month and the 301 victories of Erich Hartmann, the Luftwaffe's top-scoring Experte.

In accordance with the Teutonic penchant for precision, great effort was put into confirming (or otherwise) every 'Abschuss' (shooting down). The Luftwaffe system was impartial but characteristically inflexible. Unlike the practice in the Allied air forces, kills could not be shared, and claims were only awarded for destroyed aircraft. Every Abschuss had to be witnessed by either another pilot or someone on the ground. Alternatively, the pilot might have recorded the victory on his aircraft's cine-gun camera, if fitted. However, if the wreckage of the enemy aircraft claimed as destroyed could not be found, there were no known witnesses, or the Allied aircrew concerned were not captured, then no victory was awarded. When submitting a claim the 'Viktor' was expected to record the exact geographical position and time of the kill. He then submitted his claim to his immediate supervisory officer for either endorsement or rejection. If the former, the report was forwarded to the Geschwaderstab, which filed another report and in turn forwarded both papers to the Reichsluftfahrtministerium (RLM, German Air Ministry). The RLM would then check the circumstances of the claim and, if it was approved, notify the unit concerned. This rather drawn-out process could take up to a year. Despite this effective system, however, even the Oberkommando der Luftwaffe (High Command), was astonished by the Jagdwaffe's claims during the opening weeks of the Russian war. Eventually, however, the High Command had to accept the claims as perfectly genuine, as indeed we do today. When comparing the German combat claims with actual Allied losses, the former are found to be remarkably accurate. Conversely, that is not the case with Allied combat reports.

Returning to the Kanalgeschwader, JG26 was first numbered 234, and received its first Me 109s in November 1937. The unit's honour title was awarded in December 1938, the Geschwader being named after Albert Leo Schlageter, who had been executed by the French in 1923 after blowing up a section of railway as a protest against the Allied forces occupying the Rhineland, the area of Germany in which the Geschwader's home bases were located. On 1 May 1939 the unit was redesignated JG26 and a new badge was painted on the 'Schlageter' 109s; a black gothic 'S' on a white shield. The emblem of 8/JG26 was the cartoon character 'Adamson', after which the Staffel was named, while 9/JG26's fighters bore a bright red, fierce-looking 'Höllenhund' (Hellhound).

Instead of participating in the invasion of Poland, JG26 remained in Germany to protect the Fatherland's western flank. During the Blitzkrieg in the west it supported Army Group 'B' which invaded the Netherlands. Flying Freie Jagd ahead of the army, JG26 won air superiority on the campaign's first day. It then flew in support of the invasion of Belgium, and later engaged RAF Spitfires over Dunkirk. At the same time the Geschwader regrouped at bases in the Pas-de-Calais before supporting the army's attack in the south against the main body of the French Army. The battle won, JG26 found itself at Villacoublay, a large former French Air Force base just south-west of Paris. While the French signed the Armistice at Compiègne on 22 June 1940, Me 109s of II/JG26 patrolled overhead. After this the entire Geschwader returned to its home bases in the Rhineland to prepare for the air assault against England.

On 21 July 1940 JG26 returned to France and used bases in the Pas-de-Calais, again mostly former cornfields such as the huge one at Caffiers, home of III/JG26. Since 6 June 1940 Adolf Galland had successfully led this Gruppe, being rewarded on 22 August with command of the Geschwader. He was succeeded as III Gruppe Kommandeur by Hptm Gerhard Schöpfel, another outstanding Experte. Having been heavily committed during the Battle of Britain, JG26 withdrew south to the Abbeville area during the late autumn of 1940. On Christmas Day Adolf Hitler himself dined at the Geschwader HQ, a chateau near Abbeville. On 9 February 1941 the Geschwader again returned to Germany to rest and refit; it was the last time JG26 would be afforded such a luxury. Its place in France was taken by JG53.

The German cartoon character Adamson on an 8/JG26 Me 109.

During this period Galland's unit began re-equipping with the new Me 109F, the Geschwaderstab and III/JG26 receiving the new fighter at the end of March 1941. However, although I/JG26 also began receiving the Me 109F, there were insufficient aircraft to equip the entire Geschwader. Certain elements of JG26 therefore retained their 'Emils' until the summer of 1941.

The first Me 109Fs had entered service in November 1940, but were grounded after several unexplained crashes. Investigations revealed that in each case the tail had failed, so immediate steps were taken to strengthen the structure. Once this work was completed, deliveries were resumed. There were numerous differences between the 'Franz' and the 'Emil' it replaced, including redesigned radiators, flaps and ailerons, and it had slightly greater wingspan. The 'F' enjoyed aesthetic benefits, having rounded wingtips and a streamlined nose profile incorporating a larger spinner. The Me 109F's tailplane lacked the supporting struts of the 'E', and the new fighter also had a smaller rudder. The Me 109F was powered initially by the Daimler-Benz DB601N and then by the DB601E, which used a lower-octane fuel and gave the fighter a top speed of 390 mph at 22,000 ft. Its Service ceiling was 37,000 ft and its range 440 miles. An ingenious nitrous oxide injection pack known as 'Ha Ha' was added to the F-2, giving it exceptional boost.

The two engine-mounted MG 17 machine-guns were retained, but provision was made for a single 15 mm or 20 mm cannon firing through the propeller boss. The F-1 arrived with an engine-mounted MG FF/M 20 mm cannon manufactured by Oerlikon, but the F-2, which became available in quantity shortly afterwards, was armed with the 15 mm Mauser MG 151. To sight his target the German pilot had the Revi/12C reflector-type gunsight. A thumb button on his control column fired the cannon, and a conventional finger trigger discharged the machine-guns. In the case of the Me 109F's MG 151 cannon, which used high-explosive, armour-piercing and incendiary ammunition, the rate of fire was 700 rounds per minute. Each Rheinmetall-Borsig MG 17 fired 1,180 rounds per minute.

The Me 109E of Oblt Schöpfel on the huge expanse of cornfield from which III/JG26 operated during the Battle of Britain. Note the Staffelkapitän's pennant on the aerial mast and the Höllenhund insignia of 9/JG26.

Adolf Galland at Audembert on 24 September 1940, while Kommandeur of III/JG26, with Oblts Schöpfel and Müncheberg, the threesome being the Gruppe's first Ritterkreuzträger. (Michael Payne)

The Me 109E had been armed with two wing-mounted 20 mm cannon and two engine-mounted MG 17s. With just two MG17s and a single 15 mm or 20 mm cannon, the new Me 109F was more lightly armed, and this caused controversy among the Experten. Adolf Galland himself argued that such light armament was useless against the improved and more heavily armoured Spitfires, and that the wing-mounted cannon were better for the novice. Werner Mölders, however, favoured the lighter armament, which reduced weight and thereby increased agility. In action, some Experten chose to use only the rapid-fire MG 151 cannon, ignoring the machine-guns completely. Interestingly, across the Channel at Tangmere, discussions in a similar vein were taking place as Wg Cdr Bader opposed the cannon armament of the Spitfire Mk VB, preferring instead the eight 0.303 in machine-guns of the Mk VA. It seems that armament was down to personal preference and, indeed, ability. Overall, it appears that the Me 109F's lighter armament was not to have any negative implications for the Jagdwaffe; nor did the Spitfire Mk VB's cannon for Fighter Command.

The Me 109F undoubtedly represented the zenith of the entire 'Ein-Hundert-Neun' series, and was generally operated by the Experten with great enthusiasm on all fronts. About 2,300 were built, representing just 7 per cent of total Me 109 production. As heavier Allied aircraft entered the arena the type required further upgrading, the next variant, the 'Gustav', being developed as a slayer of four-engine bombers and even carrying anti-aircraft rockets. Reflecting the extent of Germany's later battle for survival, by comparison with the total number of 'F's produced the 'G' represented 70 per cent of the entire Me 109 production total.

Like their Fighter Command counterparts, the Jagdflieger were essentially young men who loved flying. Many had been initiated into the ways of a pilot during the 1930s as members of the Deutscher Luftsportverband (DLV), a pseudo-sporting club which trained youngsters as glider pilots, ultimately to form the basis of the new, secret Luftwaffe. Service pilots experienced *ab initio* flight at elementary flying training schools where they also studied aerodynamics, navigation, radio procedures, aviation law and other related subjects. Upon successful completion of the course the tyro passed to the next instalment of flying training, concerned with more advanced aircraft types. Bomber pilots then went to a further training school and received another 60 hrs flying, and proceeded on to a specialist school to learn instrument flying. As has already been explained, once the Jagdflieger had completed flying training his next stop was his allocated Geschwader's Ergängungstaffel, for operational training before joining a Jagdstaffel proper. On 23 May 1941 Lt Heinz Knocke joined 6/JG52 as a newly trained pilot:

My Staffelkapitän is Oberleutnant Rech. Like him, two other Staffel members, Barkhorn and Rall, have the Iron Cross. Apart from Leutnant Krupinsky who has been here a week longer than I, the other pilots are all experienced NCOs. They are good men and know their job. They watch me rather suspiciously out of the corners of their eyes, and appear to have a low opinion of young Leutnants. On learning that I am not a card-player, they ignore me completely. At times like this, the proudly gleaming new rank badges are not worth a penny.

The field blue Luftwaffe uniforms bore the eagle insignia on the right breast, in silver bullion for officers and embroidered for other ranks. The metal pilot's qualification badge was worn on the left breast. Collar patches and shoulder straps indicated rank, the background colour identifying the wearer's particular branch of service, aircrew Waffenfarbe being a golden yellow. Wings, borders and oak leaves were all in silver.

Summer-issue flying helmets were fawn in colour and had both radio earpieces and a throat microphone. Flying goggles were either ordinary or of the shatterproof

An Me 109 'Franz' of 8/JG26 on the Kanalfront during mid-1941.

Nitsche & Gunter type with dark lenses. A fawn-coloured, one-piece flying overall was also provided, although the pilot could choose to wear ordinary uniform with a leather flying jacket and boots. At the top of the boots were strapped a plentiful supply of cartridges for his Mauser flare pistol for use in an emergency, the pistol itself often being secured to the lifejacket.

In preference to the heavy, kapok-filled lifejackets often worn by bomber crews, the Jagdflieger preferred the Schwimmweste, a lightweight example which could be inflated either by mouth or by activation of a pressurised cartridge. The Schwimmweste also carried packets of fluorescine which, when exposed to sea water, automatically discharged a bright yellow dye around the floating pilot. An inflatable life-raft was stowed in the cockpit as a further precaution against ditching. German aircrew often wore bright yellow skullcaps over their flying helmets, again as a precaution if they ended up in the Kanal.

The Luftwaffe had paid great attention to air-sea rescue since 1940, the Seenotflugkommando operating Heinkel He 59 floatplanes to search for ditched aircrew. At strategic positions in the Kanal were anchored rescue buoys, known as 'Lobster Pots' by the RAF, containing four bunks and anything else a downed airman might need. With an aircrew survival time of just 1–2 hrs when immersed in sea water, even during summer, such safety measures were essential. The RAF, on the other hand, had no proper air-sea rescue organisation early in the war, operating just 18 launches to search for ditched airmen along the entire length of England's south coast. Frequently, therefore, RAF pilots were saved only by chance encounters with passing shipping, or by civilian lifeboats.

On 1 April 1941 Galland's JG26 received orders to return to France, this time joining Luftflotte 3 in Brittany. Stab and I/JG26 operated from Guipavas, near Brest, while the Second Gruppe flew from Morlaix and the Third from St Brieuc. II/JG2 was then able to leave Brest and return to its previous bases at Bernay and Beaumont-le-Roger. The object of basing the entire JG26 in Brittany was to provide cover for the

German Navy, in particular the battlecruisers *Scharnhorst* and *Gneisenau*, which had recently arrived in Brest following a successful Atlantic raid.

This period in Brittany brought little action. On 4 April 1941, however, Maj Galland and Obfwl Robert Menge flew from Düsseldorf to Brittany. Having stopped to refuel at Le Touquet, the temptation of the nearby Kent coast and the victories it might offer proved too much for the Geschwaderkommodore. Consequently the Rotte made a brief, unscheduled sweep across the Channel before flying on to Guipavas. At about 5,000 ft over Dover the Me 109s bounced two 91 Squadron Spitfires flown by Sgts Spears and Mann, who had been scrambled from Hawkinge to intercept a Ju 88. Galland and Menge despatched the two Spitfires in a single, diving pass before striking out westwards for Brest. Spears baled out safely, and Mann forced-landed his burning Spitfire back at Hawkinge. Many years later Sgt Mann achieved international fame after being taken as a hostage from his Beirut home. Having been held captive for several years, Jackie Mann died recently in Cyprus, where he had lived following his release. For Galland on that day in 1941, either Spears or Mann represented his 58th kill.

By April 1941 Oberst Theo Osterkamp was Jafu 2, and on the 15th of that month he celebrated his 49th birthday in Le Touquet. Galland decided to visit his old comrade and help him celebrate. Stowing a basket of lobsters and several bottles of champagne behind the seat of his Me 109F, he took off from Guipavas with Lt Westphal. Again, however, Galland made an unauthorised detour over the Dover Straits, this time meeting the 12 Group Wittering Wing (Spitfires of 65 and 266 Squadrons together with the Hurricanes of 402), which was undertaking a Channel patrol. The Wing Leader, Wg Cdr Coope, ordered the Wing to climb through cloud above Dover. Westphal alerted Galland to a 'single Spitfire which was on a curving course'. The Kommodore fired from astern and hit Coope's Spitfire in the wing and fuel tank, and a cannon shell also ripped through the pilot's parachute pack. With his fighter belching black smoke, Coope safely forced-landed at Manston, shocked but otherwise unharmed.

Although concerned by the disappearance of its leader, the Wittering Wing continued its patrol, only to be bounced by Galland and Westphal over Dungeness. Although the latter's guns jammed, Galland shot down Sgt Harold Whewell of 266 Squadron, who crash-landed at Hawkinge. Sergeant Barraclough, also of 266, was wounded. One of 266 Squadron's flight commanders, Flt Lt Holland, reported having seen an Me 109 dive through the Spitfires, its wheels coming down as it did so. Although Flt Lt 'Paddy' Finucane of 65 Squadron claimed an Me 109 destroyed low over the sea, both Galland and Westphal returned safely to France, where Galland correctly claimed two Spitfires destroyed. At Le Touquet he realised why his aircraft was flying sluggishly; for some reason its wheels had come down. However, he was able to present Osterkamp with his birthday gifts; delicacies which had flown in action over the Kanal.

The rest of JG26 saw little action while based in Brittany, largely spending their time dropping practice bombs on the French coast. On 31 May 1941 JG26 was not disappointed, therefore, to receive orders for a new move back to the Pas-de-Calais; as it was close to England, action could be guaranteed. The following day JG26 returned to the coastal plains around Calais, Galland's 'Führerungsverband' (lead formation) again operating from Audembert near Wissant, just two miles away from Osterkamp's Jafu 2 Operations Bunker. I/JG26, commanded by Hptm Rolf Pingel, went to Clairmarais near St Omer, and Hptm Schöpfel's Third Gruppe went to Ligescourt, north-east of Abbeville and near the mouth of the Somme Estuary. Hauptmann Walter Adolph's Me 109E-equipped II/JG26 went further north to Maldegem in western Belgium.

Unlike Wg Cdr Bader, who had chosen to lead the Tangmere Wing at the head of one particular squadron, Oberst Galland reflected a higher quality of leadership by rotating every Staffel in the Geschwader through Audembert. This meant that he came to know all of his pilots and recognise their strengths and weaknesses, which could then be acted upon.

While Oberst Galland remained the Geschwader's Experte of Experten, JG26, like JG2, boasted many more Experten within its ranks. Hauptmann Gerhard Schöpfel, Kommandeur of III/JG26, was among the Jagdwaffe's most successful pilots in 1940, receiving his Ritterkreuz on 9 September. On 18 August he had bounced 501 Squadron over Canterbury and despatched four Hurricanes in as many minutes, killing one pilot and wounding the other three. Such a feat of arms was actually unprecedented in 1940. Oberleutnant Gustav 'Micky' Sprick, Kapitän of 8/JG26, was also among the first Jagdflieger to achieve 20 victories and receive the Ritterkreuz (1 October 1940). Josef 'Pips' Priller had fought with 6/JG51 in France and during the Battle of Britain, also receiving the Ritterkreuz in October 1940. The following month he became Kapitän of 1/JG26, and was destined for a great wartime career.

The move of JG26 to north-east France, however, meant that JG2 had to stretch itself further westwards again to cover Brittany in addition to the Cherbourg area. From this point onwards, as all other Jagdgeschwader moved east for *Barbarossa*, JG2 and JG26 became the sole Kanalgeschwader, with a total force of some 150 Me 109s.

From the foregoing it is clear that the RAF faced an extremely experienced, well equipped, and motivated enemy. Contrary to popular belief, after the Battle of Britain the Luftwaffe was far from being a spent and defeated force. In any case, the Germans had only failed to gain aerial supremacy over England because of unsuitable equipment and poor leadership. The aircrews themselves had fought with great skill and courage and, when responding to numerous 'Alarmstarts' (scrambles) in 1941, they would continue to do so.

As previously explained, the Kanalgeschwader often operated from makeshift airfields, particularly during the Battle of Britain, when large numbers of Me 109s assembled in the Pas-de-Calais. Has anyone considered who prepared these fields for use? In early 1996 I was contacted by Frank Kamp, who told me he had 'been given a spade instead of a rifle'. He served in the Reichsarbeitsdienst (Labour Corps) in 1940, and his is the story of yet another who played a far less glamorous supporting role:

Almost immediately upon completing my second term at college in August 1940, I received my call-up papers and so reported to the Stadthalle (town hall) in Münster. I was posted to the Reichsarbeitdienst and we were trained along military lines, even with regard to spade drill! After the Battle of France we were marched to Bramsche railway station with full kit and accompanied by a marching band. We had no idea where we were going, but once aboard realised that we were travelling in a south-westerly direction. We crossed Holland, then Belgium, eventually arriving in France. The engine stopped and we were told to get off the train. Where were we? Someone spotted a sign, "Calais", and then we realised that we were in the Pas-de-Calais, close to the English Channel. After a wait, we were collected by lorries and driven to Marquise, on the Calais-to-Boulogne road, south of Cap Gris Nez and Wissant. During this journey we saw the first German and Allied war graves.

We were quartered in a school at Marquise. Everybody was aware that Dover was just across the Channel, and it was not long before I had my first look at England. Strangely, although we were so close to England, we were unaware that the Battle of Britain was taking place, and in fact I remained ignorant of any great aerial battle throughout the entire time I spent on the Kanalfront. We were, however, fully aware of the airfield's fighters.

Left: *Oberleutnant Gustav 'Mickey' Sprick, Kapitän of 8/JG26.*

Below: *Johann Schmid was one of the most successful Kanaljäger in 1941. Older than most of his comrades at 30, Schmid was killed on 6 November 1941; having shot down a Spitfire over the Channel north of Calais, his Me 109 crashed when he circled the impact spot at low altitude and touched the sea. His final score was 41 victories, all in the west.*

At Marquise, our commander, Hoppner, conveyed to our entire unit of 120–150 men exactly what was required from us regarding our general behaviour, not least towards the civilian population. He also explained that our work would involve building and extending, in addition to maintaining, airfields for fighter aircraft. At that stage he did not tell us that we would actually be on Adolf Galland's airfield at Audembert, near Wissant. Our commander asked for the fullest co-operation from everyone, and requested tradesmen and those of us with basic French to step forward. Qualifying on both counts, I did so and Hoppner inferred that some special assignments may be in store for us. He concluded by emphasising that we were now in "enemy territory", but stressed that every effort should be made not to offend the dignity of the local population. Disobedience to these orders would, he assured us, be severely punished.

I was then selected for special military training, which included rifle drill. On this very day. Luftwaffe steel helmets and rifles were produced. However, we were concerned as we had not received any weapons training. We were told not to worry as we would not be issued with any ammunition! Therefore we had to mount a guard, but without bullets! This ridiculous situation went on throughout our entire time in France, despite the fact that Dover was clearly visible! As a result of this experience, I formed the opinion that the Germans were clearly bluffing, the French shocked, and the British had no idea of the risks actually being taken by their adversary. Personally, at the age of 19, I had no thoughts other than perhaps being able to visit England as a civilian tourist after the war, the country of which Professor Kotteritz had often spoken of when he strayed from the content of our lessons at my grammar school.

We worked amongst Galland's "Schlageter" Geschwader and I often saw him either taking off or returning from a sortie. Initially we built service roads on the airfield, but later constructed hangars for the Me 109s and 110s. Their engines were also test-run in these constructions. It appeared as though there was something like 700 fighters in the Pas-de-Calais. The initial planned target bombing, however, seemed to degenerate as the war progressed into the deliberate terror bombing undertaken by both sides.

During our activities on the various airfields, I had many opportunities to travel in the area around Boulogne, the coast, Calais and St Omer. We acquired an abandoned British lorry, and I was usually the driver's mate. It was the first time that I had sat in a vehicle with the steering wheel on the "wrong" side. On one such trip we ended up in a large quarry. I have long since forgotten our duty that particular day, but not what we found there. The quarry was out of bounds to the local civilian population. In it was a huge railway gun, which upon our arrival appeared poised to fire. The gun had been rolled out of its bunker, and its aim was northerly, towards England. From an artilleryman I learned that Dover was their intended target. This massive artillery piece ran on its own rails, carrying its own colossal shells and gunpowder. Everything was handled by mechanical means. When the first salvo was fired the shell could actually be seen leaving the barrel. There was an incredible recoil. It occurred to me that these shells were probably not that accurate, and so this bombardment again falls into that dreadful undertaking, quite preposterous and futile, calculated to strike fear and despondency into the civilian population.

As I had been trained in rifle drill, I continued to be called upon for occasional guard duties. The guard was posted outside our school building at Marquise, facing the marketplace. Next door was the town hall. One day we were told that a British pilot had been shot down that afternoon, and that the French police had agreed to his overnight custody in one of their cells. Consequently, that night we were reminded to be particularly careful on guard duty in case of any reaction from unknown parties. That night, therefore, we held our rifles at the ready, but of course without any ammunition! Fortunately the night passed without incident and the pilot was moved on the following day, although I never saw him.

The winter of 1940–41 was severe, and so we were eventually issued with British bounty overalls to be worn over our working clothes. As February came closer we knew that the period of six months which we were required to serve in the Labour Corps would soon be over. During early February 1941, therefore, it was no surprise to bid *"au revoir"* to Marquise and Galland's airfields. I travelled by train through Belgium and Luxembourg to Münster. Within a week my call-up papers for military service arrived, posting me to the Infantrie Pioneer Ersatz Kompanie 211 (Infantry Engineer Home Company 211).

On Sunday 22 June 1941 a Sondermeldung (special announcement) was broadcast over the radio, thus making Operation *Barbarossa* public knowledge. I simply could not believe it, although I understood to some extent Hitler's thinking. Now we had a war on two fronts. I talked to a Kamerad and he agreed that this development was quite incredible and to our great disadvantage. Gone were any hopes of an early end to the war, replaced now by the prospect of a long and drawn-out fight to the death.

Let us leave Frank Kamp with his premonition of eventual doom for the Third Reich and return to the Kanalfront in 1941. As the area of France inland of Cherbourg required a much longer flight across the sea, north-east France became more frequently visited by the RAF. As this was JG26's area of responsibility, the Tangmere Wing often clashed fiercely with Galland's Me 109s. Many Experten in the Kanalfront Jagdflieger were poised to enter their most successful phase of the entire war.

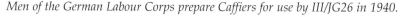

Men of the German Labour Corps prepare Caffiers for use by III/JG26 in 1940.

CHAPTER FIVE

Tangmere Wing at War

The essential background to both sides provided by the foregoing chapters will assist the reader's understanding of the remaining pages. While previous books have concentrated either upon Wg Cdr Bader's personal exploits or those of a particular squadron, this chapter offers the first overview of the Wing's offensive operations. It should be borne in mind that, throughout this time, the squadrons were also flying constant defensive patrols of base and the south coast, during which several Ju 88s were destroyed, plus convoy protection sorties. In addition they frequently provided cover for air-sea rescue operations. The basic facts of each sortie have been enhanced, wherever possible, by first-hand accounts from both sides. It is hoped that this day-to-day study, based on the operational war records, will not only be of interest to the general reader, but will also be invaluable to historians as a reference to the Wing's operations, especially when cross-referenced with the appendices relating to the Tangmere Wing's losses and claims.

18 March 1941
Wing Commander DRS Bader DSO DFC arrives at RAF Tangmere, becoming both Wing Commander (Flying) and second-in-command of this notable fighter station.

19 March 1941
At 15:20 hrs 610 Squadron took off from Westhampnett to patrol Hastings at 30,000 ft, with 616 Squadron leading and positioned slightly below. Upon reaching the patrol

A popular contemporary postcard of Wg Cdr Douglas Bader. The photograph was taken at Westhampnett during the summer of 1941.

line, the 'smoke trail height' was found to be at 25,000 ft, so 610 Squadron descended to slightly below that altitude, 616 Squadron doing likewise. This meant that any enemy aircraft positioned above the Wing would create a condensation trail and therefore be easily seen. This positioning, with 610 Squadron providing top cover and 616 flying below, was to remain the standard pattern throughout Bader's leadership of the Tangmere Wing. On this particular occasion the Wing made three sweeps out to sea and was then ordered to Beachy Head. When it was crossing the English coast at 16:20 hrs two Me 109s attacked 610 Squadron from the rear. The Spitfires' formation was pairs in vic flights line astern. Sergeant Payne saw an Me 109 in his rear-view mirror. He half-rolled, dived, and then throttled right back. The Messerschmitt fired a short burst before overshooting, but scored no hits. As he passed in front of Payne, the 610 Squadron pilot delivered a 3 sec burst, raking the bottom of the German's fuselage. He pressed home his attack, smoke and flames engulfed the Me 109's cockpit and the enemy fighter was seen to crash into the sea about five miles off the French coast. Other 610 Squadron pilots engaged in the fight against II/JG53 without conclusive results. Sergeant Eade was shot down by Hptm Bretnütz, but forced-landed in a field near Hailsham. Back at Westhampnett, Sqn Ldr Burton wrote in his log book: 'Wing patrol with 610, led by Wing Commander Bader. 'Johno' gave alarm: "Look out!"'

As the Spitfires cruised over the Channel, Pt Off Johnson sighted three Me 109s just a few hundred feet higher and travelling in the same direction; a perfect target for 145 Squadron, which was higher than the enemy aircraft. In his excitement, instead of calmly reporting the exact details of his sighting, 'Johnnie' Johnson shouted: 'Look out Dogsbody!' The effect was startling, as the entire Wing broke hard in all directions! Back at base, Wg Cdr Bader gave Johnson a public rebuke, which although hurtful was well justified. As they left dispersal, however, Bader acknowledged the smarting pilot officer with a knowing grin. It was a lesson that Johnson never forgot.

21 March 1941
Bader recorded in his log book: 'Snoop up Channel'.

24 March 1941
Another 'snoop' recorded in the Wing Leader's log book.

28 March 1941
As a result of 'hostile bombing', some 400 airmen were dispersed from Tangmere itself and billeted at Goodwood racecourse.

2 April 1941
The AOC, Air Vice-Marshal Sir Trafford Leigh-Mallory CB DSO, arrived at Tangmere during the afternoon and visited the various dispersal points and Sergeants' Mess. After inspecting both the canteen and airmen's dining hall, he dined in the Officers' Mess. Having stayed overnight in Chichester, the AOC then visited the Westhampnett squadrons. There he inspected the kitchen and Airmen's Dining Hall of 610 Squadron, and also the Sergeants' Mess. At the Officers' Mess he spoke with 610 Squadron's pilots before leaving for his Uxbridge HQ at 10:45 hrs. Before the AOC left, a success was reported to him; Flt Lt Norris and Sgt Ballard, both of 610 Squadron, had intercepted a Ju 88 at 07:00 hrs and shot it down into the sea.

3 April 1941
The Tangmere Sector entertained another VIP, Grp Capt HRH the Duke of Kent. The Poles of 302 Squadron presented their royal visitor with a Polish eagle made of Perspex from a Ju 88 destroyed by the squadron.

6 April 1941
A day of Rhubarbs, two such operations being flown by 610 Squadron. At 14:50 hrs Sqn Ldr Ellis DFC and Sgt Page took off, later crossing the French coast at St Valéry just below cloud, which was 10/10ths at 800 ft. It was raining hard and visibility was only two miles. After flying inland for 10 miles, the Spitfires turned north and split up. Ellis saw an airfield which he believed to be Bois Roubert and dived to attack, only to find it deserted. He then flew out to sea and up the Somme Estuary to find Abbeville, but he failed to locate this aerodrome and so recrossed the coast south of Boulogne. Following the coast to Cap Gris Nez, he saw no suitable targets and so returned to base without having fired a shot. Page, after separating from his CO, flew along a main road travelling south-west from Dieppe and was fired at from the ground. He fired one short burst at the gun position responsible before climbing into cloud and also returning to Westhampnett.

Flight Lieutenant Norris crossed the mouth of the Somme but found deteriorating weather ahead. He ordered Pt Off Ross not to proceed inland for that reason, and the pair flew along the coast between Dieppe and Cap Gris Nez. While passing Le Touquet they attacked a stationary trawler two miles out to sea, but had little else to report upon landing.

7 April 1941
The Polish 302 Squadron departed Westhampnett to join the Kenley Wing.

10 April 1941
At 05:55 hrs Tangmere was attacked by a Ju 88. Five airmen were killed and 14 wounded. A delayed-action bomb remained outside the Watch Office, however, and No. 8 barrack block was completely destroyed by a direct hit. In addition, No. 5 block was seriously damaged and a bomb passed clean through the Link Trainer Room, having ricocheted off the road outside (see Chapter Three).

13 April 1941
616 Squadron undertook both cine-gun and formation practice flights, the latter under the supervision of Bader.

14 April 1941
Squadron Leader H. De C.A. Woodhouse AFC assumed command of 610 Squadron, Sqn Ldr John Ellis DFC being posted on rest to 54 OTU as Chief Flying Instructor.

15 April 1941
Bader led 12 Spitfires of 616 Squadron to escort bombers returning from Brest. The sortie passed without incident.

16 April 1941
On this day Sqn Ldr Jack Leather handed over command of 145 Squadron to Sqn Ldr Stan Turner. The AOC paid another visit to Tangmere, arriving by air. After lunching in the Officers' Mess he held a conference with the Station Commander and squadron commanders before returning to Uxbridge at 16:30 hrs.

17 April 1941
Between 06:15 and 07:45 hrs the Tangmere Wing escorted bombers to Cherbourg; 'Escort carried out OK', reported the 610 Squadron diary. 145 Squadron saw two Me 109s shadowing the Beehive, but these made no attempt to engage.

Between 15:35 and 17:10 hrs Flt Lt Farmer, leading 610 Squadron, flew an offensive sweep over northern France but met no opposition.

In 1941 Bob Morton was a Sergeant Pilot with 616 Squadron. Now a retired schoolteacher, he is seen here reminiscing at the launch of the author's book A Few of the Many *at Worcester Guildhall in May 1995. (Dr Dennis Williams)*

18 April 1941
Squadron Leader Woodhouse of 610 Squadron flew a solo Rhubarb but found 'nothing worth firing at'.

19 April 1941
During the afternoon 145 Squadron's new CO, Sqn Ldr Turner, 'visited the French coast at Cap Gris Nez. Flew along the coast at 200 ft but saw no signs of enemy activity on land or sea.'

21 April 1941
The Wing escorted 18 Blenheims to Le Havre, but the bombers could not find their target, flying west of it. As the Spitfires ran low on fuel they had no option but to leave the bombers to their fate. That day, Bob Morton was a Sergeant pilot with 616 Squadron, and in 1995 he remembered:

> When our fuel was getting near danger point, Bader waggled his wings as a signal to us and set off for England. On the crossing, I fear that we concentrated more on our fuel gauges than keeping lookout. Only a stream of golden rain past my canopy, and the sight of my No. 2 rearing up out of control, alerted me that we were being attacked! I shouted a warning to the squadron before turning steeply in time to see two Me 109s haring back to France. There was no point in trying to catch them, so I concentrated on my No. 2, a Sergeant called Sellars. I saw that he had baled out, and was floating above the mass of creamy foam that I later came to associate with a ditched aircraft. I circled him for a time, to provide a fix, then made for home before my petrol ran out. I later learned that whilst I had circled Sellars, so too had Flight Lieutenant Colin Macfie been protecting me. In spite of the ASR resources, and a search of the area by the entire squadron immediately after we had been refuelled, Sellars was never found.

Sergeant Sellars had been the victim of I/JG2's Lt Votel, who claimed a Spitfire destroyed at 10:12 hrs, 50 km south of the Isle of Wight.

During the afternoon 145 Squadron was ordered on another Channel patrol with the intention of escorting returning bombers, but no contact was made.

22 April 1941
Group Captain A.B. 'Woody' Woodhall OBE arrived at Tangmere, pending his assuming command of the station two days later.

24 April 1941
Squadron Leader Woodhouse and Pt Off Gaze, both of 610 Squadron, flew on a Rhubarb, separating before crossing the French coast between Dieppe and Le Touquet. Woodhouse again found no action, but Gaze attacked some barges at Le Tréport, provoking green and red tracer before returning home. Two pairs of 616's Spitfires also went on Rhubarbs. First, Fg Off Dundas and Sgt Mabbett returned after an uneventful prowl over Abbeville, then Flt Lt Macfie and Sgt McDevette went to the Cherbourg peninsula. Macfie attacked Maupertus airfield, machine-gunning seven Me 109s which were taking off. McDevette was never seen again.

26 April 1941
Flight Lieutenant Macfie and Fg Off Dundas of 616 Squadron flew a high-altitude 'offensive patrol' over the French coast, but landed with nothing to report.

27 April 1941
145 Squadron escorted bombers returning over the Channel, but the sortie was uneventful.

Left: *Flying Officer Hugh 'Cocky' Dundas of 616 Squadron, who should really take the credit for the 'finger four' formation.*

Right: *Sergeant S.W.R. 'George' Mabbett of 616 Squadron poses with Spitfire P7827* Cock of the North, *in which Hugh Dundas was shot down on 8 May 1941 while experimenting with the new 'finger four' formation.*

29 April 1941
616 Squadron performed a sortie similar to that of 145 Squadron on the previous day.

30 April 1941
610 Squadron met and escorted six Blenheims returning from France. Nothing further to report.

5 May 1941
145 Squadron's Pt Off Offenberg, a Belgian, flew a Rhubarb to Cherbourg where he engaged two Heinkel He 60 biplane seaplanes, destroying one. During the return flight he attacked two Me 109s, one of which he claimed as a probable after seeing it dive seawards with 'smoke pouring from the engine'.

Flying Officers Roy Marples and 'Buck' Casson, both of 616 Squadron, intercepted and destroyed a Ju 88, as 'Buck' recalled in 1995:

> We intercepted a reconnaissance Ju 88 at 15,000 ft over Portsmouth. It dived south to just 100 ft over the sea. I shot the rear gunner but was hit myself and started leaking glycol. I just managed to recross the coast at 950 ft with a cockpit full of smoke. I inverted my Spitfire and baled out near Littlehampton.

7 May 1941
At 05:40 hrs Pt Off Gaze and Sergeant Warden of 610 Squadron took off to patrol Beachy Head and provide escort to a Lysander. At about 06:45 hrs the Section was at about 400 ft over the sea and travelling eastwards when they saw two aircraft moving in the same direction, slightly higher at 1500 ft and about two miles away. The Spitfires gave chase, identifying the bandits as two Me 109s. Having sighted the Spitfires, the Germans dived to sea level. The Spitfires split and chased their quarry to the French coast, but observed no hits. The enemy aircraft, however, were reported to have emitted 'clouds of black smoke'.

On this day 145 Squadron moved to Merston as a further precaution against the nuisance night bombing which had continued unabated, causing further damage. At Merston the airmen were accommodated in huts around the perimeter, while the officers remained at 'Sycamores' and the sergeants at 'Sycamore Cottage'.

8 May 1941
This day should be recorded in history as the day on which Fighter Command at last copied the Schwärm.

By this time Hugh Dundas had become second-in-command of 616 Squadron's 'A' Flight, under Ken Holden. In the evening of 7 May Bader had gathered certain of his officers in the mess, and they sat up late, discussing tactics. Sir Hugh Dundas later recalled: 'We expressed our dissatisfaction with formations adopted in the past ... the half-pints went down again and again while we argued the toss'. Dundas suggested that four aircraft flying in line abreast, each some 50 yds from its neighbour, could never be bounced from behind. Those of the right would cover the tails of the Spitfires on the left, and *vice versa*. No enemy could therefore approach unseen, but if attacked the formation could break upwards, one pair to port, the other to starboard; this was identical to the tactics developed by Werner Mölders in Spain.

Nursing a hangover at breakfast the following morning, Fg Off Dundas was to regret his inspiration of the night before: Not being a drinker, D.B. strode into the Mess with his buccaneering gait and was clearly in rude health. He told me that he had been thinking about my idea and had decided to try it out. I nodded in weak agreement but was somewhat startled when he said: "This morning"!'

The two pairs of this historic flight comprised Wg Cdr Bader and Fg Off Dundas, with Sqn Ldr Woodhouse and Sgt Maine of 610 Squadron. Bader led his Spitfires at 26,500 ft, prowling up and down mid-Channel just south of Dover with the aim of luring the Me 109s into action. Proving Dundas's theory, six Me 109s of Stab/JG51, ironically led by Maj Mölders, were seen approaching from the rear at the same height. As the Messerschmitts closed, the Spitfires flew on as though they were blissfully unaware that within seconds they might each be spiralling down towards the sea. At what he considered exactly the right moment for the pairs to break, out-turn the Me 109s and reverse the situation, Bader warned: 'Okay Boys, get ready for it', then called 'BREAK!' The Spitfires whipped round, the four pilots almost blacking out, so tight was the turn. Dundas levelled out, but there was no sign of the enemy; then as he straightened out on to the Tangmere foursome's original course he was hit hard by cannon fire. Thick smoke immediately engulfed the cockpit, and Dundas, who had only narrowly escaped a similarly traumatic experience during 1940, took what evasive action he could. After jettisoning the Perspex canopy, and with his Spitfire still pumping out smoke, Dundas was protected by Sqn Ldr Woodhouse as he limped to Hawkinge, just inland of Folkestone, and made a safe emergency landing, albeit nearly writing off a row of brand new 91 Squadron Spitfires in the process.

During the break, tracer had flashed past Sgt Mains. Shaking off his assailant, Mains then fired at an Me 109 which crossed in front of him, hitting it in the fuselage. Mains was then hit by flak, but as he broke away he fired from point-blank range at another Me 109, which plunged into the sea some eight miles out from Cap Gris Nez. This could have been one of two particular Me 109s lost by JG3 that morning. Although only Dundas had been shot down, and Mains damaged, on this occasion it was the Germans who overclaimed. Mölders claimed victory number 68, one Spitfire destroyed, and Oblt Horst Geyer two.

After Flt Lt Holden had collected his second-in-command from Hawkinge in a Miles Magister, Bader held a debrief at Westhampnett. Despite Dundas being shot down, the benefits of the line-abreast formation in preventing a surprise attack had been recognised. The fault lay with Bader, who had mistimed the break so that one or more of the Me 109s remained behind the Spitfires when they straightened out. This really was a major breakthrough in tactics for Fighter Command. At last the formation of four aircraft, operating in two pairs and flying in line abreast, not unlike the four fingertips of an outstretched hand, was to become gradually accepted as the basic tactical

Tangmere Spitfires. A 'finger four' of 610 or 616 Squadron Spitfires takes off from Westhampnett during the summer of 1941 for a penetration over France.

formation for fighters. Bader immediately ensured that the whole Tangmere Wing practised the technique, and eventually other Wings followed suit. The Biggin Hill Wing, however, led by the similarly brilliant South African, Wg Cdr 'Sailor' Malan, continued to fly sections of four in line astern. Malan was never converted, and there have been arguments since regarding the respective merits of each idea. For Tangmere the Finger Four, sometimes known as the 'Cross-over Four', was certainly to prove its worth in the battles ahead. Without this innovation by Dundas and Bader, it is impossible to say how many more RAF fighter pilots would have died unnecessarily owing to poor basic tactical formations throughout the Non-stop Offensive.

Also on 8 May, Sqn Ldr Turner and Pt Off de Hemptinne of 145 Squadron flew on a Rhubarb to Cherbourg, but returned with nothing to report.

9 May 1941
As a further precautionary measure against the night raiders, 616 Squadron moved from Tangmere to Westhampnett, there joining 610 Squadron. The squadron's airmen were accommodated in huts on the aerodrome, while the officers remained at 'Rushmans' and the sergeants at Woodfield House, Oving.

12 May 1941
During the early hours a further raid was mounted against Tangmere which again caused damage, but no casualties, thus justifying the policy of dispersal.

15 May 1941
Squadron Leader Woodhouse and Pt Off Hugill, both of 610 Squadron, were 'ordered on Rhubarb operation but did not fire'.

616 Squadron's Sqn Ldr Burton and Pt Off Johnson carried out an uneventful patrol at 4,000 ft over the French coast.

Bader wrote in his log book: 'Local snoop, squirted a Do 17'.

17 May 1941
During a Channel patrol Fg Off Dundas shot down an Me 109, three enemy aircraft having flown over the sea off Worthing before attacking the Spitfires. Sergeant Morton was practising dogfighting with two replacement pilots over Brighton:

At about 10,000 ft I put the other two into line astern prior to beginning the exercise. At that moment I saw two aircraft approaching us, about 1,000 ft above and slightly to one side. They were not Spitfires; I might have thought they were 109s except they had rounded wingtips, the well-known mark of the Me 109 being its square wingtips. As this pair of aircraft came abreast of us they turned on to their backs and dived vertically for the ground. This gave me sight of the engine cowlings – bright yellow! At that time everyone had heard of yellow-nosed 109s, which we believed were from a crack unit. Forgetting all about the accepted procedure of calling "Tally Ho", I simply yelled: "Come on, chaps, it's the real thing!". We gave chase! The 109s levelled out at about 1,000 ft, heading back across the Channel with me in hot pursuit. Although we believed that the Spitfire "had the legs" of a 109, I lost ground. By the time they reached the French coast I was at least 300 yds behind. Although I knew that they were out of range, I gave them a parting squirt before turning for home.

That was the first time I thought about the other two Spitfire pilots. There was no sign of them. I later learned that the first had tried to follow me down, but his eardrums had perforated as he had not yet learned the art of swallowing or yawning in a steep dive. The other pilot heard my shout, but then found himself alone in the sky. Unable to locate us, he returned to base and reported the mystery.

As I neared the English coast, however, I became aware that I was not alone. The 109s, or perhaps another pair, were sneaking up behind. Then began a real Biggles-style dogfight. I had first read the Biggles stories in the *Modern Boy*, and was greatly impressed by one of W.E. Johns's footnotes. He stated that in a head-on attack it was not done for the British pilot to break away; if the German also refused to break then he should be rammed. This I thought magnificent at the time, but now knew that I did not possess courage of that magnitude! This fight began with a head-on attack. Only the previous day I had heard Bader say that every pilot, in his first fight, opened fire whilst still out of range. I determined that I would not fire until I saw smoke coming out of my enemy's gun muzzles. At the instant I did so I thumbed the firing button – only to find that the 109 was no longer there! It was not courage which had prevented me from breaking, just my inability to think about more than one thing at a time! Fortunately for both of us my opponent was no less dim! The fight ended inconclusively shortly afterwards, how long it lasted I had no idea. For the first time it occurred to me that I had not informed Ground Control of the affair, and I did so. "Are you all right?", asked the Controller. "Fine thanks," I answered. "How are you?"

After examining my Spitfire the Flight Sergeant told me that he could find one bullet hole only. This seemed astonishing. This single bullet had whistled in all directions within the tailplane, clearing out all the internal structure so that the whole unit had to be replaced!

A week or two later, in one of our regular Intelligence bulletins, we were warned to look out for the new Me 109F, which had a better performance than the old 109E and could, in fact, outdistance a Spitfire. It could be recognised by its rounded wingtips... !

21 May 1941
Bader led 145 Squadron over the Channel, the object of the patrol being to cover a fighter squadron returning from France. When returning to base, Flt Lt Stevens and Fg Off Owen collided over Tangmere at 18:15 hrs, both pilots being killed.

4 June 1941
In the morning, Fg Off Clarke of 145 Squadron flew a Rhubarb to Le Havre, where he machine-gunned a searchlight post and destroyed a Junkers Ju 87 'Stuka'.

During the afternoon Bader and 616 Squadron, leading and covered by 610 Squadron with 145 providing top cover, undertook a sweep over the French coast. While crossing the Channel, 'Greenline Bus' was told to 'Fly east as friends were in trouble'. Only friendly aircraft were seen near the French coast, however, so the sortie remained uneventful. Pilot Officer Sabourin of 145 Squadron baled out over Worthing when he ran out of fuel.

On this day Sqn Ldr Woodhouse was posted to command 71 'Eagle' Squadron, Ken Holden moving on promotion from 616 to command 610 Squadron.

9 June 1941
Flight Lieutenant P.D. Macdonald MP, formerly Bader's adjutant in 242 Squadron, and a key player in the Big Wing controversy arrived from Manston to take up his new Tangmere appointment of 'Flight Lieutenant Admin.'

11 June 1941
In the morning, four Spitfires of 145 Squadron swept over France from Wissant to Berck, passing over St Ingelvert, but the patrol was uneventful.

At 11:30 hrs Bader took off from Merston, leading another four 145 Squadron Spitfires. They swept from Calais to Boulogne but again encountered no opposition.

At 16:15 hrs eight Spitfires of 610 Squadron, led by Sqn Ldr Holden, took off and were joined over base by four aircraft of 145 Squadron. The Spitfires of the latter Squadron provided top cover at 27,000 ft whilst 610 flew towards France at 24,000 ft. Over Boulogne, however, the two Squadrons lost contact. 610 Squadron flew south, just inland, to north of Le Touquet, then turned and flew north along the coast, returning inland at Cap Gris Nez. Although they orbited for 10 min there was again no action.

13 June 1941

Twelve Spitfires, four each from 610, 616 and 145 Squadrons, took off at 07:05 hrs and crossed the French coast south of Boulogne, where they turned left into the sun and proceeded eastwards. 610 and 616 lost contact for about 10 min. Subsequently, 610 Squadron came out of France at Calais and orbited off Dover before returning to Calais, where they found four aircraft above them and in the sun. These appeared to be Me 109s, but they did not engage. Recrossing the Channel, 616 Squadron was contacted near Dover. Again there was no opposition to this fighter sweep.

14 June 1941

Yet again, a Wing sweep met with no opposition.

15 June 1941

A high-altitude sweep over France by 'A' Flight of 616 Squadron again brought no response from the enemy.

17 June 1941

At 19:20 hrs the Tangmere Wing took off to participate in Circus No. 13. Bader's pilots swept from Boulogne to Cap Gris Nez, but again their presence went largely unopposed. Sergeant Beedham of 616 Squadron opened fire at a fleeting target but made no claim.

18 June 1941

Between 17:35 and 19:00 hrs the Tangmere Wing flew top cover to Circus 15, being joined by 303 (Polish) Squadron, which flew as 'top guard'. When they were five miles south of Boulogne 'A terrific flak barrage could be seen over the target area at Bois De Liques', so the Spitfires turned left to avoid this flak being put up at Boulogne. Crossing the French coast between Boulogne and Cap Gris Nez, the Wing flew over the Forêt de Guines and Marck and returned to Calais. In the Dunkirk area one section of 610 Squadron saw the Blenheims and escorted them back to the Thames Estuary. Sergeant Merriman turned back with engine trouble and was attacked by an Me 109 over the Channel. Taking evasive action and turning the tables on his opponent, he promptly shot down the Me 109, which crashed into the sea. At 18:40 hrs an Observer Corps post confirmed that a parachute was seen to fall into the sea six miles from St Mary's Bay, the location of this combat. 145 Squadron was also engaged over France, making no claim but losing Sgts Palmer and Turnbull.

19 June 1941

Tangmere Wing, again with 303 Squadron from Northolt as top cover, should have rendezvoused with 36 Blenheims over base to attack Le Havre docks. However, Operation *Derby* was not a success because only two bomber squadrons proceeded to the target, the remainder having aborted. The only engagement occurred when a handful of Me 109s were fought off by 616 Squadron. Flight Lieutenant Macfie damaged an enemy aircraft near the target area; probably a pilot from a training squadron, E/JG2, who forced-landed at Octeville.

At 20:40 hrs 'A' Flight of 610 Squadron swept the French coast between Cap Gris Nez and Gravelines. Woodhall informed Flt Lt Lee-Knight that there were six to eight bandits south-west of Le Touquet. The Spitfires hoped to intercept over Étaples, but the enemy was not sighted.

21 June 1941

During the morning the Tangmere Wing again flew as Target Support to another Circus, this time to St Omer, where a big fire was started in a wood in the target area. 610 Squadron were attacked by two Me 109s between St Omer and the French coast, and Flt Lt Lee-Knight (White 1) engaged one in a dogfight which started just inland of Calais. He attacked two Me 109s, leaving the rearmost aircraft 'smoking violently and apparently on fire'. He then turned north but was chased down to sea level by three more Me 109s which opened fire while the Spitfire pilot broke hard to port. One German overshot and Lee-Knight fired from point-blank range; the Me 109 crashed into the sea, the pilot later being seen in a yellow dinghy. White 1 was then chased by two more Messerschmitts, which he lost, but Pt Off Gaze (White 2) found himself in trouble when bounced by four Me 109s over Dunkirk. In true Biggles style he, too, made a head-on attack but saw no result because his windscreen became smothered in oil, probably as a result of hitting one of his enemies.

Sergeant Macbeth of 145 Squadron became separated over St Omer and was attacked by an Me 109 which he managed to evade, and at which he fired an inconclusive burst. The 6/JG26 Me 109E of Obfwl Luders was attacked by Fg Off Machacek (145) and Sqn Ldr Burton, and the latter reported:

> Just after take-off my hood came adrift and I landed, had it fixed in about 10 min and endeavoured to catch up the Wing. Climbed to 20,000 ft over Dungeness, could see no sign of Wing so dived down and patrolled speedboat with two other Spitfires about 10 miles east of Dover. About 12:20 hrs our fighters started to come in and I suddenly noticed two Me 109s crossing the coast NE of Dover. I then saw one Spitfire attacking. I joined in and we cut off one Me 109, the other one quickly disappeared. We dived and zoomed for several minutes over land between Dover and Manston, alternately engaging E/A with quarter and beam attacks. Finally E/A opened hood and baled out. His machine crashed into a railway embankment and blew up. Pilot landed safely and was made prisoner by a civilian. I personally cannot be sure which Spitfire pilot was responsible for destroying the E/A. It appeared that he was hardly damaged at all when he baled out. The other Spitfire attacking was of 145 Squadron, 'SO-D'.

Sergeant Frank Twitchett of 145 Squadron, however, was attacked near the English coast by Oblt Matzke of II/JG26, the Me 109s having pursued the withdrawing Spitfires across the Channel. Frank Twitchett remembers:

> The running battle started over St Omer, with several squadrons of Me 109s attacking us whilst we were at about 25,000 ft. Obviously the whole thing then broke up into a series of individual combats. Once you realise that you are separated from your squadron, the thing to do is get the Hell out of it, so I followed this normal pattern and headed for ground-level and home. By the time I reached mid-Channel, at about 500 ft, I foolishly lowered my guard slightly. The next thing I became aware of was an enormous BANG! The cockpit filled with cordite fumes and the Spitfire lurched wildly sideways. My immediate reaction was to throw the aircraft into a violent left-hand turn and look into my rear-view mirror. There I saw the unmistakable shape of an Me 109. To use the famous expression, I had really been caught with my trousers down. I subsequently learned that the German pilots were

Sergeant Frank Twitchett of 145 Squadron.

well briefed on our defensive tactics, so when I broke left my assailant was prepared for this. We circled round for several minutes, during which time my petrol supply began getting very low, and finally I lost the 109 in the haze. I then set course for England and worked my way along the south coast towards Merston, where I became aware of blood coming from my battledress jacket, and my knee. I damage checked my aircraft, saw damage to the right-hand wing, and when I pushed the rudder bar, the rudder went over to "full" with hardly any effort! Luckily the engine was still running perfectly and I was still flying. I landed safely, and was taken to the Station Sick Quarters, from where I went to St Richard's Hospital in Chichester. There I had stitches put in my knee and was told that I was going to be out of action for the next few days.

During this sortie 616 Squadron lost their first officer pilot of the year when Pt Off Brown's Spitfire dived, out of control, over France.

Between 15:50 and 17:10 hrs Bader led the Tangmere Wing on Circus 17. The Wing orbited the target area, Desvres, at 22,000 ft. Twenty Me 109s were seen in the Hardelot area, so one section of 610 Squadron broke away to engage a Schwärm, approaching from behind. A dogfight ensued and Pt Off Scott shot down an Me 109, which crashed into the sea about seven miles off Le Touquet. Flight Lieutenant 'Crow' Milling also fired at the enemy aircraft as it flashed across his sights, only to find Pt Off Scott already latched on to its tail. He was, however, able to confirm that pieces of the enemy aircraft were shot away and fell into the sea. Pilot Officer Hugill confirmed that the Me 109 crashed into the sea. During the return flight 145 Squadron's Sgt Grant encountered an Me 109E which he promptly shot down into the sea. Despite violent evasive action, Flt Lt Newling (145) was shot up and forced landed at Dungeness. 616 Squadron was also engaged, Fg Off Marples claiming one Me 109 and Flt Lt Casson and Sgt Beedham sharing another.

Across the Channel, Adolf Galland, JG26's Kommodore, would remember 21 June as a remarkable day. Just 8 min after responding to the morning's Alarmstart,

Dave Horne pokes his head through the cannon-shell-holed rudder of Frank Twitchett's Spitfire, P8341. This shows the significant damage that even one round of 20 mm ammunition could inflict on a Spitfire's tail.

Galland destroyed a Blenheim which crashed near its target, the airfield at St Omer-Arques. Just 4 min later he dispatched another bomber, but was then hit himself. Trailing glycol, the Kommodore forced-landed at Calais-Marck. Galland soon returned to Audembert, and took off again at 16:00 hrs, this time minus his Rottenflieger, Obfwl Hegenaur, who had also been shot down during the morning's action. Galland attacked a formation of Spitfires, shooting one down in flames, but without his wingman to act as a witness to this victory the Kommodore himself had to watch the fate of this 'Tommy' to obtain the necessary detail for the Abschussmeldung (combat report). In doing so, however, he committed the fighter pilot's cardinal sin, and was hit hard. The Me 109F burst into flames, plunging earthwards. Galland narrowly escaped with his life, but was wounded.

22 June 1941
Tangmere Wing went on a sweep which crossed the French coast north of Le Touquet, sweeping round St Omer to Dunkirk, where the Beehive proper was seen coming in from the coast. The Beehive was then attacked by Me 109s and, as other enemy fighters had turned behind the Wing, a general dogfight ensued from 18,000 ft to ground level. Squadron Leader Holden destroyed an Me 109, which crashed south of St Omer, and as he recrossed the French coast north of Dunkirk he machine-gunned a sandbagged gunpost. As the CO of 610 Squadron zoomed out of France at 500 ft, ground gunposts and ships opened up on him, although their aim was fortunately poor. Over France, Pt Off Horner, also of 610, saw an Me 109 preparing to attack a Spitfire. He hurried to his comrade's assistance and the enemy fighter was forced to break away before firing a shot. After a long burst from Horner, the Me 109 burst into flames, this being confirmed by Pt Off Scott. Sergeant Raine had been left behind when 610 Squadron had first broken left, so dived and found an airfield which he strafed. He then engaged an Me 109 which subsequently crash-landed in the Merville-Béthune area, somersaulting on to its back in a 'terrific cloud of smoke'.

Sergeant Robillard of 145 Squadron was attacked by three Me 109s, one of which he was to claim as destroyed when it exploded in mid-air.

On this day Adolf Hitler unleashed Operation *Barbarossa* on the unsuspecting Russians. The effect on the Kanalfront air war was the stepping up of RAF operations clearly evident in this diary's remaining pages.

23 June 1941

On a sweep between 12:45 and 14:30 hrs the Tangmere Wing crossed the French coast at Le Touquet, sweeping to the south of St Omer. A 'cluster of bombers was seen in the target area', and flak was seen between Boulogne and Le Touquet, 'although not intensive'.

Between 19:50 and 21:30 hrs the Tangmere Wing again swept over France and over Calais, and were told that bandits were in mid-Channel. Climbing into the sun, the Wing swept the centre of the Dover Straits, but was then informed of a dogfight in progress off Dover itself. Although the Wing proceeded east of Dover and orbited, nothing was seen.

Among the German pilots engaged in the combat off Dover was Oblt Heinz Gottlob, a former enlisted man, of 1/JG26:

I flew as the protection Rotte of our Staffel, as our Staffelkapitän, Oberleutnant Priller, engaged a Spitfire. Then I saw that three other Spitfires tried to get behind the Staffel. I engaged them with my Rotte. The Spitfires went into a tight turn. I turned also and climbed above them. I saw one Spitfire flying in a north-westerly direction. The Spitfire was over land at 19,680 ft altitude. I flew behind him at a range of about 70 ft and the pilot did not take evasive action. I fired all guns from behind and below. I saw a lot of smoke and parts falling from his fuselage and wings. The plane climbed, slowed and rolled over the left wing. It rolled two or three times. Then the Spitfire dived down. I dived after it and fired again. I pulled out of my dive and gained altitude. I turned into a bank and saw the Spitfire hit the water. The pilot did not escape.

Despite the Luftwaffe claiming seven Spitfires destroyed in this combat, and although Fighter Command suffered several Spitfires damaged, only one was lost; 616 Squadron's Sgt Beedham, who was rescued from the Channel by air-sea rescue. It is therefore likely that he, in fact, was Gottlob's victim. It would not be long before Oblt Gottlob and Wg Cdr Bader clashed in those dangerous skies.

24 June 1941

On this day the Tangmere Wing operated from Redhill. Over North Foreland Bader's Wing connected with Malan's Biggin Hill Spitfires, and together the RAF fighters crossed the French coast at Gravelines. Shortly afterwards ten Me 109s 'painted all black' were sighted travelling west at 19,000 ft. Unfortunately the bandits were too far ahead to be intercepted. After five minutes orbiting over Lille the Spitfires returned home, encountering 'heavy and accurate flak' in the St Omer area. Squadron Leader Burton recorded in his log book: 'Odd squirt here and there at 109s which disappear downwards at fantastic speeds. Majority appear to be 109Fs.'

25 June 1941

Tangmere Wing provided cover on Circus 22, between 12:00 and 13:00 hrs. Having crossed the French coast, the Wing was warned of 30 plus 109s approaching from the south-east. Contact was made near Gravelines, where Pt Off Scott of 610 Squadron destroyed an Me 109, which crashed into the ground. Flight Lieutenant Milling attacked two Me 109s, leaving one streaming 'thick black smoke coming from underneath and just in front of the pilot's seat'. Sergeant Davies was slightly wounded, however, and forced-landed at Manston in Kent. Bader claimed one Me 109 destroyed, and another shared with Sgt Jeff West (616). Other 616 Squadron pilots were also successful, claiming between them a further two probables and two damaged.

Between 15:45 and 17:40 hrs the Tangmere Wing flew on Circus 23, crossing the French coast at 23,000 ft over Le Touquet. About 15 miles inland, 12 Me 109Fs were seen approaching from the east, 'in rough formation'. Wing Commander Aitken, flying with 610 Squadron, attacked an Me 109, which crashed into some trees just behind Le Touquet. Sergeant Raine, also of 610 Squadron, inconclusively engaged an Me 109E which escaped into cloud, but he caught it emerging and shot off a large portion of its port wing, leaving it shrouded in smoke. Hedge-hopping his way to the coast, east of Calais he machine-gunned an Me 109E on the tarmac of an aerodrome which he roared over at just 30 ft; 'Four or five ground staff working on the aircraft were hit'. Raine was then chased by an Me 109 but was fortunate to escape with just one bullet-hole through an elevator. Squadron Leader Holden was also in action, leaving an Me 109 streaming white smoke over France. 145 Squadron's CO, Sqn Ldr Turner, engaged an Me 109E which was last seen diving, pouring smoke and glycol fumes. Sergeant Grant (145) destroyed an Me 109 over Le Touquet, and Flt Lt Arthur (145) destroyed another, the pilot of which baled out. Sergeant Camplin (145) damaged an Me 109E, and both he an Fg Off Scott also fired at flak ships.

For 616 Squadron this sortie was not a success. Having been bounced, Sgts Jenks and Brewer were both lost. Sergeant Bob Morton was also attacked:

I was flying as No. 2 to Flying Officer Marples when jumped from behind by a pair of 109s. There was the usual display of golden rain accompanied by sundry bangs as cannon shells exploded inside the machine. Instinctively I rolled on to my back and went vertically down. The first thing I noticed was – nothing; the cockpit was so full of smoke that I couldn't even see the instruments. We had recently been advised that if smoke came into the cockpit we should unfasten our Sutton harness and unplug both our radio and oxygen leads ready to bale out and before opening the canopy, as the extra draught would suck in the flames causing the smoke. I deliberately – and foolishly – ignored this sound advice; my immediate desire was to see. I put up a hand to open the canopy but it was jammed. At very high speeds – and I was certainly moving – the aerofoil shape of the canopy tended to hold it in the closed position. At last, using both hands and all my strength, I pulled it back. The smoke eased as if by magic, and as I pulled out of the dive I surveyed the damage. A couple of machine-gun panels were missing from my starboard wing, indicating that a shell had exploded inside it, and there was a bullet-hole in the engine cowling. Although that was the only visible damage, the engine sounded like a cement mixer! I quickly throttled back and surveyed the instruments. The radiator temperature was jammed against the upper stop, as was the oil temperature indicator. The oil pressure needle had dropped below the scale. Obviously damage to the radiator had caused loss of all glycol coolant, which accounted for the white smoke.

My only hope was to hold a northerly course towards the Channel; ditching there I would at least have a chance of being picked up by our ASR. I chose coarse pitch for the propeller, to nurse the engine, which sounded worse every minute, and willed it to keep turning over until I had crossed the French coast. Then came what I had dreaded: a lone 109 coming up from behind. Reluctantly I went into the defensive circle, whilst this was held neither pilot could gain the advantage. The first to break away, however, would have the other on his tail, and my time was rapidly running out. Suddenly I discovered that my opponent had broken away and was zooming inland. I have, in fact, often since wondered whether this was amongst the last acts of true chivalry in modern warfare. My Spitfire was obviously quite damaged, and by then was pouring black smoke from its exhausts. It would have taken little effort to shoot me down, thus adding an easy kill to the German's score. Instead, like a true aerial knight, he gave me a sporting chance to reach the Channel.

Neither of us had allowed for the magnificent Rolls-Royce Merlin engine in our estimation of my chances of survival. Against all reason, the engine, the moving parts of which must have been near red-heat, kept going, not just to the Channel, but across it to Hawkinge! My circuit attracted all eyes, so fortunately I made a copy-book approach, although I was unaware that my right tyre had been burst by the cannon shell in my right wing. My landing, therefore, was a series of ungainly hops, with a tight little circle at the end of it!

Bader attacked an Me 109F in the Boulogne area:

I attacked four Me 109Fs, with my No. 2, which were climbing in a slightly left-hand turn. I gave a short burst at one from close range, from inside the turn, and saw white, black and orange-coloured smoke envelope the aircraft which went down in an increasingly steep dive which finished up beyond the vertical.

Bader's victim was Oblt Heinz Gottlob of I/JG26, who was shot down near Marquise but baled out:

Priller led one Schwärm, and I led the other. We saw about 18 Spitfires over the Channel. They had apparently already seen us, since they were flying in a defensive circle. We were at about 8,500 m. The Indianer were about 500 m below. Priller banked left to reach a firing position. My Schwärm cut behind him. Suddenly there was an explosion in my aircraft. Holes appeared in the cockpit floor, between my legs. I actually saw the fur of my flying boots ripple as several bullets ripped through them. Then several cannon shells hit the right side of my cockpit. I tried to dive away using my elevators, but they were unresponsive. As I was already in a left-hand bank I kicked the rudder and commenced a wingover towards the ground – I had to decrease my altitude to a height at which I could bale out and not suffocate due to lack of oxygen. During the dive, however, I noticed that my oxygen cylinder was empty, shrouded in blue fumes – shot through! I ripped my mask off at 4,200 m and prepared to bale out when I was hit again, although this could have been my own ammunition exploding as all the shrapnel came from beneath my instrument panel and flew back, above my head. Everything was now happening very fast indeed. Suddenly I was struck on the chin with such force that my head was flung back to the right, I felt a terrible pain in my nose, eyes and skull.

I began to lose both my will and consciousness. I squinted at the release lever, but could not summon the strength to bale out. As everything was turning black, a voice inside my head called out "Get out, now!" I have no further memory, I do not know whether my parachute deployed itself, or whether I struck the tail, thus causing it to open. Although the fight had started over the Channel, I was now over French soil, fortunately near the Naval hospital at Hardinghem. At 21:05 hrs I landed at the feet of a surgeon from the hospital who was out taking a walk – I regained consciousness eight days later.

Gottlob was so badly wounded that he was never to return to JG26 or increase his score of five kills.

26 June 1941
Again the Tangmere Wing operated from Redhill, on Circus 24. Crossing the coast at Gravelines, Bader was warned of 24 plus Me 109s to the south-east. Simultaneously

the enemy aircraft were seen in front of the Wing and in loose formation. The Messerschmitts then swung behind and upwards to attack 610 Squadron from behind. Pilot Officer Gaze consequently sent one Me 109 into the sea, just off the coast. Going down to sea level, the Spitfire pilot saw his vanquished foe in the water, inflating his yellow dinghy. Squadron Leader Holden shot pieces from an Me 109's tail unit but then lost control of his own aircraft. When he looked again a parachute had opened some 5,000 ft below, although it was impossible to say if this was Holden's victim. Flight Lieutenant Lee-Knight had the misfortune to be chased 'a long way out to sea by four to six enemy aircraft, he turned two or three times on the way out, firing snapshots. One enemy aircraft was smoking badly when he broke away so he considers it to be damaged'. 145 Squadron's Sgt Johnson destroyed an Me 109F near Dunkirk, but Sgt Macbeth was reported 'missing'.

616 Squadron was also in action, Pt Off Johnson destroying an Me 109. Having previously shared a Do 17 with Fg Off Dundas several months before, this was his first complete victory, and the first of a long score:

> I became detached from Wing Commander Bader's Section at 15,000 ft through watching three 109s immediately above me. I saw them dive away to port and almost immediately afterwards saw an Me 109E coming in from my starboard side and which flew across me about 150 yds away, turning slightly to port. I immediately turned inside the enemy aircraft (E/A) and opened fire, closing to 100 yds. After two one-second bursts the E/A jettisoned its hood, rolled over and the pilot baled out, his parachute opening almost immediately. I then broke away as there were other E/A about. I estimated I was over Gravelines when in combat. On landing I heard that several pilots of 145 Squadron had witnessed this. After the combat I joined up with Flying Officer Scott of 145 Squadron and we landed at Hawkinge to refuel, returning to Westhampnett at 13:25 hrs.

Flight Lieutenant Casson damaged another Me 109, but Sergeant Morton again found himself in trouble, although not because of the enemy on this occasion:

> It grieves me to have to report an incident worthy of the notorious "Pilot Officer Prune", who at the time, in fact, had yet to be introduced via the pages of our training manual, *Tee-Em*. We had been on a sweep in the morning; whilst returning across the Channel alone, I kept the sun over my right shoulder, saving continuous study of my compass. In the afternoon we carried out another sweep. Again I became separated from my companions, though no action came my way, and again I set out for home – with the sun again over my right shoulder! Consequently it seemed to take longer to reach the eastern end of the Isle of Wight. What in fact I eventually reached was the Naze, near Clacton, but this, like my intended point, had a sunken ship with masts and a funnel showing above the water. I was satisfied, so struck inland for the aerodrome having not looked at my compass.
>
> When my fuel began to run low, I selected a suitable field for a precautionary landing. It looked like a grass field. In fact it was ploughed and full of growing wheat. The first touch sheared off my undercarriage legs. The Spitfire dug its nose into the ground, rotated laterally through 180 degrees, smashed down travelling tail first, reared up on its tail and turned through another 90 degrees before coming to rest. Sometime during this performance the fuselage had snapped in half. As a few hundred (or perhaps just a dozen!) soldiers came running up, I turned my attention to the panel over the radio set in the fuselage, mainly to hide my red face.
>
> "Are you all right?", asked one of the soldiers.
>
> "No," I replied savagely, "I've swallowed my chewing gum!"

As the 616 Squadron ORB recorded, Bob had 'mistaken the northern part of the Thames Estuary for the south coast near the Isle of Wight'.

27 June 1941

Between 13:00 and 14:30 hrs 12 Spitfires of 610 Squadron and seven of 616 flew on a sweep, operating from Friston. Although a penetration of some 30 to 40 miles was made there was no action.

Operating from Westhampnett between 20:55 and 22:20 hrs, the Tangmere Wing again swept 40 miles within France. Some 15 Me 109s were seen, but refused to engage. The flak was found to be 'very accurate over Boulogne'. 145 Squadron lost the other Wing squadrons in the haze, and formated on 12 fighters which they believed to be 616 Squadron. The Spitfire pilots were, however, amazed to see that their new companions were actually Me 109s! As the 109s dispersed into the sun, Flt Lt Newling engaged a pair of them, sending one earthwards 'shrouded in black smoke'.

28 June 1941

Between 07:45 and 09:40 hrs the Tangmere Wing flew on Circus 26, sighting bombers leaving the coast at Dunkirk. Ten miles inland from Dunkirk Sqn Ldr Holden reported two Me 109Fs going inland and 5,000 ft below. He dived to attack, but the enemy aircraft dived away inland. The only other enemy aircraft seen were 'a long way off'. Flying Officer Machacek (145) became separated from his squadron but engaged an Me 109E over Cassel which he later claimed as a probable.

On this day JG26 suffered a hard loss when Oblt Gustav 'Micky' Sprick, Kapitän of 8/JG26, was killed in action against Spitfires near St Omer. One of the first Experten with 20 victories, Sprick had received his Ritterkreuz on 1 October 1941. His final score was 31.

30 June 1941

Between 17:40 and 19:35 hrs the Tangmere Wing was on a sweep over France. Near Le Touquet 50 plus bandits were reported to the east. These were sighted by 610 Squadron about 20 miles east of Le Touquet, flying in pairs and numbering between 16 and 20. These enemy aircraft being well out of range, the Wing proceeded to St Omer, which it orbited for some 30 min. Over the Channel a pair of Me 109s were seen, but again these refused to engage. 145 Squadron, however, encountered six Me 109s over Le Touquet, Flt Lt Arthur and Fg Off St Pierre sharing the destruction of one. Sergeant Robillard machine-gunned a flak gun position near Boulogne. Sergeant McCairns of 616 Squadron was shot at, his cockpit being hit, but fortunately he was uninjured and returned safely to base.

On this day 'Buck' Casson of 616 Squadron was promoted to Acting Flight Lieutenant and took command of 'A' Flight.

1 July 1941

At 17:39 hrs the Tangmere Wing took off on a sweep, later orbiting Béthune for 25 min. Again there was no opposition to speak of, although 145 Squadron's Sgt Smith fired a short burst at an Me 109 without any apparent effect.

The nightfighter Hurricanes of 1 Squadron arrived at Tangmere. In addition to those Hurricanes and the Sector's Spitfire squadrons, Tangmere now boasted the Beaufighters of 219 Squadron, various aircraft of No. 1455 Special Flight, the AA Co-operation Unit and an Air Sea Rescue Flight. 'Pop' Elvidge was with 1 Squadron's groundcrew:

> We arrived in the blackout and were given the camp cinema as sleeping quarters. The next day I realised why; the Other Ranks' quarters had been bombed, together with

several hangars. The routine from then on was 24 hours at Tangmere, 24 at Goodwood racecourse, sleeping in the open stands. The squadron was on night intruder operations, but in the daytime we would assist with the refuelling and rearming of the Polish Wing from Northolt which used our airfield for sweeps over the Channel. All we groundcrew knew of the intruder ops was the friendly rivalry which existed between the squadron's two flights, their commanders being Flight Lieutenants Kuttelwascher and Jimmy Maclachlan. The latter was, I understood, formerly a pilot of one of Malta's Gladiators, *Faith*, *Hope* and *Charity*, and in one particular combat had his arm blown off by a cannon shell. The cockpit of his Hurricane Mk IIC had been specially adapted to accommodate his artificial arm. As I have indicated, however, little was known of their nocturnal operations, our only source of information being our riggers, who used to record on the aircraft their sorties: red swastikas for aircraft destroyed, and little red steam trains for locomotives. The squadron was also experimenting with a Turbinlite Havoc, a Boston Havoc (*sic*] with radar and a searchlight mounted in the nose. This was abandoned, however, as the light's batteries were found to be of insufficient duration.

I remember once that the "All Clear" had sounded following a raid on Portsmouth when our Ops 'phone rang, informing us that an unidentified plot remained on the board. A Flying Officer Parsons scrambled to investigate, a relatively inexperienced pilot. He returned sometime later having destroyed the bandit, but the Ops 'phone rang again: a Bomber Command Stirling had been shot down over Midhurst. Our celebrations stopped immediately for this was Parsons' victim, although at least the entire crew baled out safely.

I also remember the comings and goings of a Lysander which used to appear at our dispersal from time to time. We would see an RAF pilot and civilians board the aircraft; we had our suspicions, but it was not until after the war that these where confirmed when the story of SOE operations was told.

On a lighter note, the station band was that of the famous "Snake Hips Johnson", who had been bombed out of the Café de Paris in London before joining the RAF *en masse*.

2 July 1941

Between 11:45 and 13:50 hrs the Tangmere Wing participated in Circus 29, to Lille. Near the target all three Gruppen of JG26 intercepted the Beehive and a general dogfight ensued. One Me 109F was destroyed by Sgt Mains and another damaged by Pt Off Gaze (both of 610). 145 Squadron, which had received Spitfire Mk VAs this day, lost the Canadian Sgt Robillard. Bader claimed one Me 109 destroyed and another damaged, as did his No. 2, Sgt Alan Smith, who also machine-gunned some

Pilot Officer Philip 'Nip' Heppell of 616 Squadron.

workshops and German soldiers on a beach. Pilot Officer 'Nip' Hepple also destroyed an Me 109, the pilot of which baled out. The Wing Commander's combat report makes fascinating reading:

> I was leading 616 Squadron's first section. Sighted approximately 15 Me 109Fs a few miles SW of Lille, so turned south and attacked them. They were in a sort of four formation climbing eastwards. They made no attempt to do anything but climb in formation so I turned the squadron behind them and attacked from about 200 ft above and behind. I attacked an Me 109F from quarter astern to astern, and saw his hood come off – he probably jettisoned it – and the pilot started to climb out. Did not see him actually bale out as I nearly collided with another Me 109 that was passing on my right in the middle of a half-roll. Half-rolled with him and dived down on his tail, firing at him with the result that glycol and oil came out of his machine. I left him at about 12,000 ft, as he appeared determined to continue diving, and pulled up again to 18,000 ft. My ASI (airspeed indicator) showed rather more than 400 mph when I pulled out. Found the fight had taken me west a bit so picked up two 610 Squadron Spitfires and flew out at Boulogne, round Gris Nez and up to Gravelines where we crossed the coast again and found an Me 109E at 8,000 ft, and at which I fired from about 300 yds. No damage, but this one is claimed as 'Frightened'! The first 109 is claimed as destroyed since, although I did not actually see the pilot leave the aircraft, I saw him preparing to do so, and several pilots of 616 saw two parachutes going down, the pilot of one of which was shot down by Pilot Officer Hepple. The second 109 was seen by Pilot Officer Hepple and is claimed as damaged.

On this day Wg Cdr D.R.S. Bader DSO DFC was awarded a Bar to the DSO, and Sqn Ldr Holden a DFC.

Across the Channel, the Kanalgeschwader had suffered its first serious individual loss of the year, JG2's Kommodore, Maj Wilhelm Balthasar, having been killed by Spitfires near Aire. JG26 also suffered a serious casualty, and recorded the death of another Staffelkapitän, Oblt Martin Rysavy of 2/JG26, who was killed by German 88mm flak in an unfortunate incident of 'friendly fire'.

3 July 1941

Circus 30 saw the Tangmere Wing airborne between 10:0 and 12:5 hrs, providing close escort to bombers attacking Hazebrouck. The Beehive was intercepted by Me 109s over the target and numerous individual combats then took place. Flight Lieutenant Lee-Knight of 610 Squadron destroyed an Me 109, which crashed south-west of Lille. When attacked by more Me 109s, Lee-Knight sent another 'diving vertically down, smoking violently'. By then he was at nought feet, and machine-gunned a group of German soldiers near a searchlight at Cap Gris Nez. Sergeants Merriman and Bowen, the latter of 616 Squadron, attacked, and shared as a probable, an unfortunate Henschel Hs 126. As he broke away, however, Merriman's port wingtip struck the wing strut and port tailplane of the Henschel.

Circus 31 was next, the Tangmere Wing being airborne between 15:10 and 17:00 hrs. The Wing orbited St Omer, but although odd Me 109s were seen they dived away and refused to engage. 616 Squadron's Sgt Beedham claimed an Me 109 as probably destroyed.

4 July 1941

Circus 32 again found the Tangmere Wing orbiting St Omer. Only one 'odd enemy aircraft' was seen which dived to ground level upon being attacked'. Pilot Officer

Johnson and Sgt Morton, both of 616, each damaged an Me 109, however. Bader destroyed an Me 109 near Guines:

Intercepted one Me 109E some miles south of Gravelines at 14,000 ft, while with a section of four. Turned on to its tail and opened fire with a short, 1-second burst at about 150 yds. I found it very easy to keep inside him during the turn and closed quite quickly. I gave him three more short bursts, the final one at about 20 yds range; as he slowed down very suddenly I nearly collided with him. I did not see the result except one puff of smoke half way through. Squadron Leader Burton in my section watched the complete combat and saw the Me 109's airscrew slow right down to ticking over speed. As I broke away the 109 did not half-roll and dive, but just sort of fell away in a sloppy fashion, quite slowly, as though the pilot had been hit. Having broken away, I did not see the 109 I attacked, since I was trying to collect my section together. I am, however, satisfied that I was hitting him and so is Squadron Leader Burton, from whose evidence this report is written.

Bader's victim was Lt Joachim Kehrhahn of I/JG26, who was killed when his Me 109E-7 (6476) crashed at St Pol.

On Circus 33 the Tangmere Wing orbited Lille, seeing three Stirling bombers withdraw, leaving the target smoking. The Wing then wove behind the bombers back to the French coast, which was recrossed at Gravelines. 610 Squadron's Flt Lt Lee-Knight escorted a Spitfire with a 'dead propeller', but approaching Margate the pilot baled out. Lee-Knight then sent a 'fix' on the pilot and covered a Lysander to the downed pilot's position, some 10–15 miles east-south-east of Manston. Over the target area Sgt Mains, also of 610, destroyed an Me 109E, the pilot of which baled out, although the Spitfire pilot discovered his oil temperature to be 97°. Forced to break off, Mains landed at Hawkinge. 145 Squadron reported that 'the usual difficulty was experienced in coming into close contact with the enemy'. 616 Squadron suffered a significant loss when 'A' Flight commander Flt Lt Colin Macfie was shot down over France and captured. The squadron diary recorded: 'We are all very sad at his loss as he had been with the squadron since the beginning of September 1940, and had endeared himself to everyone despite his taciturnity'.

6 July 1941

During the morning 11 Spitfires of 145 Squadron patrolled the Channel uneventfully, except for an aborted attack by a single Me 109F.

Between 13:30 and 15:30 hrs Bader led the Tangmere Wing on a target support sortie to six Stirlings bombing Lille. The Wing orbited over the target until the Beehive arrived, bombed, and withdrew over Hardelot. The Tangmere Wing then proceeded towards the coast, just behind and to the Beehive's east. A running battle then ensued and the Wing claimed four Me 109s destroyed. The enemy fighters were reported as having 'adopted their usual tactics of trying to get a surprise attack and rushing away when Spitfires turned on them'. The bombing was noted by the Wing as being 'extremely impressive. Bombs fell in a factory area east of a railway line running roughly north and south.' Interestingly, two 145 Squadron pilots reported 'being actually shot at by a Spitfire over the target area'. Pilot Officer Arthur, also of 145, fired at an Me 109 but had not selected both cannon and machine-guns on his gun button, so only the latter were discharged, with little effect. Sadly, however, Flt Lt Michael Newling DFC, a stalwart and long-standing member of 145 Squadron, failed to return. He remains missing to this day, and is remembered on panel 29 of the Runnymede Memorial.

Bader and 616 Squadron became embroiled with Me 109s, various claims being made by members of 'Dogsbody Section'. Sergeant McCairns failed to return, although his Spitfire was seen on Dunkirk beach, where he had forced-landed.

7 July 1941

Between 09:40 and 11:30 hrs Bader led his Tangmere Spitfires on Circus 37, during which four Stirlings attacked Albert. Bombs were seen to burst in the target area, but although 'odd Me 109s were seen, no attack was made'. Some 16 E-Boats were seen off Le Touquet and attacked by the Spitfires, but without any noticeable result. One aircraft was seen to crash into the sea off Berck, and aircraft wreckage, together with patches of oil, were seen in the Channel. Another aircraft was also thought to have crashed in the sea off Le Touquet.

Bader next led the Wing on Circus 38, from 14:30 to 16:20 hrs, the Tangmere Spitfires operating from Redhill. Again bombs were reported falling in the exact target area at Choques, and there was little opposition. Sergeant Silvester of 145 Squadron was badly shot about and slightly wounded, but fortunately managed to make base. 616 Squadron's Sgt Bowen was shot about but crash-landed unhurt at Hawkinge.

On this day Hugh Dundas was promoted to Acting Flight Lieutenant, and succeeded the captured Macfie as 'A' Flight commander.

8 July 1941

Between 05:40 and 07:20 hrs Bader led the Tangmere Wing on another target support sortie, Circus 38. Four Stirlings split into two pairs to attack two targets, the 'main target being left in flames and the second with large volumes of smoke issuing from it'. On the return journey a Stirling was hit by flak and blew up, crashing on buildings below; only two of the crew baled out. 616 Squadron reported that 'it was not a very pleasant sight to watch'. While returning to the French coast, 'a Spitfire was seen spinning down very fast with glycol fumes pouring from it'. Although some Me 109s shadowed the Wing, they did not attack.

At 11:55 hrs Sgts Merriman and Doley of 610 Squadron were scrambled from Westhampnett. After several vectors they sighted two Me 109s at 15,000 ft, flying towards Portsmouth. The Spitfires gave chase, Sgt Merriman shooting one down into the sea. On the return flight to base he met another Me 109F which he left trailing smoke and diving towards the sea.

Between 14:35 and 16:40 hrs Bader led the Wing on Circus 40. The Wing, again target support, orbited the target, but was 'embarrassed by another Wing which was flying at the same height of 22,000 ft. As the Beehive recrossed the French coast at Gravelines several Me 109s were seen, one of which attacked 610 Squadron's Flt Lt Lee-Knight of 610 Squadron, who consequently claimed a probable. Pilot Officer Horner of the same squadron failed to return. A Spitfire was reported spinning down slowly, and a parachute was reported descending from 26,000 ft north of Lille. Another aircraft was seen to go down in flames near Dunkirk. Three Me 109s were seen near Lille, 'camouflaged grey with black crosses'. Three Spitfire Mk VAs of 145 Squadron returned to base before the French coast was reached, and the nine remaining aircraft of that squadron became separated later when taking evasive action. Two of their number, Fg Off Machacek and Pt Off Pine, failed to return.

9 July 1941

From 13:05 to 14:45 hrs Bader led the Wing on Circus 41, crossing the English coast over Rye and making landfall at Hardelot. Me 109s then approached in 'pairs and larger formations but not close enough to attack effectively, adopting instead their usual tactics of trying to lure the Spitfires away'. Squadron Leader Turner of 145 Squadron managed an inconclusive burst at a fleeting Me 109, but Sgt McFarlane, who made a solo attack, was last seen on fire and diving over France. Wing Commander Bader and Sergeant Smith made claims, Bader's including more 'Frightened' Me 109s: '...Several others were frightened and I claim one badly frightened who did the quickest half-roll and dive I've ever seen when I fired at him!'

However, 616 Squadron lost two pilots, Sqn Ldr E.P. Gibbs, a former aerobatic pilot, and Sgt Bob Morton. By flying inverted close to the ground, Gibbs managed to fool his assailants into thinking that he was finished. At the last minute he righted his Spitfire, popped down the undercarriage and made a perfect landing. He evaded capture, and was one of several Tangmere Wing pilots who made 'home runs' that summer.

Bob Morton was probably shot down by Oblt Eickhoff of I/JG26. He remembers the day's events vividly:

On 8 July our first Spitfire Mk VB was delivered, with two cannon instead of eight machine-guns. To my delight the CO asked me to take it out over the sea and test the cannon. Why I was chosen was a mystery; none of our officers, except Wing Commander Bader, had ever used cannon, and all would have liked the chance. I went straight down to the hangar and sought out the Flight Sergeant. "I know what you've come for," he said. "We're having a bit of trouble lining up the cannon. Can you come back after lunch?" I said that I would, but during lunch an afternoon sweep was ordered. I flew with my heart in my mouth, fearful that someone else should be testing the new Spitfire. Immediately we landed I went straight to the hangar but the work was still not finished, nor was it after tea, when I was asked to return in the morning. Again a sweep intervened, and after lunch, another. On that occasion I flew as No. 2 to a new pilot, Flying Officer Gill. As soon as we got over France he commenced imitating the Blackpool Big Dipper. My maps kept being flung from their storage pocket, and it was all I could do to remain in contact with him. Looking behind was out of the question. The result was inevitable; again the golden rain, again the explosions within my Spitfire.

This time, as I levelled out, the whole aircraft was vibrating. I discovered later that a shell inside my port tailplane had opened it up like a baked potato. As before, I made for the coast, but this time the engine stopped completely, one propeller blade sticking up in front of me in silent immobility. I tried to call up the other aircraft, as Macfie had done a few days before when he too was shot down, but I knew that nothing was getting through. I also knew that I had five engine starter cartridges left. With great concentration, I went through the whole starting procedure with each one. Each time the propeller kicked over, but stopped again. I looked at my altimeter; all prisoners of war begin to go "round the bend" eventually, but I started early: the altimeter read 3,000 ft, the minimum safe height for baling out being 300 ft. For some reason I decided that it was already too late. However, the aircraft was still under control and I had no sure knowledge that my parachute was undamaged following the cannon shells exploding within the fuselage. Fortunately there was a huge expanse of ripening wheat below, near St Omer, with a large house in the middle of it. I steered away from the house, not wishing to give the occupants the danger of sheltering me or the embarrassment of refusing, and landed gently with wheels up. Some German soldiers then captured me and took me to St Omer in a lorry which only had one tyre.

I never returned to Tangmere, but I would like to think that if I ever do I shall find a new Spitfire Mk VB still awaiting my test flight.

In Sgt Morton's enforced absence Sqn Ldr Burton tested the new Spitfire Mk VB, P8707, and wrote in his log book: 'Cannon firing. Nearly hit a boatload of fishermen!'

10 July 1941

At 11:35 hrs Bader led his Wing on Circus 42. Over the target 'Dogsbody' and 616 Squadron had several combats with Me 109s. 145 Squadron investigated a flight of aircraft approaching from the rear but found these to be Spitfires. Owing to the haze, 145 then lost the Wing. Six of the squadron's Spitfires had already aborted shortly after crossing the French coast, although the reason is unknown, and two more Spitfires turned back at St Omer. One Spitfire of 610 Squadron returned to base after being airborne for just five minutes, due to an unserviceable airspeed indicator. Combats took place as the Wing withdrew, 610 losing three pilots, among them Sgt Peter Ward-Smith: 'I felt a pain in my leg and the aircraft became uncontrollable. Realising that I could not get home, I baled out: the parachute worked perfectly.' One of 14 Spitfire pilots who failed to return that day, Ward-Smith spent the rest of the war as a prisoner.

Bader claimed an Me 109 probable in the Béthune area, before destroying an Me 109E near Gravelines:

> Was flying with section of four northwards over 10/10ths between Calais–Dover. Sighted three Me 109Es below, flying south-west over the cloud. Turned and dived to catch them up, which we did just over Calais. The three 109s were in line abreast and so were my section, with one lagging behind. I closed in to 150 yds behind and under the left-hand one, firing a two-second burst into its belly beneath the cockpit. Pieces flew off the 109 exactly under the cockpit and there was a flash of flame and black smoke, and then the whole aeroplane went up in flames. This was seen by Sergeant West and Pilot Officer Hepple of my section. Time approximately 12:50 hrs, height 7,000 ft, position either south of Calais or over Calais.

The Wing Commander's victim on this occasion was Lt Herbert Reich of II/JG26, who crashed, wounded, near Guines.

Stab I/JG26 was to suffer a more significant loss when the Gruppenkommandeur,

Sergeant Peter Ward-Smith of 610 Squadron.

Hptm Rolf Pingel, was captured. Having watched the 7 Squadron Stirling of Pt Off Fraser explode some five miles off Hardelot, killing everyone on board, Pingel stalked another bomber back to the English coast:

I followed one of these big planes back to England, hoping for an opportunity to attack. Whether I was hit by machine-gun fire from the Stirling, or from a Spitfire, I do not know. Maybe both! My engine cut, and both my oil and water overheated. I tried to escape close to the ground, as I had done many times before, but close to Dover there were many English planes. I was unable to bale out due to my low altitude, so I made a pancake landing at St Margaret's Bay, Dover.

The Gruppenkommandeur had in fact been shot down by a Pole, Sgt J. Smigielski of the Northolt Wing's 306 Squadron. Unwittingly, Pingel had presented the RAF with the first Me 109F it had captured intact. It was subsequently repaired and evaluated by the Air Fighting Development Unit at Duxford. Rolf Pingel, himself an Experte and Ritterkreuztrager with 26 victories (four of them scored in Spain), was an expensive loss to the Germans. He was succeeded as Kommandeur of I/JG26 by 25-year-old Hptm Johannes Seifert, formerly Kapitän of 3/JG26.

11 July 1941
610 Squadron had an early start, sweeping the Channel uneventfully between 06:40 and 08:40 hrs. Circus 43, however, between 11:10 and 12:20 hrs, provided more action. This sortie was out of the ordinary, as Tangmere's Station Commander and controller, Grp Capt Woodhall, actually flew a Spitfire with 610 Squadron; definitely unusual practice! The Wing was led by Sqn Ldr Burton of 616 Squadron. Over France 610 Squadron briefly engaged some Me 109Es, Sgt Merriman claiming a probable and Pt Off Grey one damaged. 616 Squadron's Sgt Smith experienced oxygen trouble, which could prove fatal at high altitude, so he dived down, crossing the French coast at zero feet. Flying over a Luftwaffe airfield, he destroyed two Ju 87s and damaged several others, finally having a squirt at a hut and an E-Boat.

The Me 109F of Hauptmann Rolf Pingel, Gruppenkommandeur of II/JG26, being dismantled by the RAF.

Bader resumed the lead for Circus 44, from 14:50 to 16:40 hrs. Eight Me 109s were seen over France, but these withdrew into cloud as the Beehive approached and no engagements took place.

12 July 1941

With Bader leading the Wing again, Circus 46 was a little more eventful. Near Dunkirk, 20 Me 109Fs were seen climbing. These were bounced by Bader's section while the remainder of 616 Squadron duelled inconclusively with other Me 109s.

14 July 1941

Circus 48 saw Bader and the Tangmere Wing crossing the French coast near Hardelot. South of St Omer ten Me 109s were seen approaching from the Dunkirk area, but refused to engage when challenged by 610 Squadron. More Me 109s were seen hanging higher up, but these too would not engage, although a section of 610 Squadron Spitfires was attacked, head-on, over St Omer, fortunately without loss. Squadron Leader Turner's section of 145 Squadron Spitfires was attacked, his own aircraft being hit by 'soft-nosed cannon shells'. Turner himself engaged three different Me 109s, damaging one.

Pilot Officer Johnson of 616 Squadron destroyed an Me 109F, probably that flown by Uffz R. Klienike of III/JG26, whose Yellow 3 was reported missing. Johnson reported:

I became separated from the squadron when over the target, so decided to fly with the Beehive during the return flight. When about 25–30 miles from the French coast and flying at 1,500 ft above and behind the Beehive, I saw three aircraft in line astern to the south-west. I then turned inland, above and behind the three aircraft which I then identified as Me 109Fs. I made a quick aileron turn and attacked No. 3 from below and behind when I was climbing. I gave a second burst with cannon and machine-gun at 150 yds range and saw the tail unit blown off and the E/A went into an uncontrollable spin. I am claiming this E/A as destroyed. I then broke away as my No. 2 had lost me.

When over the French coast at 10,000 ft, I saw an Me 109E over Étaples, diving steeply. I gave chase. It pulled out at 2,000 ft and flew straight and level. I drew up and gave a short burst at 150 yds range. I thought I saw something break away from the starboard wing of the E/A, but cannot be certain as my screen was covered with oil from the E/A in the first engagement. I therefore make no claim in this second engagement.

Squadron Leader Burton recorded: 'Chased out by 109s over Gravelines with D.B. and Cocky'.

17 July 1941

During the evening the Tangmere Wing flew a pure fighter sweep, crossing into France over Hardelot. Just inland, five Me 109Fs approached on the Wing's port side, in a slight dive and from the direction of Boulogne. A combat ensued, Wg Cdr Bader and Sqn Ldr Holden selecting one each but being unable to press home the attack due to more 109s diving on them. The Spitfires quickly withdrew back over the Channel, regrouped and then returned inland. Two Me 109s were seen approaching, but these were considered to be a decoy. Another engagement then took place at 20,000 ft over Le Touquet, during which 610 Squadron's Pt Off Tony Gaze claimed a probable.

19 July 1941

Circus 51 again found Bader and his Spitfires flying target support. Only one brief engagement took place, near Dunkirk, in which 610 Squadron's Sgt Raine claimed a

Squadron Leader 'Billy' Burton of 616 Squadron walks in at Westhampnett after a sweep. Observant readers might have noticed that, in most photographs of him, Burton is wearing a German lifejacket or Schwimmveste, as he is here. This was a popular souvenir of a combat victory, and one wonders whether Burton took his example from the Me 109 pilot he shot down near Canterbury on 21 June 1940?

probable. Bader claimed an Me 109 destroyed, sharing another with Flt Lt Dundas. 'Dogsbody' also claimed a probable, as did his No. 2, Sgt Smith. 145 Squadron's Sgt Smith machine-gunned a gunpost near Gravelines on his way out of France, but otherwise the sortie passed without incident for that squadron.

On this day, Flt Lt Hugh Dundas received the DFC.

20 July 1941
Between 11:40 and 13:10 hrs the Tangmere Wing provided escort to another Circus, but no engagements took place, largely owing to poor visibility over France.

21 July 1941
Between 07:40 and 09:35 hrs Bader led the Wing on Circus 54. Landfall was made at Le Touquet at 08:14 hrs, after which the Wing's squadrons split up and acted independently. 610 Squadron orbited Béthune before following the Beehive out of France. Sergeant Merriman chased five Me 109s, one of which blew up while another went down in flames. 610 Squadron reported that one of the four Stirling bombers involved appeared to have one engine stopped. 616 Squadron clashed briefly with some Me 109s, inconclusive claims being made by Pt Off Hepple and Sgt Beedham. According to 616 Squadron the sweep was 'disappointing as the enemy refused to fight'. Although it was apparently unrecorded elsewhere, Sqn Ldr Burton's log book states: 'One enemy pilot baled out before we fired. 1/3rd of an Me 109 destroyed, claim agreed by 11 Group.' After the sweep, as usual, Spitfires put down to refuel at just about every airfield on the South Coast, the Tangmere Wing's pilots taking on petrol at Hawkinge, Friston, Redhill, and Shoreham before returning to base.

Above: *Sergeant S.W.R. 'George' Mabbett poses with 616 Squadron Spitfire 'QJ-D'. Photographs of coded aircraft are rare indeed. Mabbett was killed in action over St Omer on 21 July 1941.*

Right: *Sergeant Mabbett's grave in Longuenesse cemetery, where the Germans buried him with full military honours.*

Before the day's end Bader led his Wing on Circus 55. In contrast to the day's first sweep, a number of dogfights ensued. Wing Commander Bader and Flt Lt Dundas each claimed an Me 109 damaged, and Pt Off Hepple one damaged. So far as 610 Squadron were concerned, however, the sortie was uneventful apart from eight Me 109Es approaching the Wing over France but not engaging. Squadron Leader Burton wrote in his log book: 'Should have shot down a 109, but failed to open fire till too late owing to uncertainty of identity'.

Oberleutnant Hans 'Assi' Hahn of JG2 (in forage cap). On 21 July 1941 he claimed two Spitfires destroyed; one of them might have been Sergeant Mabbett's. (Chris Goss)

Unfortunately 616 Squadron suffered a casualty; Sgt S.W.R. 'George' Mabbett, 'Johnnie' Johnson's No. 2, was undoubtedly a victim of JG2. Oberleutnant Hans 'Assi' Hahn of III/JG2 claimed two Spitfires destroyed, while Schellback and Mayer, both of 7/JG2, claimed one each. Brian Mabbett, Sgt Mabbett's younger brother, wrote to me in 1995:

> My brother, whom we all called "George", was, and is, my hero. We came from a very poor background in Charlton Kings, Gloucestershire, but George, who was a gentle and kindly person, passed for the Grammar School. I remember him as a great brother who excelled at sport and was extremely popular in our village. Between 1936–39 he played rugby for Cheltenham, from 17 onwards, and then, at only 19, he played for both Gloucester and Gloucestershire County. The telegram officially notifying my mother of his death arrived on what would have been my brother's 22nd birthday. My father had died just a few months before, and I was just 15. The Germans buried George with full military honours at St Omer cemetery. As I have said, he was a great brother, and no-one else could ever compare to him.

22 July 1941
Between 12:05 and 13:50 hrs Bader led the Wing on a close-escort sortie to six Blenheims attacking Le Frait. Although bombs were seen bursting in the target area,

neither flak nor enemy aircraft showed any response. Bader recorded the reason for the sortie in his logbook: 'Looking for *Scharnhorst*'.

During the evening the Westhampnett squadrons were joined by the Spitfires of 306 and 308 Squadrons, both units being elements of the Polish Wing based at Northolt. Bader then led all five squadrons over France, providing escort to 11 Beauforts from Thorney Island. In the direction of Le Havre, however, 616 Squadron lost contact with the Wing and failed to encounter the enemy despite sweeping Le Havre to Cherbourg. The Poles, however, in their truly aggressive style, strafed German airfields at Guines and St Omer, but were attacked on the return flight. Pilot Officer Surma of 308 Squadron destroyed an Me 109F which he saw crash into the ground, and others were claimed by Flt Lt Janus and Sgt Kremski.

On this day most of the Spitfire Mk Vs arrived to complete an update in aircraft which had begun on 1 July.

23 July 1941

The Tangmere Wing's first commitment of the day was to escort six Blenheims, but Bader and his pilots arrived five minutes late and the bombers were seven minutes early, so no rendezvous was made. Instead all landed at Manston, from where the Beehive took off collectively and struck out on a 'Roadstead' to attack enemy shipping off the Belgian coast. 145 Squadron contacted Me 109s, and Sqn Ldr Turner and Sgt Grant each destroyed an enemy fighter. Flying Officer Forde's target was believed to have taken hits in the tail, but he made no claim. Over enemy occupied territory 610 Squadron drove off several Me 109s, but on the way out only four Blenheims could be found. One of these lagged behind and eventually crashed into the sea some 40 miles from Deal, sinking immediately. Although the Spitfires orbited, none of the crew came to the surface. Again the Wing's Spitfires had to land at various airfields to refuel before returning to base, making Friston, Hawkinge and Lympne busy airfields.

During the evening Bader led the Wing on another Circus. After crossing the coast at Le Touquet the Wing was constantly engaged by Me 109s, which almost immediately split the Spitfires into sections of four or pairs. Another 50 Me 109s were seen holding back, their leader clearly timing the moment to attack. The 610 Squadron diary records that 'all engagements were terrific dogfights'. One of 610's pilots crash-landed at Bexhill with a shrapnel wound to his arm and a cut left eye, but Wg Cdr Bader and Sgt Raine (610) shared an Me 109 destroyed and Pt Off Grey (610) claimed a probable. 145 Squadron's Sgt Frank Twitchett, back in action after being wounded on 21 June, damaged an Me 109E. Sergeant Breeze's Spitfire was damaged and his engine cut, but fortunately he managed to glide to the English coast, crash-landing at Beachy Head. Flying Officer Forde was with Sgt Twitchett when they attacked the enemy, but the officer pilot did not return to base. 616 Squadron 'met plenty of enemy fighters'. Bader and Flt Lt Dundas shared an Me 109 destroyed, Flt Lt Casson destroyed another and damaged two more, and Pt Off Johnson damaged a third. 'Buck' Casson's claim put up the squadron's half-century. Squadron Leader Burton's log recorded: 'Had two squirts. Found 109 beating up a Spitfire. Sent 109 quickly back to France!'

24 July 1941

Escort to bombers over Cherbourg, uneventful.

26 July 1941

The Tangmere Wing took off on an early-morning escort, but the sortie was cancelled by Bader before crossing the English coast owing to poor visibility.

28 July 1941
This is a most important date in the history of Wg Cdr Bader's Tangmere Wing, as on this day the Wing's identity changed because 145 Squadron was relieved at Merston by 41 Squadron from Catterick. The squadron was commanded by Donald Finlay, a pre-war Olympic hurdler and a career officer. Squadron Leader Bob Beardsley DFC was then a recently commissioned Flying Officer. He recalls:

From March 1941 onwards, our squadron, which had been heavily engaged during the Battle of Britain, remained at Catterick, in Yorkshire, where we "oldies" trained new pilots. The more senior pilots amongst us were slowly being rested and posted away to other units. I was actually posted to a nightfighter squadron at Ayr, but this was cancelled as someone with experience was needed to shepherd the new young pilots (I was just 21 myself!). We also took part in a number of convoy patrols and scrambles, plus night flying, a very unpopular practice in Spitfires. I was commissioned in June and stayed with the squadron, moving to Merston and the Tangmere Wing in July 1941.

Air Commodore Sir Archie Winskill KCVO CBE DSO DFC* was also with 41 Squadron:

On arrival at Tangmere as a young Flight Lieutenant, I found Bader a very charismatic leader and a truly impressive individual. A Wing briefing went something like this: Wing Commander Bader would waddle into the briefing marquee in his usual pin-legged style, halt in front of the 35 pilots present, stare at us for a few seconds, take his pipe out and in a loud, confident voice say: "OK, chaps, St Omer today – return tickets only! Press tits 13:00 hrs." Then he would waddle out. We would have followed him to the ends of the earth!

   After taking off, the squadrons of the Wing would gradually form up whilst climbing easterly along the south coast, reaching Wing formation at 20,000 ft over Beachy Head. We would then head south to the target area. As we crossed the French coast the Me 109s were waiting for us. As Sweeps were usually flown at mid-day, the 109s usually had the added advantage of the sun's position. To keep a Wing of 36 Spitfires together, pilots can only fly at no more than three-quarter throttle, thus the 109s had both height and speed advantage. Harry Broadhurst's theory for Sweeps at that time was to fly high and at full throttle once you had crossed the French coast – a much sounder principle.

   With Bader, once he had spotted the enemy, there was a semblance of directing his squadrons and deploying them in the air for the attack, but on the whole when he sighted the first 109s he was after them, the Wing just breaking up and it being every man for himself!

A member of 41 Squadron's groundcrew was 1253818 LAC P.A. 'Jack' Younie, who remembers:

I joined the RAF in June 1940. After basic training and a course at RAF Cranwell I was eventually posted to 41 Squadron at RAF Fairlop in Essex. We spent one day there when the whole squadron was transferred to Catterick in Yorkshire, the reason being that the squadron had to replace pilots who had been lost during the Battle of Britain. Our job at Catterick was just getting the pilots trained for the usual routine of that time. We were then posted to the Tangmere Wing, being based at Merston, and later, Westhampnett. When we arrived we were billeted in huts dispersed around the airfields and at various locations outside. We used to use pushbikes to

Left: *Flight Lieutenant 'Archie' Winskill, a 41 Squadron flight commander. On 14 August 1941 he was shot down near Calais by Feldwebel Bigge of 8/JG2, but evaded and made a 'home run'. Now Sir 'Archie' Winskill, he is presently collaborating with the author on the publication of his fascinating escape story.*

Right: *Jack Younie, a member of 41 Squadron's groundcrew at Merston during 1941.*

travel back and forth. The Spitfires were also dispersed around trees along the edge of the airfield. Mainly the job there was sweeping the French coast; as you are probably aware, that year there was two hours' British Summer Time, meaning that we were on duty from 03:30 to 23:30 hrs, which did not leave us much time for sleeping! However, the Spitfires were usually away on their sweeps for about two hours, and that time was used for catching up on a bit of sleep or playing football etc. with pilots who were on standby for the next sortie. The pilots were also on standby, of course, for any defensive scramble over our own coast.

For us it was a very busy time as we also had to keep up with our weapons training, aircraft recognition and other lectures we had to attend. We did have one very intense month, during which we were almost constantly on duty non-stop. We also had to put on a night guard, although this was shared with other squadrons. At the end of this non-stop month, we were, however, granted a 48 hr leave – I spent most of the time in bed!

A couple of incidents spring to mind. We had a new Spitfire delivered and a Sergeant pilot took it up but discovered that the undercarriage would not come down, even despite using the emergency gear. The CO then went up and guided him down, the Sergeant made a perfect belly landing and survived the incident unscathed. We had Spitfires coming back damaged all the time, it was hectic.

I first met Wing Commander Bader when he once flew over from Tangmere to lead our squadron on a patrol over France. I did not know who he was, but I directed the aircraft in. He called me over but then turned his back on me when I reached the Spitfire; I wondered what on earth was going on, but then realised who he was as he put his hand on my shoulder and lowered himself down to the ground. I think he picked me because I just happened to be the right height for him to put his hand on my shoulder!

At Cranwell I had qualified as an RTO operator and my main job was servicing the radios and radar equipment in the aircraft, in addition to the pilot's microphones and headsets. This was done on a daily basis and also between sorties. We also helped out with rearming and were also used by the fitters as ballast to hold the aeroplanes down whilst their engines were run up. All in all it was a hard year, on the go all the time.

29 July 1941
An uneventful Rhubarb due to poor weather.

31 July 1941
The AOC again visited the station, 'conversing with most of the pilots'.

1 August 1941
Two pairs of 41 Squadron Spitfires undertook Rhubarbs, but nothing of note was subsequently reported.

An important move took place in 41 Squadron when its CO, Don Finlay, was promoted to Acting Wing Commander and posted to become the 11 Group Engineering Officer, his successor being a Canadian, Sqn Ldr L.M. 'Elmer' Gaunce DFC. Gaunce, from Alberta, had first served in the army before joining the RAF in 1936. Throughout the Battle of France he was a flight commander with 615 Squadron, and was awarded the DFC after the destruction of four Me 109s between 20 July and 26 August 1940. On the latter date, having already been shot down on 18 August, Gaunce baled out of a blazing Hurricane over Herne Bay. At the end of the Battle of Britain he was given command of 46 Squadron, leading the squadron into action against Italy's disastrous aerial attack on England on 11 November 1940. In December 1940 he was rested from operations until he took command of 41 Squadron at Merston.

Also on this day, Bader's adjutant, Flt Lt P.D. Macdonald MP, was posted away from Tangmere.

2 August 1941
Five pairs of 41 Squadron Spitfires undertook Rhubarbs throughout the day, but again there were no results to report back at Merston.

3 August 1941
At 14:30 hrs 41 Squadron undertook a three-aircraft Rhubarb, and subsequently reported attacking with cannon a railway engine, a signal box and a factory at Le Tréport.

At the same time, a singleton 41 Squadron Spitfire also flew on a Rhubarb, but nothing of consequence was reported.

4 August 1941
Six Spitfires of 610 Squadron undertook a sweep from 11:30 to 12:45 hrs but, apart from seeing six aircraft of 616 Squadron over France, reported an uneventful sortie owing to poor visibility.

7 August 1941
Between 17:10 and 18:55 hrs Bader led the Tangmere Wing on a Circus to Lille power station, orbiting between Merville and Le Touquet. A large formation of Me 109s dived out of the sun, but when the Wing turned to attack they mostly dived away, not pressing home their attack. Dogfights ensued, 41 Squadron's Sgt Mitchell damaging an Me 109F over Béthune. Flight Lieutenant Gilbert Draper (41 Sqn), was shot down over Fruges, near Lille, and was captured. Sergeants West and Brewer of

616 Squadron each claimed a damaged Me 109. The Germans persisted in using these probing tactics over Hazebrouck, Merville, and Lille, only breaking away over the French coast.

In his log book Bader wrote: 'Damned good bombing – blown to hell'.

Bob Beardsley of 41 Squadron remembers that sortie:

This was our first sweep proper since January, and we went to Lille, losing Graham Draper, who was to be a PoW until 1945. On this sortie I was leading a section of four, our rear cover. We were the low squadron of the Wing, and as I looked to my rear left I saw an Me 109 closing on my port sub-section, so close that the cannon orifice in the propeller boss was very apparent! I called "Break port!", and we all went hard at it. The attacking aircraft had not fired, but I called the Wing Leader to tell him that we had been attacked by 109s. To my amazement, Wing Commander Bader responded: "Only Hurricanes, old boy!" I, however, failed to see the joke! The next second the whole Wing was engaged – I saw no more "Hurricanes". When the lead squadron was attacked, Bader did actually say: "Sorry old boy!".

9 August 1941
On this day the 616 Squadron ORB records the end of an era:

This was a very sad day because we lost our much admired Wing Leader, Wing Commander Bader, and Flight Lieutenant Casson, "B" Flight commander and one of the "originals" of the squadron. Both these leaders were very popular with everyone and they will be sadly missed. They are both prisoners of war. In this offensive operation our squadron claimed four destroyed enemy fighters and one probably destroyed, a very good effort.

The following two chapters deal with the events of that day in great detail. No stone has been knowingly left unturned in an effort to solve the controversy regarding Bader's capture, which has raged for more than half a century.

Officers of 41 Squadron outside Shopwyke House, the Officers' Mess. Left to right: Babbage, Draper, Winskill, Gaunce (CO), Finlay (former CO), Williams, and Ranger.

CHAPTER SIX

Break! For Christ's Sake Break!

On the morning of Monday 9 August 1941 the teleprinter clattered away at Tangmere as the Form 'D' came through from 11 Group HQ, detailing the Tangmere Wing's task for the day. This was to be another complex Circus, No. 68, involving many aircraft to Gosnay. The Tangmere Wing was to provide target support. Directives issued that August stipulated that the Target Support Wing's role was to:

> ... clear the road to the target area, also to cover the withdrawal of the bombers and escort Wings. There are usually two Target Support Wings, one being routed the same direction as the bombers, to arrive over the target three minutes earlier, and the other is given a different route, but also arriving three minutes in advance of the bombers.

For Wg Cdr Bader and the Westhampnett Spitfire squadrons, 616 and 610, Target Support was a routine sortie, although not, of course, without the usual hazards. While Sqn Ldr 'Elmer' Gaunce DFC's 41 Squadron had arrived at Tangmere satellite Merston only two weeks previously, the squadron had already flown numerous practice sweeps out of Catterick, and at least one over France from Redhill.

Alan Smith, Bader's usual 'Dogsbody 2', had a head cold and was unable to fly, being grounded in accordance with regulations. He was shortly to be commissioned and, as his name was not 'on the board', Sgt Smith prepared to go into London to buy a new uniform. His place as the Wing Leader's wingman was taken by New Zealander Sgt Jeff West, a pilot with one-and-a-half Me 109s destroyed and one damaged to his

Sergeant Jeff West, left, and Sgt Brewer, both of 616 Squadron, open their post. As Sgt Alan Smith, Bader's usual No. 2, was in London buying a new uniform on 9 August 1941, West took his place on Circus 68.

Squadron Leader Ken Holden, Officer Commanding 610 Squadron. The Spitfire is a presentation aircraft, Observer Corps II, *although its serial number is unknown.*

credit. West was not inexperienced; frequently that summer he had flown as No. 2 to Flt Lt E.P. Gibbs, until that officer was shot down over France on 9 July 1941.

For this Target Support sortie to Gosnay, Dogsbody Section therefore consisted of:

Dogsbody: Wg Cdr Douglas Bader DSO* DFC

Dogsbody 2: Sgt Jeff West

Dogsbody 3: Flt Lt Hugh Dundas DFC

Dogsbody 4: Pt Off 'Johnnie' Johnson.

Also leading 'Finger Fours' within the 616 Squadron formation of three sections would be the CO, Sqn Ldr 'Billy' Burton (Yellow Section), and the 'B' Flight commander, Flt Lt 'Buck' Casson (Blue Section). On the other side of the airfield Sqn Ldr Ken Holden DFC and 610 Squadron also prepared for the morning sortie.

Take-off occurred at 10:40 hrs, 'Dogsbody' Section leading Westhampnett's Spitfires for yet another sortie into very hostile airspace. High over Chichester, Sqn Ldr Holden swiftly manoeuvred 610 Squadron into position above and slightly to port of 616 Squadron. As the Wing was Target Support, it had no bombers to meet before setting course for France, although the Spitfires were still routed out over Beachy Head. As the Wing left Chichester, however, there was no sign of 41 Squadron.

The Beachy Head Forward Relay Station recorded the Tangmere Wing's R/T messages that day (reproduced here by kind permission of AVM J.E. Johnson). As the Wing neared 'Diamond', 41 Squadron had still not appeared. Group Captain Woodhall, at Tangmere, was the first to speak, making a test call:

'Dogsbody?'

DB: 'OK, OK.'

Bader then made R/T test calls to the commanders of both 610 and 41, using their

Flight Lieutenant Hugh 'Cocky' Dundas DFC, commander of 616 Squadron's 'A' Flight, outside his Westhampnett office with his Labrador, Robin.

Christian names, as was his usual practice:

DB: 'Ken?'
KH: 'Loud and clear.'
DB: 'Elmer?'

There was no response from Sqn Ldr Gaunce, which provoked an acid remark from the Wing Leader to 'Woody'. Unable to wait, 616 and 610 Squadrons set course for France and Gosnay, adopting their battle formations in the process. Still climbing, Bader waggled his wings insistently, indicating that 'Dogsbody 3', Flt Lt Dundas, should take the lead. Dundas slid across, tucking his wingtip just two or three feet from Bader's. From this proximity Dundas saw the Wing Leader mouth two words: 'Airspeed Indicator', meaning that the instrument on W3185 was unserviceable. The Wing had to climb at the right speed to arrive over the target at the appointed time, which was crucial. Dundas gave a thumbs-up and moved forward to lead the Spitfires to France. On the rear of his hand he had fortunately written the time at which the Wing was due over the French coast, as well as the speed which had to be maintained. The 21-year-old flight commander then 'settled down to concentrate on the job'.

Sir Hugh Dundas later recalled that 'the sun was bright and brilliant, unveiled by any layer of high haze or cirrus cloud'. Realising that the white cumulus cloud below provided a background which would immediately reveal the silhouettes of any aircraft, Dundas correctly anticipated that under such conditions 'Dogsbody' would wish to climb as high as possible, so he adjusted both his throttle setting and rate of climb accordingly, taking the Spitfires up to 28,000 ft. Then came more radio messages:

DB: 'Ken and Elmer, start gaining height.'
KH: 'Elmer's not with us.'
Unidentified, garbled voice on the R/T, believed to be Sqn Ldr Gaunce.
DB: 'Elmer from Dogsbody. I cannot understand what you say, but we are on our way. You had better decide for yourself whether to come or go back.'
A further garbled message, followed by "Woody" advising 41 Squadron: "Walker leader, Dogsbody is 20 miles ahead of you".

Following the last radio transmissions, at least the Wing was now aware that more Spitfires were bringing up the rear, even if they were some distance away. The Spitfires now cruised over the Channel and towards France with 610 Squadron above and behind 616. Dundas led the Wing over the French coast right on cue (although there is conflicting evidence regarding whether the coast was crossed south of Le Touquet or between the 'Golf Course' and Boulogne, slightly further north). This

Squadron Leader 'Elmer' Gaunce, DFC, of 41 Squadron with his flight commanders, Flt Lts Roy Bush, DFC, (left) and Roy Marples, DFC. On 9 August 1941 Marples was still with 616 Squadron, and it was he who sighted the Me 109s first.

crucial timing observed, Bader accelerated ahead and informed 'Dogsbody 3' over the R/T that he was resuming the lead. The Spitfires' arrival over the coastal flak belt was greeted by dangerous little puff-balls of black smoke which made the formation twist and turn. 'Beetle' then called 'Dogsbody', informing him that the beehive itself was 'on time and engaged'. As the Spitfires forged inland, therefore, some distance behind them the bombers and various cover Wings were now bound for France and action.

Slightly below the condensation trail level, a 610 Squadron pilot reported seeing contrails 'above and to our left'. Squadron Leader Holden consequently led the squadron higher still while 'Beetle' (B) reported:

B: 'Dogsbody from Beetle. There are 20-plus five miles to the east of you.'
DB: 'OK, but your transmitter is quite impossible. Please use the other.'
B: 'Dogsbody is this better?'
DB: 'Perfect. Ken, start getting more height.'
KH: 'OK, Dogsbody, but will you throttle back? I cannot keep up.'
DB: 'Sorry Ken, my airspeed indicator is u/s. Throttling back, and I will do one slow left-hand turn so you can catch up.'
KH: 'Dogsbody from Ken, I'm making "smoke" at this height.'
DB: 'OK, Ken, I'm going down very slightly.'

'Beetle' then advised 'Dogsbody' of more bandits in the vicinity. Flying Officer Roy Marples (RM) of 616 Squadron saw the enemy first:

RM: 'Three bandits coming down astern of us. I'm keeping an eye on them, now there are six.'
DB: 'OK.'
B: 'Douglas, another 12-plus ahead and slightly higher.'
RM: 'Eleven of them now.'
DB: 'OK, Roy, let me know exactly where they are.'
RM: 'About one mile astern and slightly higher.'
B: 'Douglas, there is another 40-plus 15 miles to the north-east of you.'
DB: 'OK Beetle. Are our friends where they ought to be? I haven't much idea where I am.'
B: Yes, you are exactly right. And so are your friends.'
RM: 'Dogsbody from Roy. Keep turning left and you'll see 109s at nine o'clock.'
DB: 'Ken, can you see them?'
KH: 'Douglas, 109s below. Climbing up.'

By this time, 616 and 610 Squadrons had progressed into a very dangerous French sky indeed. 'Beetle' had already reported some 72 bandits, representing odds which outnumbered the Spitfires by nearly 3:1. Clearly this was not to be an uneventful sortie. Apprehension mounting, the Spitfire pilots switched on their gunsight reflectors and set gun buttons to 'Fire'. Anxiously the sky was searched, an ever-watchful eye being kept on the Me 109s positioned 1,000 ft above the Wing and waiting to pounce. Bader himself dipped each wing in turn, scrutinising the sky below for the Messerschmitts reported by Ken Holden.

DB: 'I can't see them, will you tell me where to look?'
KH: 'Underneath Bill's section now. Shall I come down?'
DB: 'No, I have them. Get into formation. Going down. Ken, are you with us?'
KH: 'Just above you.'

As Dogsbody Section dived on the enemy, Flt Lt Casson followed with three other aircraft of 'B' Flight.

'Dogsbody 3', Flt Lt Dundas, had 'smelt a rat' with respect to the Schwärm of Me 109s that Dogsbody Section was now rapidly diving towards. Finding no targets to the Section's right, 'Dogsbody 4', Pt Off Johnson, skidded under the section and fired at an Me 109 on the left. By this time the whole of Dogsbody Section was firing, although Dundas, still unhappy and suspecting a trap, had a compelling urge to look behind. Suddenly Pt Off Hepple shouted over the R/T: 'Blue 2 here. Some buggers coming down behind, astern. Break left!'

The Spitfire pilots hauled their aircraft around in steep turns. The sky behind Dogsbody Section was full of Me 109s, all firing; without Hepple's warning the Spitfires would have been nailed. As the high Me 109s crashed into 616 Squadron, Sqn Ldr Holden decided that it was time for his section to join the fray and reduce the odds. Informing Flt Lt Denis Crowley-Milling of this decision, Holden led his Spitfires down to assist. Buck Casson, following Bader's Section, was well throttled back to keep his flight together. Also attacking from the rear, Casson managed a squirt at a Rotte of Me 109s. Flying Officer Marples, No. 3 in Casson's section, then shouted a warning of even more Messerschmitts diving upon the Wing, while Sqn Ldr 'Billy' Burton urged the Spitfires to 'Keep turning' to prevent the Me 109s getting in a shot, as they could not out-turn the Spitfires. Suddenly the organised chaos became a totally confused maelstrom of twisting, turning fighters:

'BREAK! FOR CHRIST'S SAKE BREAK!'

The Spitfires immediately 'broke' – hard. 'Johnnie' Johnson remembers:

There was this scream of "Break!" – and we all broke, we didn't wait to hear it twice! Round, then a swirling mass of 109s and Spitfires. When I broke I could see Bader still firing. Dundas was firing at the extreme right 109. There was some cloud nearby and I disappeared into it as quick as possible! I couldn't say how many aircraft were involved, suffice to say a lot. It seemed to me that the greatest danger was a collision, rather than being shot down, that's how close we all were. We had got the 109s we were bouncing and then Holden came down with his section, so there were a lot of aeroplanes. We were fighting 109Fs, although there may have been some Es amongst them. There was an absolute mass of aeroplanes just 50 yds apart, it was awful. I thought to myself: "You're going to collide with somebody!" I didn't think about shooting at anything after we were bounced ourselves; all you could think about was surviving, getting out of that mass of aircraft. In such a tight turn, of course, you almost black out, you cannot really see where you are going. It was a mess. I had never been so frightened in my life, never!

Chased by three Me 109s, the closest just 100 yds astern, Pt Off Johnson maintained his tight turn, spiralling down towards the safety of a nearby cloud, into which his Spitfire dived with over 400 mph on the clock. He pulled back the throttle and centralised the controls. The altimeter stabilised but, the speed having dropped to less than 100 mph, the Spitfire stalled. Beneath the cloud 'Dogsbody 4' regained control. Having requested and received a homing course for Dover, he headed rapidly for England. Over the R/T, Pt Off Johnson could still hear 616 and 610 Squadrons' running battle:

'Get into formation or they'll shoot the bloody lot of you!'
'Spitfire going down in flames, ten o'clock.'
'YQ-C (616 Squadron Spitfire). Form up on me, I'm at three o'clock to you.'
'Four buggers above us' (from 'Nip' Hepple).
'All Elfin aircraft (616 Squadron) withdraw. I say again, all Elfin aircraft withdraw.'
'Use the cloud if you're in trouble' (from 'Billy' Burton).
'Are you going home, Ken?' (also from Burton).
'Yes, withdrawing' (from Holden).
'Ken from Crow. Are you still about?'
'I'm right behind you, Crow.'
'Are we all here?'
'Two short.'
'Dogsbody from Beetle. Do you require any assistance?'
'Beetle from Elfin Leader. We are OK and withdrawing.'
'Thank you Billy. Douglas, do you require any assistance? Steer three four zero to the coast.'

The silence from 'Dogsbody' was ominous.
Flight Lieutenant Casson remembers:

I watched Wing Commander Bader and "A" Flight attack and break to port as I was coming in. I was well throttled back in the dive, as the other three had started to fall

Flight Lieutenant L.H. 'Buck' Casson,
commander of 616 Squadron's 'B' Flight.

behind and I wanted to keep the flight together. I attacked from the rear, and after having a squirt at two 109s flying together, shot down another. The other three "B" flight machines were in my rear and probably one of the lads saw this.

I climbed to 13,000 ft and fell in with "Billy" Burton and three other aircraft, all from "A" Flight. We chased around in a circle for some time, gaining height all the while, and more 109s were directly above us. Eventually we formed up in line abreast and set off after the Wing.

"Billy's" section flew in pairs abreast, so I flew abreast but at about 200 yds to starboard. We were repeatedly attacked by two Me 109s which had followed us and were flying above and behind. Each time they started diving I called out and we all turned and re-formed, the 109s giving up their attack and climbing each time.

About 15 miles from the coastline I saw another Spitfire well below us and about half-a-mile to starboard. This machine was alone and travelling very slowly. I called up "Billy" on the R/T and suggested that we cross over to surround him and help the pilot back, as he looked like a sitting duck. I broke off to starboard and made for the solitary Spitfire, but then, on looking back for "Billy" and the others, was amazed to see them diving away hard to the south-west for a low layer of cloud, into which they soon disappeared. I realised then that my message had either been misunderstood or not received. Like a greenhorn, I had been so intent upon watching "Billy's" extraordinary disappearance to the left, and the lone Spitfire to my right, I lost sight of the Me 109s that had been worrying us. I remember looking for them but upon not discovering their position assumed that they had chased "Billy" instead. I was soon proved wrong, however, when I received three hits in both fuselage and wing. This occurred just as I was coming alongside the lone Spitfire, which I could not identify as it was not from Tangmere. I broke for some cloud at 5,000 ft, which I reached but found too thin for cover, and was pursued by the 109s.

I then picked out two more 109s flying above me and so decided to drop to zero feet, fly north and cross the Channel at a narrow point, as I was unsure of the damage sustained and the engine was not running smoothly. I pressed the teat and tried to run for it, but the two Me 109s behind had more speed and were rapidly within range, whilst the other two flew 1,500 ft above and dived from port to starboard and back, delivering quick bursts. Needless to say I was not flying straight and level all this time.

In the event I received a good one from behind which passed between the stick and my right leg, taking off some of the rudder on its way. It passed into the petrol tank, but whether the round continued into the engine I do not know. Petrol began leaking into the cockpit, oil pressure was dropping low, and with the radiator wide open I could smell the glycol overheating.

As the next attack came I pulled straight up from the deck in a loop, and on my way down, as I was changing direction towards the sea, my engine became extremely rough and seized up as white glycol fumes poured forth. There was no option but to crash-land the aircraft.

I tried to send "Dogsbody" a hurried message, then blew up the wireless and made a belly landing in a field some 10 miles south of Calais. The "Goons", having seen the glycol, were decent enough not to shoot me up as I was landing, but circled about for a time and gave my position away to a German cavalry unit in a wood in a corner of the field. One of the pilots waved to me as he flew overhead, and I waved back just before setting fire to the aircraft. Due to the petrol in the cockpit, and because I was carrying a port-fire issued for this purpose, igniting the aircraft was easy. No sooner had I done this than a party of shrieking Goons armed with rifles came chasing over and that was the end of me!

What eventually happened to the lone Spitfire which I went to help out I have no

'Buck' Casson's Spitfire after his forced landing near Marquise on 9 August 1941. The centre section has been destroyed by the Portfire device fitted for such circumstances. (Schöpfel via Caldwell)

idea. As the 109s followed me I assume that he got away okay; I certainly hope so. I will never forget that day, one which I have gone over so often in my daydreams.

Flight Lieutenant Casson was the victim of Hptm Gerhard Schöpfel, Gruppenkommandeur of III/JG26. Now 84, Herr Schöpfel recalls:

My IIIrd Gruppe attacked a British bomber formation, after which my formation was split up. With the British on their homeward flight, I headed alone for my airfield at Ligescourt, near Crécy. Suddenly I saw a flight of Spitfires flying westwards. I attacked them from above and after a short burst of fire the rear machine nosed over sharply and dived away. Whilst the other aircraft flew on apparently unaware, I pursued the fleeing Spitfire as I could see no sign of damage. The British pilot hugged the ground, dodging trees and houses. I was constantly in his propwash and so could not aim properly. Because of the warm air near the ground my radiator flaps opened and so my speed decreased; it thus took me a long time to get into a good firing position. Finally I was positioned immediately behind the Spitfire and it filled my gunsight. I pressed the firing button for both cannon and machine-guns, but – click! I had obviously exhausted my ammunition in the earlier air battles. Of course the British pilot had no way of knowing this and I still wanted to strike terror in him for so long as he remained over French soil. I thus remained right behind him, at high speed. Suddenly I was astonished to see a white plume of smoke emit from the Spitfire! The smoke grew more dense and the propeller stopped. The pilot made a forced landing in a field east of Marquise. I circled the aircraft and made a note of the markings for my victory report, watched the pilot climb out and waved to him. Just before being captured by German soldiers, he ignited a built-in explosive charge which destroyed the centre-section of his aircraft.

I returned to my field and sent my engineering officer to the site to determine the reason for the forced landing. He found, to my amazement, that the Spitfire had taken a single machine-gun round in an engine cylinder during my first attack. Had

Gerhard Schöpfel, who shot down 'Buck' Casson, in his Me 109E while Kapitän of 9/JG26 during the Battle of Britain.

I not pressed on after running out of ammunition, and therefore forcing the pilot to fly at top speed, he would probably have reached England despite the damage. Just a few weeks before, in fact, I myself had made it back across the Channel after two of my engine's connecting rods had been smashed over Dover. On this occasion over France, however, the British pilot, a Flight Lieutenant, now had to head for prison camp whilst I recorded my 33rd victory.

While 'Buck' Casson was to spend the rest of the war as a prisoner, his life had clearly been saved by Gerhard Schöpfel running out of ammunition. With petrol splashing into the cockpit, another hit would no doubt have turned the Spitfire into a fireball. Luck, it appears, played no mean part in survival.

Returning to the French coast, Pt Off Johnson saw a lone Me 109 below. Suspecting it to be one of the three which chased him into the cloud just a few minutes previously, 'Johnnie' anxiously searched the sky for the other two. The sky was clear. From astern, 'Dogsbody 4' dropped below the Me 109 before attacking from its blind spot, below and behind. One burst of cannon shells sent the enemy fighter diving earthwards, emitting a plume of black smoke.

Johnson came 'out of France on the deck, low and fast', his Spitfire roaring over waving peasants, just feet above their fields. At the coast, German soldiers ran to their guns, but in a second the fleeting Spitfire was gone. Climbing over the Channel, 'Dogsbody 4' realised that something might have happened to Wg Cdr Bader:

As I was crossing the Channel, Woodhall, who obviously knew that there had been a fight from the radar and R/T, repeated: "Douglas, are you receiving?" This came over the air every five minutes or so. I therefore called up and said: "Its 'Johnnie' here Sir, we've had a stiff fight and I last saw the Wing Commander on the tail of a 109". He said: "Thank you, I'll meet you at dispersal".

The silence from 'Dogsbody' over the R/T clearly meant one of two things; either his radio was u/s or he had somehow been brought down. Air Marshal Sir Denis Crowley-Milling, then a flight commander in Ken Holden's 610 Squadron, recalls:

> The greatest impression I have of 9 August 1941 is the silence on the R/T. Douglas always maintained a running commentary. Had the worst happened? The colourful language and running commentary had suddenly ceased, leaving us all wondering what had happened. Was he alive or dead? Had his radio failed? I know we were above thick cloud on the way home and asked the Tangmere Controller to provide a homing bearing for us to steer. This was way out in accuracy, however, and unbeknown to us we were flying up the North Sea, just scraping in to Martlesham Heath with hardly any fuel remaining – it was indeed a day to remember!

So confused had been the fighting, so numerous the aircraft in this incredible maelstrom over St Omer, that only Bader himself had the answers to the questions regarding his present state and whereabouts. After the first downwards charge, 'Dogsbody' had found himself alone after levelling out at 24,000 ft. In front of him were six Me 109s flying in a line-abreast formation of three pairs. Flying alone, Bader knew that he should ignore this enemy formation and adhere to the instructions which he had even issued to his pilots as formal instructions; get out and get home. However, he considered that these Me 109s were 'sitters', and in a split second greed overcame discipline and good judgement. Alone over France, Bader stalked the middle Rotte. He later reported:

> I saw some more Me 109s. I arrived amongst these, who were evidently not on the lookout, as I expect they imagined the first formation we attacked to be covering them. I got a very easy shot at one of these which flew quite straight until he went on fire from behind the cockpit – a burst of about three seconds.

As two Me 109s curved towards him, 'Dogsbody' broke right violently, although he anticipated with some bravado that his course would take him between a pair of Messerschmitts. Suddenly something hit Spitfire 'DB'. Owing to the proximity of the enemy aircraft, Bader assumed that he had collided with an Me 109. The Spitfire went completely out of control, diving earthwards with its control column limp and unresponsive. Looking behind, Bader gained the impression that the entire fuselage aft of the VHF aerial had disappeared, although he was later to report that it was 'probably just the empennage' that was missing.

Bader was unable to consider baling out at 24,000 ft, owing to the lack of oxygen outside the cockpit at that height. His dilemma was that the doomed fighter was already exceeding 400 mph, and would soon be subjected to forces so great that escape would be impossible. He yanked the canopy release mechanism and the hood was whipped away, the cockpit immediately being battered by the airflow. Without legs, would he be able to thrust his body upwards to get out? As he struggled to get his head above the windscreen he was nearly plucked out of the cockpit, but he became stuck halfway. The rigid foot of his artificial right leg was jammed in the cockpit, held in a vice-like grip. Ever downwards the fighter plunged, its helpless pilot trapped half in and half out of his crashing aeroplane, battered by the rushing wind. Desperately gripping his parachute's D-ring, Bader struggled furiously to get out. Eventually, at about 6,000 ft, the restraining strap of the offending artificial leg broke. Free at last, Bader was plucked out into mid-air. As the Spitfire continued its dive, he experienced a brief sensation of floating upwards. The terrible buffeting having ceased, in the sudden silence he was able to think. His hand still gripped the

D-ring, so he pulled; there was a slight delay before the parachute deployed and then he really was floating, gently descending to earth beneath the life-saving silk umbrella.

At 4,000 ft Bader passed through a layer of cloud, emerging below it to see the ground still far beneath him. Alarmed by the roar of an aero engine, he saw an Me 109 fly directly towards him, but the bullets he must have half-expected never came as the enemy fighter flashed by just 50 yds away.

It might surprise many people to know that a parachute descent resulting from enemy action or some other mishap whilst flying was the first a pilot would make, there being no formal parachute training. Consequently, Bader had never before had to consider the practicalities of landing with artificial legs, or indeed one such leg. He had some minutes to ponder this matter as he drifted earthwards, then French soil suddenly rushed up to meet him and he hit the ground hard in an orchard near Blaringhem, south-east of St Omer (see Prologue). For Wg Cdr Douglas Bader the air war was over, his personal period of operational service having lasted just 18 months.

'Johnnie' Johnson recalls the scene back at Westhampnett:

> Group Captain Woodhall was waiting for me on the airfield, and when Dundas, West, Hepple, and the others came back the consensus of opinion was that the Wing Commander had either been shot down or involved in a collision.

In his flying log book Johnson wrote that on this penetration over France there had been 'more opposition than ever before'. Squadron Leader Burton's log book recorded: 'Had a bad time with 109s on way out and had to get into cloud'.

As the clock ticked on it became clear from fuel considerations that the two Spitfires reported missing during the radio chatter over France were not going to return to Westhampnett. Reasoning that if they were flying damaged machines the pilots might land at one of the coastal airfields, Tangmere control telephoned each in turn, receiving negative responses from them all.

Douglas Roberts was a Radio Telephone (Direction Finding) Operator at the Tangmere 'Fixer' station located, perhaps oddly, on West Malling airfield in Kent:

> It was there that on 9 August 1941 we were told that Wing Commander Bader was missing and so listened out for several hours. Our system was basic when compared to modern equipment today, but nevertheless very efficient. The aerial system was a double dipole which, when rotated, would indicate either a true bearing or a reciprocal. Despite our diligence, nothing was heard from "Dogsbody".

Had either of the two missing pilots reached mid-Channel, there was an excellent

Douglas Roberts at work. He waited hours for a radio transmission from 'Dogsbody' on 9 August 1941, but without result.

chance that they would be picked up by air-sea rescue. If their dinghies drifted closer to the French coast, it was more likely that the Germans would reach them first, unless their positions could be discovered and a protective aerial umbrella established. Consequently Dundas, Johnson, Hepple, and West were soon flying back over the Channel, searching. At Le Touquet Dundas led the section north, parallel to the coast and towards Cap Gris Nez. Avoiding flak from various enemy vessels, especially near the port of Calais, the Spitfires made a steep turn at zero feet to return to Le Touquet. At one point Hepple broke away to machine-gun a surfacing submarine, but otherwise the only item to report was an empty dinghy sighted by Sgt West. To 'Johnnie' Johnson that empty life-saving rubber boat was somehow symbolic of their fruitless search. With petrol almost exhausted, the section landed at Hawkinge. No news had yet been received of either missing pilot. Immediately their aircraft were refuelled, the 616 Squadron pilots took off, intending to head back across the Channel to France. Shortly after take-off, however, Grp Capt Woodhall cancelled the sortie, fearing that a second trip was too risky, as the enemy might now be waiting. Swinging round to the west, Dundas led the Spitfires back to Westhampnett.

For Hugh Dundas, the thought that Bader might be dead was 'utterly shattering'. Having narrowly escaped with his life after being shot down during the Battle of Britain, Dundas, aged 20, had been totally inspired by Douglas Bader when 616 Squadron later provided pilots to fly with the Duxford Wing. In November that year his brother, Flt Lt John Dundas DFC of 609 Squadron, was killed in action over the Solent. His brother's loss affected him deeply, so when Bader arrived at Tangmere he no doubt helped fill a great void in this young man's life. The two were certainly close, and Dundas was to remain devoted to Douglas Bader until his own death in 1995.

'Buck' Casson's loss was also a serious blow to Dundas's morale. They had joined the squadron together at Doncaster and, until that day, were the last remnants of the old pre-war pilots. When it dawned on him that he was now the only surviving member of the old guard, Dundas found this a 'terrifying thought'. Regarding Bader, as a loyal lieutenant Dundas felt some degree of responsibility. He drove back to Shopwyke House 'alone and utterly dejected'.

With no news to impart other than the fact that her husband had apparently vanished, Grp Capt Woodhall had the unenviable duty of driving over to the Bay House and informing Thelma Bader. John Hunt, a young Intelligence Officer, was already there, having arrived to give some support only to discover that Thelma had not yet received the bad news. 'Woody' tempered this by stating that Douglas Bader was 'indestructible and probably a prisoner'. Later, Hugh Dundas arrived and with Jill, her sister, persuaded Thelma to take some sherry, which she only brought up again. As Dundas drove back to Shopwyke House he cried. Back at the mess, he and 'Johnnie' Johnson shared a bottle of brandy, but desolation had overtaken the inner sanctum.

Just as the Target Support detail had been 'routine' for the Tangmere Wing, so too was 9 August 1941 for JG26's pilots, dispersed around various airfields in the Pas-de-Calais, who responded urgently to the 'Alarmstart'. It was Me 109s from the 'Schlageter' Geschwader that the Tangmere Wing fought that day, high above Béthune. After the action, which developed into a running battle between Béthune and the French coast, the German pilots claimed a total of seven Spitfires destroyed. In reality the figure was five; three Spitfires of 452 (Australian) Squadron had also failed to return (one pilot being killed), lost somewhere between Béthune and Mardyck. Although JG26, the sole Luftwaffe unit to engage the Spitfires that day, lost only two Me 109s (and one pilot killed) as a result of the engagement, the RAF pilots claimed a staggering 22 Me 109s destroyed, 10 probables, and 8 damaged.

Flight Lieutenant 'Paddy' Finucane, DFC, of 452 Squadron (second from left) congratulates Sgt Chisholm 'on getting two'. The date is unclear, however, as Chisholm was given a 'half' of two 109s destroyed on 9 August 1941, but destroyed two himself on 16 August. On the former date Finucane claimed an Me 109E destroyed, possibly a machine of II/JG26 which crashed near Merville.

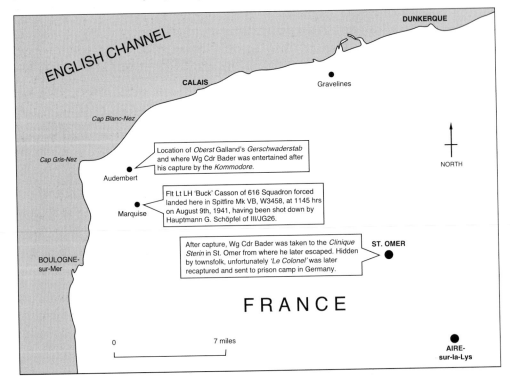

Among the successful German pilots was JG26's Kommodore, Oblt Adolf Galland, who had recorded victory number 76, a Spitfire north-west of St Pol, at 11:32 hrs. Shortly afterwards, Oblt 'Pips' Priller, Staffelkapitän of 1/JG26, arrived at Audembert to tell Galland about the captured legless 'Adler', urging: 'You must come and meet him'. While he was hospitalised at the Clinique Sterin in St Omer, Bader was actually visited several times by two JG26 pilots. He shared a bottle of champagne with them in the doctor's room and concluded that they were 'types' whom he would have liked in the Tangmere Wing.

Previous accounts have stated that the Germans recovered Bader's missing leg from his Spitfire's crash site, but in fact French eyewitnesses confirm that the artificial limb in question fluttered down on its own and landed close to Bader's parachute (see Prologue). The villagers handed the article in to the German authorities, and Galland's engineers made running repairs on the leg to afford its owner some mobility. A few days later Galland sent his Horsch staff car to fetch Bader for a visit to the Geschwaderstabschwärm.

While visiting JG26, Bader was keen to discover what had happened when he was brought down. His own explanation was a collision with an Me 109, although he had not actually seen the aeroplane with which he had supposedly collided. Galland was puzzled, as none of his aircraft had been involved in such a collision. One Me 109 pilot had been killed, however. This was Uffz Alfred Schlager, who crashed at Aire, some 10 miles south-east of St Omer. The Germans therefore conceded the possibility that Bader collided with Schlager, who had not survived to make a report. So far as Galland was concerned, however, it seemed more likely that Bader had been shot down by one of two pilots, either Obfwl Walter Meyer of 6/JG26 or Lt Kosse of 5/JG26, who had recorded their 11th and 7th victories respectively above the area of St Omer that morning.

According to Galland, for Bader it was an 'intolerable idea' that his master in the air had been an NCO pilot. Tactfully, therefore, a 'fair-haired, good-looking flying officer' was selected from the victorious German pilots and introduced to Bader as his champion. Kosse was the only officer of that rank to make a claim that morning, so it is likely that it was he whom Bader met at Audembert. However, neither German pilot's victory report was conclusive, and Galland later wrote that 'it was never confirmed who shot him down'. Had Bader's victor been identified, the Gefechtsberichte (the Luftwaffe publicity machine) surely would have made a great story of it.

Among the officers present at the reception was Hptm Gerhard Schöpfel. In 1995 he recalled the occasion:

My meeting with Wing Commander Bader was memorable and one which I well recall. Our Oberst, Joachim-Friedrich Huth, had lost a leg in the First World War, and when the report about Bader being shot down reached him he was sure that spare artificial legs existed in England. There followed a number of telephone calls, during which Bader's capture was reported to the Red Cross, and it was decided that an RAF aircraft should be offered free passage to deliver the spare legs to our airfield at an appointed time and date. So far as I know, this was initially confirmed by England.

When the Red Cross announced that Bader was a prisoner, on 14 August 1941, there was absolute euphoria within Fighter Command, and particularly at Tangmere, where Grp Capt Woodhall broadcast the news over the station Tannoy. Sir Denis Crowley-Milling remembers:

The loss of Douglas Bader had left us all stunned. A few of us, including Dundas and

Mrs Thelma Bader: 'Douglas is safe and a prisoner'.

Johnson, were with Thelma Bader in their married quarters at Tangmere when the telephone rang. After speaking, Thelma came back to join us and very calmly said: "Douglas is safe and a prisoner".

When the signal was received from Germany offering free passage for an RAF aircraft to deliver Bader's spare legs, Woodhall responded so enthusiastically that he even offered to fly a Lysander to Audembert himself. However, the Air Ministry rejected the proposal out of hand.

Gerhard Schöpfel continues:

> On the appointed time and date for an RAF aircraft to arrive with the legs, I was at the Geschwader-gefechtsstand in Audembert, having flown in from my base at Ligescourt, home of my III/JG26. Soon after our meeting, Bader wanted to inspect one of our Me 109s. Galland invited him to climb into a Geschwader-maschine and Bader commented that he would like to fly it, but of course this could not be allowed.

The Germans took many photographs of this visit, which many non-flying JG26 members would later name as the most memorable incident of their entire war. Among the snapshots is a photograph of Bader sitting in the cockpit of an Me 109 with a German officer standing on the wing adjacent. In *Reach for the Sky* and other books the object in this officer's left hand has been described as a 'pistol', but other photographs from the same series show that Oberst Huth is actually holding his gloves!

Gerhard Schöpfel recalled:

> When told of our arrangement via the Red Cross regarding his spare legs, he was not surprised when no plane arrived, as he felt that high authority in England would take

Left: *Oberst Joachim-Friedrich Huth. An Experte in both wars, Huth lost a leg himself during the First World War. Popular legend has it that when Adolf Galland showed Douglas Bader the cockpit of an Me 109, Huth stood on the other wing, pointing his pistol at Bader 'in case he tried to take off'. In fact Huth was holding a pair of leather gloves.*

Right: *Douglas Bader is shown the cockpit of an Me 109F by Oberst Adolf Galland, Kommodore of JG26.*

time to sanction such things. He hoped, however, that his own Wing would find a way.

One or two days later our radar announced a Beehive approaching. The Blenheims flew over St Omer, where they dropped a few bombs on our I Gruppe. Also dropped, however, was a crate containing Bader's legs, which was attached to a parachute.

The 'Leg Operation' took place on 19 August 1941, when, during a Circus to Longuenesse, an 82 Squadron Blenheim dropped the spare legs by parachute. The Tangmere Wing flew close cover, as Ron Rayner recalled:

I flew with 41 Squadron on that particular sortie and I remember it distinctly. The legs were dropped over St Omer and not without ceremony, it being announced over the R/T that Wing Commander Bader's legs had been delivered. We were weaving around the Blenheims and we were acting as individual aircraft, not a cohesive formation as was usual. Then we continued on to the target before turning round for home.

Woodhall signalled the Germans, so consequently the crate in question was recovered and the legs duly presented to Bader. Galland, however, was most upset that the British had responded so unchivalrously. To his mind, 'bombs and charity did not go together'. For Galland, however, his meeting with Bader was to acquire an even more bitter aftertaste.

On 17 August 1941, while Bader still occupied Chambre 21 in the Clinique Sterin,

Wing Commander Bader being received by Oberst Galland at Audembert. Hauptmann Schöpfel is on the extreme left, and Oberst Huth on the extreme right.

Oberst Galland and his officers take Bader on a tour of their airfield at Audembert. (Buchmann via Caldwell)

Left: *The dog appears to be the focal point of attention, but of more interest to us is the officer fifth from left, Hauptmann Johan Schmid, who claimed a Spitfire destroyed 10 km east of St Omer at 1125 hrs on 9 August 1941. (Buchmann via Caldwell)*

Right: *Bader takes his leave of the Geschwaderstab. Many non-flying JG26 personnel were later to identify this incident as their most vivid memory of the entire war.*

Luftwaffe NCOs remove the parachute harness from the crate containing Bader's replacement artificial legs.

a local French girl who worked at the hospital in an auxiliary capacity, Lucille Debacker, handed Bader a note. Its content was astonishing. A Frenchman would wait outside the hospital every night from midnight until 02:00 hrs, poised to guide 'Le Colonel' to a local 'safe' house. Incredibly the note was even signed by a Frenchwoman, Mme Hiècque, in her own name. The Hiècques were a working-class French family who lived at the quai du Haut-Pont in a long row of terraced houses overlooking the St Omer canal. Gilbert Petit, a young friend of the Hiècque family, was employed at the SNCF railway station in the town. Each night he waited patiently in the shadows of an alleyway across the road from the hospital, risking being caught out after curfew. Within, Bader had received bad news. He was imminently to be taken to Germany. Having been given his new legs, on the night of 20 August he knotted bed sheets together, lowered the makeshift rope out of a window at the rear of the building and climbed down. Squeezing through a small gap between the chained gates, Bader met Petit and together they made their way through the cobbled streets, darkness cloaking them. Having avoided at least one German patrol, the fugitives eventually reached the sanctuary of the Hiècque household, Bader in great pain from his stumps. 'Le Colonel' was given a bed upstairs, and before drifting off into sleep he thought: 'That's foxed the bloody Huns. I'll be seeing Thelma in a couple of days!'

The following day Mme Hiècque walked to the hospital and saw many German soldiers searching for the escaped prisoner. Upon her return she told Bader: 'Les Boches sont tres stupides!' Bader, however, appreciated the consequences for these French patriots if he was found in their house. Mme Hiècque was supremely confident, however, that the Germans would never find him, and awaited word from Gilbert that the Underground had been contacted and an escape plan formulated. That afternoon 'Le Colonel' was taken out into the back garden, and watched a tangled mass of contrails overhead as yet another drama took place above St Omer. The Hiècques and their neighbours shouted enthusiastically, 'Vive les Tommies! Vive les Tommies!', giving Bader another view of the sweeps he had flown so often.

The Hiècques' canalside house was some distance from the Clinique Sterin, and the Germans, convinced that Bader could not walk far, cordoned off the area of St Omer around the hospital, which they now searched intently. The hospital staff were questioned, and one female lacked Lucille Debacker's courage and resolve. Hélène Lefevre betrayed the conspirators. At about 17:30 hrs there was an urgent bang at the Hiècques' door; 'Les Boches!' M Hiècque bundled Bader into the back garden, hiding him in a chicken run. Within a minute the Germans were in the house, and seconds later a bayonet was thrust repeatedly into the straw covering the escapee. Realising that the next stab would probably penetrate his neck or back, Bader stood up, raising his hands. As the Germans escorted him out of the front door to a waiting car, he tried to persuade the Stabsfeldwebel who had arrested him that the old couple had no knowledge of his presence, his arrival having been during the night via a back garden gate. It was then that he saw Hélène Lefevre leave the German vehicle, and realised that they had all been betrayed.

Bader's escape attempt made life 'very unpleasant' for Oblt Galland. There was an inquiry into the escape, and even Bader's visit to Audembert, for which Galland had not requested permission, came under scrutiny. For the Germans, however, this was a taste of just how unmanageable and implacable Wg Cdr Bader was going to be in captivity, even as a disarmed prisoner.

Gerhard Schöpfel continues with the German view:

After Wing Commander Bader received his new legs, we heard that he had escaped by knotting some bed sheets together and climbing out of an upstairs window. For a man with two artificial legs this must have taken incredible guts and willpower. Really, however, in view of the strenuous activity involved, which included hiking over the Pyrenees, he actually had little chance of getting away with it. He was soon found in a house by the canal in St Omer. Our Geschwader was told that, on a subsequent train journey into captivity proper, the guards took both his legs away to prevent another audacious escape attempt!

At the end of August, 616 Squadron's ORB concluded that the month had been:

> ...a disappointing one from the operational point of view owing to the poor weather conditions. Although 16 offensive sweeps were carried out over France, their effectiveness was in several cases hampered by too much cloud, making it difficult for the squadrons in the Wing to keep together. Wing Commander Bader DSO (& Bar) DFC, and Flight Lieutenant Casson were shot down on 9 August and are now prisoners of war. This was a serious loss to the RAF, the Wing and the squadron.

In the overall scheme of things, August 1941 was indeed a disappointing month for Fighter Command; 98 Spitfires and 10 Hurricanes were lost. However, JG2 and JG26 together lost just 18 pilots, i.e. the loss ratio was exactly six to one in the Luftwaffe's favour.

Following the loss of its first Wing Leader, the Tangmere Wing itself would never be the same again. It is appropriate to allow Air Vice-Marshal 'Johnnie' Johnson, Bader's No. 4 on 9 August 1941, the last word:

> When Douglas was shot down it really was his own fault. He was tired, ready for a rest. Leigh-Mallory had asked him to come off Ops, as "Sailor" Malan, leader of the Biggin Hill Wing, had already done, having recognised in himself the signs of strain. Douglas wouldn't go, of course, and so the AOC agreed to let him stay on until the end of what was called the "season", the end of September when the weather started failing. Peter Macdonald, our adjutant, a former MP who had served with Douglas in 1940, also recognised the signs of strain and had insisted that Douglas, Thelma, and he go off on a week's golfing to St Andrews – they were, in fact, booked to go on 11 August. Douglas was tired and irritable, he couldn't see things quickly enough in the air. On the day in question, when Ken Holden sighted the 109s and Bader was unable to see them, he should have let Ken come down and attack as he had suggested. In not allowing this, he lost us six, maybe even seven seconds, by which time the high 109s were down on us. But of course Douglas was a bit greedy and would not therefore allow this. When I was a Wing Leader later in the war, such a situation often arose and it made sense for me, if I couldn't see the enemy, to stay put and cover those who could whilst they attacked. This is what should have happened.

A Luftwaffe NCO shows the crate to the camera.

CHAPTER SEVEN

An Open Verdict

When I began the research for this book, a priority was to gather as much information as possible concerning the events of 9 August 1941 as they affected the Tangmere Wing. It appeared that no previous work had assembled and considered all of the available facts; these I fully intended to analyse and report on accordingly. Having already researched detailed accounts of many other days of intense combat, I knew that previously published and accepted accounts were frequently incorrect, even for incidents concerning the famous. For example, I feel privileged to have discovered the true sequence of events leading up to the capture of Oblt Franz von Werra, later to become famous as the only German prisoner of war successfully to escape from Allied custody. The correct story was published for the first time in my third book, *Through Peril to the Stars* (Ramrod Publications, 1993). I found it amazing that a best-selling book, *The One That Got Away*, on which a film was based, and indeed many other publications, had got it wrong. It was therefore with some confidence that I embarked upon my quest to discover what had really happened to Wg Cdr Douglas Bader that day high above France.

On 9 August 1941 Circus 68 was directed against Gosnay, near Béthune, an oft-visited target some 20 miles south-east of St Omer. The first thing to go wrong for the Tangmere Wing was that, as 616 and 610 Squadrons took off and made for the English coast, Bader discovered that his airspeed indicator was unserviceable. It was accepted practice that any pilot whose aircraft developed a defect should turn back, but of course Bader did not. Indeed, the 610 Squadron diary records that on 10 July 1941 one of its pilots returned 'after five minutes with a u/s ASI'. On this occasion, however, Bader pressed on, although he handed over the lead to Flt Lt Dundas upon reaching Beachy Head.

By that time, though, his actions had probably contributed to the next problem; 41 Squadron failing to make the rendezvous. A former 41 Squadron pilot, Ron Rayner, has pointed out that, although the squadron had arrived at Merston just two weeks earlier, it had previously flown many practice sweeps from Catterick and, indeed, a number over France already. The squadron commander, Sqn Ldr Gaunce DFC, was an experienced and exceptional fighter pilot and leader. It was unusual for a squadron not to arrive at its appointed position on time. In this case, however, 616 and 610 Squadrons had taken off from Westhampnett and 41 from Merston, the intention being that the three squadrons would join over Chichester. However, it is likely that, as Bader had no ASI, between taking off and handing over to Dundas he had actually flown too fast for 41 Squadron to catch up. There is evidence, in the form of the transcribed radio messages, that after Bader resumed the lead over France he flew too fast. Squadron Leader Holden asked 'Dogsbody' to 'slow down'. The unserviceable ASI, coupled with the fact that the Wing Leader did not turn back as he ought to have done, no doubt explains why the Tangmere Wing went into action that day as 24 Spitfires instead of 36.

On Circus 68 Fighter Command lost five Spitfires: Wg Cdr Bader and Flt Lt Casson from the Tangmere Wing, and three from 452 (Australian) Squadron. In addition, 452

Squadron suffered two more aircraft damaged. Two of 452 Squadron's pilots were captured and one was killed. Available information records their attack as having been: 'Delivered about 11:30 hrs between Mardyck and Béthune, mostly above 20,000 ft but some at 10,000 ft'. Mardyck is virtually part of Dunkirk, Béthune being some 30 miles to the south-east; a lot of sky in which to pinpoint a combat 55 years later.

Both 315 and 603 Squadrons also suffered one Spitfire damaged each. The sole German opposition to Circus 68 was provided by JG26, the Geschwaderstab and all three Gruppen making contact with the enemy. This amounted to between 100 and 120 Me 109Es and Fs, a substantial force. Consequently the German pilots made claims for seven Spitfires destroyed, a figure which tallies closely with the actual RAF losses of five Spitfires destroyed and four damaged. The JG26 claims were as follows:

Pilot	Victory No.	Unit	Opponent	Time & location
Oblt Schmid	16	Geschwaderstab	Spitfire	1125 hrs, 10 km E of St Omer
Obfwl W. Meyer	11	6/JG26	Spitfire	1125 hrs, St Omer
Obfwl E. Busch	6	9/JG26	Spitfire	1125 hrs, location n/k
Uffz H. Richter	n/k	Geschwaderstab	Spitfire	1130 hrs, N of Dunkirk
Oblt A. Galland	76	Geschwaderstab	Spitfire	1132 hrs, NW of St Pol
Lt Kosse	9	5/JG26	Spitfire	1145 hrs, St Omer
Hptm G. Schöpfel	31	Stab III/JG26	Spitfire	1145 hrs, E of Marquise

(n/k = not known)

German losses are sourced from the Luftwaffe Quartermaster General's Returns, which were not for propaganda purposes but for internal audit. This original source can therefore be considered as complete and accurate as our own records. On the day in question an Me 109F-2 of III/JG26 crashed on take-off at Ligescourt, and an Fw 190 crash-landed near Le Bourget, the latter an incident not believed to be combat-related. The only other losses are as follows:

3/JG26: Me 109F-4 (8350) crashed near Aire. Uffz Albert Schlager killed.
II/JG26: Me 109E-7 (6494), pilot unknown, baled out near Merville.

As we have seen, Bader's impression was that he had collided with an enemy aircraft. Certainly 'Johnnie' Johnson has graphically described the close proximity of the enemy, the maelstrom of fighters being just '50 yds apart', but Bader was not lost during these initial seconds of mayhem. Having levelled out from the diving charge, Bader then went off alone, stalking a section of Me 109s. Again he had broken the rules. As Frank Twitchett of 145 Squadron once explained to me: 'If separated over France, the only sensible thing to do was get down on the deck and get home fast'.

When he was repatriated in 1945, Bader reported that, after his subsequent attack,

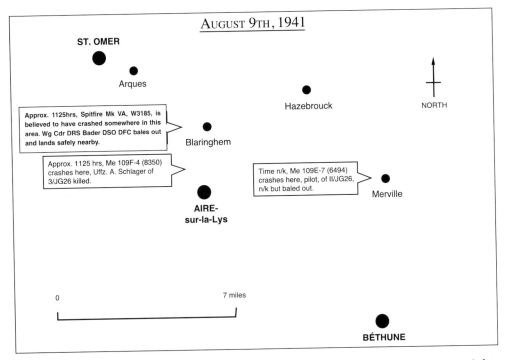

during which he set an Me 109 alight aft of the cockpit: 'In turning away right-handed from this, I collided with an Me 109 which took my tail off, it appeared as far up as the radio mast but was actually only the empennage'.

However, in a letter dated 5 August 1981, Grp Capt Sir Douglas Bader wrote: 'My impression was that I turned across a 109 and that it collided with the back of my Spitfire, removing the tail. On the other hand, if the pilot of the Me 109 had fired his guns at that moment, he could have blown my tail off. The result would have been the same.' The question that must therefore be asked is: did Wg Cdr Bader collide with an Me 109, or was he actually shot down?

None of Galland's pilots had been involved in a collision during the combat in question, but a candidate could be Uffz Albert Schlager whose machine crashed at Aire-sur-la-Lys. Bader's Spitfire is believed to have crashed somewhere between St Omer and Aire, probably closer to the latter. If a collision occurred, the locations of the two fighters' crash site would probably not rule out this possibility completely. Clearly, as Schlager was killed, and is therefore unable to report on his demise, it is unlikely that we will ever know his fate for sure. However, Squadron Leader 'Buck' Casson's description of events suggests that the German pilot fell to his guns. In 1996, 'Buck' recalled that the pilot of the 109 he attacked baled out but his parachute did not open. This information is consistent with eye-witness evidence that Schlager's body lay several hundred yards from the crash site of his aircraft. If these accounts are relied upon, one could conclude that Schlager fell to 'Buck's' guns and was therefore not involved in a collision with Wing Commander Bader. The only other Me 109 lost on 9 August 1941, an Emil, was shot down at Merville, some miles to the SE of Aire. The pilot baled out and was not involved in a collision. Two pilots of 452 Squadron claimed Me 109Es destroyed in their fight, Flight Lieutenant Brendan 'Paddy' Finucane DFC (Gosnay–Bethune area) and Flight Lieutenant 'Bluey' Truscott (between Mardyck–Bethune).

Both the Me 109F and Spitfire Mk VB were armed with two 20 mm cannon, heavy-calibre aircraft armament which often had a devastating effect. Whereas the use of small-calibre ammunition such as 0.303 in required either a sustained attack or a lucky strike, the cannon-armed Me 109s in the Battle of Britain were often able to cause significant damage to their opponents in quick-fire passes. Bader had found his control column useless and his aircraft hurtling earthwards out of control. However, the fact that he was not pitched forward violently indicates that not all of his tail unit became detached, and certainly not the entire fuselage aft of the radio mast, as he at first believed. When Pt Off Hugh Dundas was shot down over Kent by Maj Mölders on 22 August 1940, he said: 'The explosions were so unexpected, so shattering, their effect on my Spitfire so devastating, that I thought I had been hit by our own heavy ack-ack'.

Bader himself has conceded that he did not see the Me 109 which he thought he had struck, a collision being simply his 'impression' of the destructive forces acting upon his Spitfire at the time. He has suggested himself that 20 mm cannon ammunition could have achieved the same effect. It has been established that a collision was only a possibility if Bader had collided with Schlager, something which cannot be conclusively proven. If Bader was shot down, as previous authors have also suggested, who, then, was responsible?

Looking at the table of German combat claims, and bearing in mind that 'Dogsbody', although not lost in the initial charge, was nevertheless hacked down within the opening few minutes of the engagement, only one claim stands out; that of Obfwl Walter Meyer of 6/JG26, who claimed his 11th victory over St Omer at 11:25 hrs. However, the suggestion that Meyer was Bader's victor is slightly discounted by the claim for a Spitfire destroyed at the same time but at an unknown location by 9/JG26's Obfwl Busch. However, 9/JG26 was a part of Hptm Schöpfel's IIIrd Gruppe which, according to the Kommandeur's account, had actually intercepted the beehive proper, some minutes after the initial skirmish in question.

When researching Douglas Bader's biography, his brother-in-law, Wg Cdr 'Laddie' Lucas, working with Henry Probert, the head of the Ministry of Defence's Air Historical Branch at that time, examined the German claims and was sufficiently satisfied with the timing of Meyer's claim to conclude that he was Bader's victor. Although they made the connection between Bader and Mayer (incorrectly referring to the German pilot as 'Max Mayer'), Lucas and the AHB wrongly assumed that Flt Lt Casson had been shot down in the same area as Bader. Thus they assumed that Lt Kosse, who claimed a Spitfire over St Omer at 11:45 hrs, had shot down Casson. In reality, as we have already seen, Casson was shot down by Hptm Schöpfel, who even had a photograph taken of the downed Spitfire.

Those who have previously attributed Casson to Kosse have not approached Sqn Ldr L.H. Casson DFC AFC for his account, but have assumed that he was shot down in the action over St Omer. It is never a safe course to assume anything in such an investigation, however, and had any of these authors asked 'Buck' for themselves, they would have discovered that he was shot down some minutes after the Tangmere Wing's St Omer skirmish, while heading back towards the French coast. Together with Don Caldwell in Texas, USA, a published author and an accredited JG26 historian, we were able to connect 'Buck' Casson's loss with Schöpfel's claim, timed at 11:45 hrs over Marquise, near the French coast.

Regarding Lt Kosse's claim, it is unlikely that this pilot even fought the Tangmere Wing, the Spitfires of which, as the Target Support Wing, were first to arrive over the target area. Kosse recorded that his combat had occurred at 11:45 hrs, some 20 min after the initial 'bounce', during which Obfwl Meyer destroyed a Spitfire at 11:25 hrs. A timespan of 20 min represents a long interval, considering the speed at which these fighters flew. By 11:45 hrs the Tangmere Wing was recrossing the French coast, this

Oberfeldwebel Walter Meyer claimed a Spitfire destroyed at 1125 hrs over St Omer on 9 August 1941. He died in 1943. (Don Caldwell)

being confirmed by the fact that 'Buck' Casson was shot down near Marquise, just three miles from the coast, at exactly that time. As Hptm Schöpfel went to some trouble to obtain evidence for his victory report, even flying low over the crashed Spitfire to record its code letters, it is reasonable to accept his timing as accurate. In view of these times, and the fact that the Tangmere Wing was heading home at 11:45 hrs, I believe that Kosse actually engaged Spitfires of 452 Squadron. Incidentally, Leutnant Kosse, who was possibly the JG26 pilot introduced to Bader, did not survive, being killed late in the war with an RVT unit (Reichsverteidigung, the organisation responsible for the air defence of Germany).

While Obfwl Walter Meyer's claim could fit, the fact that a claim has been made is inconclusive in any case. As stated previously, the Germans lost only two Me 109s that day, those of Schlager, who was killed at Aire, and an unidentified pilot who baled out near Merville, though the Spitfire squadrons engaged claimed a staggering 22 Me 109s destroyed, 10 probables and a further 8 damaged. In *Flying Colours*, 'Laddie' Lucas concluded that the German losses tallied fairly closely with the Tangmere Wing's claims of five Me 109s destroyed and two probables, but he did not take into account the fact that JG26 was the only Jagdgeschwader to suffer losses, and then offset these statistics against all of Fighter Command's claims that day. A rigorous analysis puts a totally different complexion on the matter; the RAF overclaimed by more than ten to one!

In respect of German combat claims, today we have for each reference only the most basic of details, such as the pilot's name, the type of enemy aircraft claimed, and the location, date, and time. Unfortunately the majority of German pilots' personal combat reports have not survived. Therefore, with merely 'Spitfire destroyed, 11:25 hrs, St Omer' as evidence, it is impossible to conclude with certainty that Obfwl Meyer shot down Wg Cdr Bader. Whatever the accuracy of Meyer's claim, however, I would again refer to Adolf Galland's statement: 'It was never confirmed who shot down Douglas Bader'. Shooting the tail, or much of it, off a Spitfire is fairly significant damage to observe. If Bader was shot down by one of the JG26 pilots, why were their reports therefore inconclusive? In a letter to me dated 19 February 1996, 'Laddie' Lucas summed up the situation perfectly:

> When having dinner at Douglas Bader's house in the country, Adolf Galland told me categorically that D.B. had been shot down over the Pas-de-Calais in 1941. Galland stated that there had not been a collision. I can say in fact that, in my own humble experience, receiving a volley or two of cannon shells from an Me 109 could certainly sound like a collision with a London bus! I put this view to Douglas, who responded: "In that case, old cock, because it was me, why didn't they have the bugger responsible goose-stepping down the Under-den-Linden?"

In the final analysis of the available evidence, another possibility cannot be ignored (and I emphasise the word *possibility*). During the action concerned just two aircraft were brought down, Bader's Spitfire and Schlager's Me 109F. The Tangmere Wing, however, claimed eight destroyed and two probables, and Obfwl Meyer claimed one Spitfire, the total number of claims representing overclaiming (in terms of aircraft destroyed) of nearly five to one. In view of that overclaiming, as the German combat reports were inconclusive, and a collision unconfirmed, could it be that Wing Commander Bader was the victim of 'Friendly Fire'? Unpalatable though this prospect may be, particularly to Tangmere Wing veterans, in the confusion of battle such incidents were not, in fact, uncommon; the prospect cannot therefore, be ignored. 'Friendly Fire' may go a long way towards explaining the mystery surrounding Bader's loss that day. Perhaps an RAF pilot pressed the gun button at the wrong time, totally unaware of his mistake? I doubt, however, that we will ever know.

'Friendly Fire' presents an interesting and, indeed, topical subject in itself. In recent years the public have become accustomed to the term, such tragedies now being known to have occurred on countless occasions. A recent and much publicised example happening during in the Gulf War, when British soldiers were killed during a strafing run by an American A-10 fighter. In fact, such incidents were far more common during the Second World War than most people realise. The so-called 'Battle of Barking Creek' of 6 September 1939, when Hurricanes and Spitfires fought each other over the Thames Estuary, is an oft-quoted example, but just three days into the war pilots lacked experience, and such hard-earned lessons were inevitable. By the end of the Battle of Britain, however, no fewer than 20 front-line British fighters,

Left: *A Spitfire Mk V under fire from Gerhard Schöpfel on 26 June 1941.*

Right: *An Me 109F about to explode over France in 1941. Its similarity to a Spitfire cannot be discounted.*

Left: *Spitfire pilot Sqn Ldr Brian Lane, DFC, shot down by a Hurricane on 8 November 1940.*

Right: *Flying Officer Franek Surma, VM, KW, a Polish pilot of 308 Squadron, shortly after baling out of Spitfire R6644 at Madresfield, Worcestershire, on 11 May 1941. He engaged another Spitfire, which he identified as an Me 109F, in a protracted dogfight on 20 September 1941.*

bombers, and transport aircraft (but mainly Spitfires, Hurricanes, and Blenheims) had been mistakenly shot down by 'friendly' anti-aircraft fire, and a further nine had been mistakenly shot down by RAF fighter pilots. At the time, such information was suppressed, but the loss of the equivalent of more than two squadrons of aircraft to 'Friendly Fire' could not be ignored. For example, official records state that on 7 October 1940 Pt Off Dennis Adams of 41 Squadron was shot down by 'return fire from a Do 17 near Folkestone'. The truth is somewhat different, however, as (the now late) Sqn Ldr D.A. Adams recalled for me:

I let the chaps think that I had been a clot and let the Dornier's rear gunner get me. In fact we had a new boy flying as my number three, and he was trying to get himself a squirt. As I turned to attack he let fly and took out my controls plus half the instruments, and also put bullets into the fuel tank. When I got back to Hornchurch, I had quite a talk with this young man the following morning!

Another mishap occurred on 8 November 1940, when Sqn Ldr Brian Lane DFC and Sgt 'Jimmy' Jennings of 19 Squadron were patrolling in their Spitfires over Canterbury, as Wg Cdr Bernard Jennings AFC DFM remembered in 1989:

As we neared the cloudbase an Me 109 dived out of the cloud a short distance in front of us, followed by a Hurricane which opened up on us. Sandy's engine was hit, packed up and he lost height. As his Number Two, and because there were obviously some unfriendly people about, I stayed with him until he eventually forced-landed at Eastchurch.

Furthermore, as already mentioned in Chapter Five, on 6 July 1941 two pilots from the Tangmere Wing's 145 Squadron reported 'actually being shot at by a Spitfire over the target'.

On 20 September 1941 the Polish Wing at Northolt, comprising 306, 308, and 315 Squadrons, flew as Escort Cover Wing on Circus 100. Among the Polish Spitfire pilots was Fg Off Franek Surma VM KW, one of the Few and a rising ace with four destroyed confirmed, two probables and several damaged to his credit. Over the target, Rouen, Surma closed and attacked an Me 109F from just 20–30 yds range. The enemy aircraft burst into flame and plunged earthwards. Attacked himself, Surma broke, losing his No. 2, Sgt Jan Okroj, in the process. Alone, Surma then followed the Beehive at a distance, trying to rejoin the nearest squadron. As he made progress a yellow-nosed Me 109F was sighted manoeuvring to attack the bombers. Surma chased the Messerschmitt, getting in a long burst from 80 yds, and this enemy also caught fire and went down. By now Surma was down to 6–7,000 ft, so he flew low to the Channel. The remainder of his combat report makes fascinating and relevant reading:

About 10 miles out to sea I caught sight of the bombers – they were on my starboard side. As it was quiet I managed to join a squadron on the port side, by which time I could see the English coast, and saw an Me 109F making off after attacking a Spitfire. Behind the Me were three Spitfires in line astern. I manoeuvred to cut off the Me 109's escape, but the Spitfires abandoned their quarry for some unknown reason. The enemy aircraft climbed and I tried to get on his starboard side and into the sun. At that moment the German turned to port and looked back – as I was at the same height he saw me. This Me had its undersurfaces painted in the same blue as our Spitfires, and the upper surfaces were camouflaged in green and brown as our aircraft used to be, no doubt to confuse us.

The German pulled over on his back, I followed and got him below me. We started a dogfight but he kept on circling and made several attempts to reverse our positions. The Me was superior in engine power and climbed away very easily. My only possible tactics were to turn either to port or starboard to cut in on him. All this time the E/A was gaining height on me and attempted to shoot me down. However, his ammunition was wasted as I took care to keep out of his axis of fire. I was unable to fire at him as I could not get in a sufficiently favourable position to do so. As the position became a stalemate we both broke off at the same time.

Contrary to my suspicion when I wrote about this combat in *The Invisible Thread: A Spitfire's Tale* (Ramrod Publications, 1992), German pilots did not paint their machines to represent Spitfires. Of that there is absolutely no doubt, so one can only conclude that the 'Me 109F' engaged by this experienced young Polish fighter pilot was in reality another Spitfire. German aircraft masquerading in RAF colour schemes would have had everything to lose and nothing to gain. Even the Luftwaffe's Rosarius Circus of captured Allied aircraft bore crosses and swastikas, and British examples of captured Luftwaffe aircraft likewise bore RAF markings.

These incidents were not confined to the early stages of the war. On 10 June 1944, just four days after the Allied invasion of Europe, Pt Off Tony Minchin, a young Mustang pilot with 122 Squadron, wrote in his diary:

20 Me 109s with RAF roundels and our invasion markings "bounced" some of our boys who were taken by surprise and had a hell of a job to extricate themselves.

Flight Lieutenant Hayward was badly shot up, receiving a cannon shell through his leg, but he turned away smartly on his adversary, shot him down and brought the plane back to land. He had to be lifted out of his cockpit and taken to hospital immediately. Damned good show on his part.

Research now indicates that the likelihood is that 19 Squadron, also operating Mustangs, had attacked those of 122 in yet another incident of 'friendly fire'. On this occasion, moreover, the Mustangs all wore distinctive black and white 'invasion stripes' intended to assist aircraft identification in the air. The truth relating to this incident was only discovered by post-war researchers.

Other pilots agree that such mistakes did happen in the heat and confusion of fighter-to-fighter combat, as confirmed by the foregoing examples and statistics. Aircraft recognition in combat could sometimes be questionable. During 1940, for example, RAF fighter pilots frequently reported combat with 'He 113s', Flt Sgt George 'Grumpy' Unwin DFM being credited with the 'first of this type shot down by Duxford' on 5 November 1940. We now know, however, that the existence of He 113-equipped units was merely a piece of German propaganda, as the type never entered service. Unwin's adversary was probably a JG26 Me 109. Even more frequently, the identities of German bombers engaged by Spitfire and Hurricane pilots were incorrectly reported. On 30 September 1940 the last great daylight battle of the Battle of Britain took place when a large force of KG55 He 111s, escorted by Me 109s and Me 110s, were briefed to attack Westland Aircraft at Yeovil (see the author's *Angriff Westland*, Ramrod Publications, 1994). However, a number of intercepting RAF fighter pilots that day incorrectly identified the German bombers in their combat reports. They included such experienced men as Sqn Ldr Herbert Pinfold, 56 Squadron's CO, who reported 'God knows how many Do 215s', and Flt Lt Ian 'Widge' Gleed DFC, a flight commander in 87 Squadron, who wrote of '70 Ju 88s'.

On 9 August 1941 the Tangmere Wing fought Me 109Fs. The 'Franz' had entered service in early 1941 and, unlike its angular 'Emil' predecessor with its square wingtips, had rounded wingtips, smooth lines and no tail struts. In a split second, as an image jockeyed into the reflector ring, it would have been easy to make a mistake. Again referring back to Chapter Five, on 17 May 1941 Sgt Morton of 616 Squadron mistook Me 109Fs for Spitfires, a mistake which could have cost him his life. Furthermore, the difficulty of making split-second decisions in combat is emphasised by the following entry in Sqn Ldr Burton's log book, written on 21 July 1941: 'Should have shot down an Me 109, but failed to open fire till too late owing to uncertainty of identification'.

Another thing which cannot be overlooked is that a pilot frequently fired at a target at the same time as another pilot of whose presence he was unaware, both pilots acting totally independently so far as they were concerned. Such situations had led to the gross overclaiming of Bader's Big Wing during the Battle of Britain. An example is a combat fought on 8 November 1941, during Circus 110. Pilot Officer Jurek Poplawski of 308 Squadron saw a Spitfire being attacked by an Me 109F over the sea near Dunkirk. He hastened to assist, shooting pieces off the Me 109, which broke away, though not before it had destroyed the Spitfire, whose pilot, Fg Off Surma, was reported missing and remains unaccounted for to this day. Pilot Officer Stabrowski had likewise come to his comrade's assistance, with a result similar to Poplawski's. Back at Northolt the Poles filed their combat reports and were each awarded an Me 109F damaged. Nearly half a century later my research for *The Invisible Thread: A Spitfire's Tale* indicated that Poplawski and Stabrowski had attacked the same Me 109F, which was probably flown by Hptm Johannes Seifert, Gruppenkommandeur of I/JG26. However, in this instance, as so often happens, it

Hauptmann Johannes Siefert, Kommandeur of I/JG26. As Siefert shot down Fg Off Surma on 8 November 1941, he was attacked simultaneously by two Spitfire pilots, each acting independently and unaware of the other's presence.

proved impossible to further my enquiries beyond tracing Jurek Poplawski in Buenos Aires, as both Seifert and Stabrowski were killed later in the war. Bearing the foregoing in mind, it would not be beyond the realms of possibility that, if Obfwl Walter Meyer did fire at Wg Cdr Bader, another pilot might also have done so, each being unaware of the other's presence.

With all of the known available evidence regarding the bringing down of Bader examined, it transpired that, rather than resolving the mystery as originally intended, my research not only presented the case for each traditional theory, but added a further and similarly inconclusive possibility. Over half a century later, however, we shall never know whether, yet again, the speed of combat deceived the human eye. Most of the participants in that combat are now deceased, including Bader himself. It can only be left for the reader to decide which possibility seems the most likely, based upon the available evidence.

As if the fascinating mystery surrounding Wg Cdr Bader's capture near St Omer was not enough, in 1981 the tale took yet another twist.

In *Flying Colours*, 'Laddie' Lucas states that, in March 1981, Sir Douglas Bader opened the Schofield Air Show in Sydney, Australia, where, by chance, he was introduced to former Luftwaffe fighter pilot Max Mayer, who had long been domiciled in the Dominion. The pair exchanged pleasantries, but no more. The following day Bader was apparently astonished to read in the press an article based upon an interview which Mayer had given an Australian journalist after his meeting with Sir Douglas, in which he claimed to have shot him down on 9 August 1941. Bader's biographer, having researched the German records to some extent, assumed that this was actually Obfwl Walter Meyer (note the different spelling of the surname), who had claimed the destruction of a Spitfire above St Omer at 11:25 hrs on the day in question. What 'Laddie' Lucas did not know was what had happened to Obfwl Meyer. On 11 October 1942 Walter Meyer collided with his No. 2 and was hospitalised. He never left hospital, dying of tuberculosis in January 1943.

Another Bader book, using the aforementioned biography as source (as I had done when writing *A Few of the Many* (Ramrod Publications, 1995)), accepted as fact the information that Mayer had shot down Bader. This account also claimed that the 'Australian Fighter Mafia' had unsuccessfully attempted to trace Mayer. I cannot understand why there should have been any difficulty.

Who was Max Mayer? Having contacted the *Sydney Daily Telegraph Mirror* in Sydney, I received a copy of the article in question, written by C.J. McKenzie. Mayer claimed to have shot Bader down with 'one cannon burst, which ripped away the tail of Bader's Spitfire'. He continued: 'I saw him spiralling down, I saw his face. I followed him down because I had to confirm the kill. When I saw his parachute coming up I turned away. I reported where he had crashed.' McKenzie was advised by one of Bader's entourage not to 'bring that up or you'll get an argument'. Mayer claimed that it was the second time he and Bader had shaken hands, the first occasion having been in the Clinique Sterin in St Omer: 'He was surprised when he found it was me. He was a Wing Commander. I was a mere Leutnant. He was very warm towards me and we shook hands strongly.'

Already it was possible to identify major inaccuracies in Max Mayer's story, notwithstanding the fact that Walter Meyer had died in 1943. Firstly, it would be impossible to identify a pilot's face in the circumstances described, and in any case, while in the Spitfire Bader would have been wearing goggles and an oxygen mask. Secondly, Mayer gives the impression that at the time, so far as the Germans were concerned, his claim was accepted. Yet Adolf Galland said: 'It was never confirmed who shot down Douglas Bader'. Furthermore, whereas Mayer claims to have been a Leutnant, Walter Meyer was an NCO.

In C.J. McKenzie's article Martin Maxwell Mayer also claimed to have destroyed 34 enemy aircraft, a tally including victories not only on the Kanalfront but also over Russia and North Africa. This score, he stated, had won him the coveted Knight's Cross. Anyone checking the list of fighter pilots who were Ritterkreuzträger would discover no reference to a Martin Max Mayer. Oberstleutnant Egon Mayer received both the Knight's Cross and Oak Leaves, but was killed in action on 2 March 1944. Hauptmann Hans-Karl Mayer received his Knight's Cross on 3 September 1940, but was lost over the Channel on 17 October 1940. Leutnant Wilhelm Mayer's Knight's Cross was awarded in March 1945, by which time he was already dead, having been killed by Spitfires on 4 January 1945. Leutnant Eduard Meyer's 'throat ache' was cured in 1941, but the following year he collided with a comrade over Russia and was also killed. Therefore no Ritterkreuzträger named Mayer or Meyer survived the war.

Martin Maxwell Mayer claimed to have flown with the French Air Force in Algiers after the Second World War, but my friend and colleague Dr Bernard-Marie Dupont, himself a former French army officer, confirms that there is no record of such a pilot, a non-French national, having flown with the French Air Force.

Kerry Taylor of the *Sydney Daily Telegraph Mirror* was able to put me in contact with C.J. McKenzie himself, now retired. In a letter to me dated 31 August 1995, McKenzie enclosed a copy of a letter from Sir Douglas Bader, then aged 71, to Max Mayer, dated 5 August 1981:

Dear Max Mayer,
    You will recall that we met on Saturday 28 March at the Schofields Air Show near Sydney. We were both pleased to meet each other because we were ex-fighter pilots (on opposite sides) and we had an agreeable conversation for some minutes.
    The next morning, 29 March, I read an article in one of the newspapers quoting an interview with you, during the course of which you said that you had shot me down over France on 9 August 1941 and had followed me down until you saw me bale out.

Having read that, I was hoping to see you that day, so that we could discuss it. None of us could find you on Sunday. We tried on the Monday to contact you, but were unsuccessful. Then I left to go elsewhere in Australia. Dolfo Galland, who commanded JG26, has become a great friend of mine since the war. He cannot tell me about the incident on 9 August 1941.

My impression was that I turned across a Me 109 and that it collided with the back of my Spitfire, removing the tail. On the other hand, if the pilot of the Me 109 had fired his guns at that moment, he could have blown my tail off. The result would have been the same.

Please write and tell me your account of this incident, if you can remember it. You told the Australian press that you followed my Spitfire down until you saw me bale out. I imagine you knew it was me because you saw, when I baled out, that one leg was missing. I know that you had lived in Australia for 25 years but cannot think why you did not tell me all this when we talked to each other on 28 March. We could have had a tremendous laugh about it and really enjoyed it.

I shall greatly look forward to hearing from you,
Best wishes,
Yours sincerely,
Douglas Bader.

My letter from C.J. McKenzie was also interesting:

Dear Dilip,

I enclose a copy of a letter Bader wrote to Max Mayer, dated 5 August 1981, which you might find interesting. I must say that he has put more "spin" on his meeting with Mayer than Shane Warne puts on a "leggie"!

Bader met Mayer at Mascot Airport (our Sydney Kingsford Smith International), not at the Schofields Air Show. It had taken me some time to tee-up the meeting and Bader knew precisely who he was meeting and why. I introduced Mayer in those terms. He knew also why I was there, why the photographer was there, yet he seems to express surprise at the story of 29 March.

He says, after reading the story: "I was hoping to see you that day so we could discuss it". What day does he mean? And discuss what? He says further that he tried to find Mayer on the Sunday and Monday. He had only to phone *The Sunday Telegraph* to have been put in contact with Mayer.

The meeting between the two was brief, not as Bader says: "an agreeable conversation for some minutes".

Max Mayer died some years ago.

I hope that some of this might be of interest to you and wish you well with your project.

I remain etc ...
C.J. McKenzie.

As Kerry Taylor said: 'The weaving of the web becomes even more intriguing!'

There is no doubt, however, that Martin Maxwell Mayer was certainly not the man he claimed to be, nor indeed the man who shot down Douglas Bader. Lady Joan Bader (Sir Douglas's second wife, whom he married in 1973 following Thelma's death two years previously) has no knowledge of any response from Mayer to her late husband's letter. Is there to be no end to this intrigue?

CHAPTER EIGHT

Postscript

When considering such a remarkable story, it would perhaps surprise no-one that, according to *Reach for the Sky*, when Wg Cdr Bader was hiding in St Omer, so too was his friend Flt Lt Denis Crowley-Milling DFC of 610 Squadron. The 610 Squadron flight commander had been shot down near St Omer on 21 August 1941, and was just one of 18 Spitfire pilots lost by Fighter Command that day. Furthermore, Brickhill states that when 'Crow' was told of the Resistance's plan to break Bader out of the Clinique Sterin, he had immediately agreed to stay and help. Again the truth is slightly different. According to Flt Lt Crowley-Milling's subsequent report to MI9 regarding his ultimately successful evasion, he did not actually arrive in St Omer himself until 27 August, by which time Bader had already been taken to Germany. Crowley-Milling was more fortunate than his Wing Leader, however, and after hiking across the Pyrenees he landed in Plymouth on 2 December 1941.

Although Bader's own escape attempt was unsuccessful, it was also remarkable, for it had been orchestrated by ordinary citizens of St Omer. This indicated to the Germans the strong anglophobic support existing in France. The Hiècques and Lucille Debacker were arrested and interrogated by the Gestapo at the town's Kommandanteur. Remanded in custody, all were inevitably found guilty at a military

Sir Denis Crowley-Milling when he was a Pilot Officer with 242 Squadron during the Battle of Britain.

tribunal on 9 September 1941 and sentenced to death. However, local feeling ran high, and after many pleas for leniency, including one from none other than Marshal Petain, the leader of Vichy France, the Germans commuted the sentences to 15 years for Debacker and 10 years each for Leon and Maria Hiècque. Thereafter, Leon was detained at Diez Lahn prison, the two females being incarcerated at the Fortress d'Anrath. Remarkably, they all survived the experience and were released in 1945, fortunate indeed not to have been shot in 1941 or sent to a death camp. The Germans never discovered the involvement of Gilbert Petit, who continued working at St Omer railway station as though nothing had happened (he did not 'disappear' in 1943, as *Reach for the Sky* would have it).

Having also been captured on 9 August 1941, Flt Lt 'Buck' Casson was brought before a German General and then spent his first night as a prisoner of war in a room guarded by two German soldiers. The following day his guards drove him to Lille, from where he was conveyed by rail, via Cologne, to the Dulag Luft interrogation centre at Oberusal, near Frankfurt. His third night in captivity was spent in the 'cooler' while his clothes were thoroughly searched. On 21 August he was joined by Douglas Bader, 'but not for long', the Wing Commander being moved swiftly to Oflag VIB at Lübeck. 'Buck' himself arrived at Oflag XC, also at Lübeck, on 24 August. There, on 16 September 1941, he received the news that he had been awarded a well deserved DFC. His period of captivity (throughout which he recorded a 'Kriegie Diary', published in the author's *A Few of the Many*) ended on 2 May 1945.

Much has been written about Douglas Bader's time as a somewhat unappeasable prisoner, almost obsessed with the prospect of escape, and I do not intend to add much to that existing literature. However, while certain other prisoners resented Bader's almost constant 'Goon baiting', it should perhaps be remembered that while able-bodied prisoners were able to let off steam by playing sport or at least walking endlessly around the wire, Bader could only be a spectator, there being no outlet for his intense spirit. Can any of us imagine what a torture this must have been to a man like him?

Furthermore, his stumps also caused problems, having shrunk slightly, and no appropriate medical supplies were available. I spoke at length with a disabled friend, Terry Morse, who has one artificial leg, and he confirmed that, even with the much advanced medication and technology available in 1996, during the summer months the pain from his stump frequently becomes so unbearable that the only remedy is to refrain from walking for several days. Throughout the summers of 1940 and 1941, of course, Bader was flying fighters continuously. What pain must he have suffered then?

The late Wg Cdr Roger Boulding, a 74 Squadron Spitfire pilot shot down over France and captured on 17 June 1941, once related a Bader morale booster from their days together at Stalag Luft III at Sagan:

> It was snowing hard, and we were playing snowballs. Wing Commander Bader was enthusiastically joining in the fun. A young German Leutnant then came rushing over with a note from the Kommandant for the "Ving Commander". Bader, quick as a flash, said: "Be a good chap and just hold that for me will you?", holding out his snowball for the German. Instinctively the young officer took the snowball, and then, not knowing what to do and realising that he had made a complete fool of himself, just stood there holding it whilst several hundred prisoners had hysterics! It was little things like that that made you realise what kind of a man Douglas Bader really was.

The next stop was Stalag VIIIB at Lamsdorf, a huge camp of 20,000 PoWs. Peter Fox was also a prisoner there, and recalled:

> Douglas Bader and I were frequently in adjacent cells in what the Germans called

"Protective Custody", but known to us as the "Cooler". We devised a way of passing cigarettes to each other, but on one occasion, as I passed some through the hatch to Douglas, the cigarettes were accepted but a German voice said "Danke"!

After even more trouble, the Germans sent Bader to the notorious Offizierlager IVC at Colditz. There he was reunited with Geoffrey Stephenson, his friend from Cranwell days whom he had later found it difficult to serve under in 19 Squadron. Stephenson had been shot down near Calais on the squadron's first full-formation combat, on 26 May 1940. For him, the years behind the wire must have seemed endless. Captivity for both men, however, ended at last on 14 April 1945.

One of Bader's first thoughts upon liberation was the possibility of getting hold of a Spitfire, just to get a couple more trips in before it was all over; or even of getting command of another Wing, perhaps one in the Far East, where the fighting was still bitterly continuing. No doubt finding the prospect incomprehensible, Thelma Bader was less enthusiastic, to say the least. By this time, however, Bader's former ally and AOC, Leigh-Mallory, was dead, having been killed together with his wife in a flying accident during 1944. A telephone call to Air Cdre 'Tubby' Mermagen at Reims, his old Cranwell chum and former 222 Squadron CO, indicated that Douglas Bader was only going one place; home. Again in contradiction to the account given in *Reach for the Sky*, he did not jump straight back into the cockpit of a Spitfire and fly to St Omer for a reunion with the Hiècques; they were not to meet again until 1964.

Group Captain Douglas Bader pictured with Madam Hiècque, then aged 80, in St Omer, 1964. The French authorities invested her with the Legion d'Honneur and made Bader an honorary citizen of St Omer.

'Johnnie' Johnson: Bader's Bus Co. Still Running.

For Wg Cdr Douglas Bader DSO* DFC* the war was over, even if only reluctantly on his part.

What did those who served under Bader at Tangmere in 1941 really think of their buccaneering leader, with his unquenchable thirst for action? Four survivors have given their views.

Air Marshal Sir Denis Crowley-Milling:

> When Douglas Bader was lost over France, so ended our time with "Dogsbody" leading and encouraging us all in the air. For some of us ex-242 Squadron it was 15 exciting months from early June 1940 to August 1941. An unforgettable experience which stood us in good stead until we were rested from operational flying.

Air Vice-Marshal 'Johnnie' Johnson:

> I certainly found Douglas Bader awe-inspiring when he arrived at Tangmere, the great man, Wing Commander, DSO, DFC, legendary and so on, and of course by comparison I was just a Pilot Officer. But he treated us all as equals, he was a great leader. I learned a great deal from him regarding qualities of leadership. You can, in fact, learn 90 per cent of the skills required for leadership, man management, being straightforward with your subordinates and so on, but that last 10 per cent, which wins the hearts and minds, is an indefinable gift given to but a few, such as the gift of a great artist or writer. Bader had that gift, make no mistake. When I later became a Wing Commander, I always tried to remember the things I had learned from him, model myself upon him really.

George Reid, groundcrew, 616 Squadron:

> So far as I am concerned, after Wing Commander Bader was shot down, a happy feeling settled on 616, Westhampnett, Tangmere and, I daresay, Chichester. Good days arrived, the sun came out and life was grand, the war in the air was being won as our pilots took the attack to enemy-held France.

Flight Lieutenant Frank Twitchett:

> Whilst our 145 Squadron CO, Stan Turner, was enormously popular, I cannot say
> the same for Wing Commander Bader. Obviously we admired the man
> tremendously, but he did cause problems by persistently basing himself at
> Westhampnett with 616 Squadron. Based at Merston, I can, in fact, only recall
> having seen him on two occasions. On the downside of this man he was quite
> arrogant and there was a rumour that he was trying to create an all-officer pilot
> Wing at Tangmere. This was prevented by the NCO pilots, certainly on 145
> Squadron, putting in requests for postings. Of course Group wanted to know
> what it was all about and that was the end of that.

Mrs Jean Allom adds:

> I think that the brash, arrogant exterior was a front, as it can be with so many similar
> people. Douglas Bader had an inferiority complex regarding his lack of legs and was
> driven by having to constantly prove himself. I also found him to be very kind,
> however, and my friendship with the Baders only ended with their deaths.

Douglas Bader's story not only captivated the general public during the Second
World War, but also inspired a new generation during the 1950s, when Brickhill's
book and Danny Angel's film of the same name were released. After the war, Gp Capt
Douglas Bader became a great example to disabled people the world over, and he
strove to help whenever possible. In 1976 he was knighted for his services to the
public and the disabled, making him Gp Capt Sir Douglas Bader KBE CBE DSO*
DFC* DL RAF Retd. Thelma, however, had died in 1971; two years later Douglas
married Joan Murray, now Lady Bader. On 4 September 1982 this great man, for great
he undoubtedly was, had a massive heart attack and died in a car being driven by his
wife.

Even after death, however, the man's charisma still reaches out and engulfs the
public, and this was graphically illustrated by the media storm which brewed
following our discovery of the St Omer Spitfire, initially thought to be Bader's in
early 1996. It was only then that I fully appreciated this quite incredible and
apparently all-consuming general fascination with Douglas Bader. Many of the Few,
particularly those who fought in 11 Group, resent Bader's fame and recognition,
which, in the eyes of the general public, is almost to the exclusion of all others. A
comparison can also be drawn with the acclaim and popularity accorded to the
Spitfire; the less charismatic Hurricane, despite its many superb qualities, has always
been overshadowed by its contemporary.

During the more recent Gulf War, Flt Lts John Peters and John Nichol of XV
Squadron were shot down during their first sortie. The account of their subsequent
ordeal as prisoners of war in Iraq, *Tornado Down*, became a bestseller, and consequently
some other Tornado crews who completed numerous sorties successfully came to
resent the popularity of the 'two Johns'. However, would they have changed places
with Peters and Nichol and experienced the hell on earth they survived? Ask a man in
the street to name a Tornado pilot, and the chances are he will answer 'John Peters'.
John Peters, the reluctant hero, has become an inspiration to a generation. Heroes are
needed in wartime, and the legless Douglas Bader, a charismatic and ambitious
professional fighter leader, provided the media with such a figure. The incredible thing
is that this fascination with Douglas Bader seems likely to last for ever.

Just as Bader's story had captivated both the British public and media, so too did
his enemies respect him; Gerhard Schöpfel recalled:

Some time after Wing Commander Bader's capture, I visited the interrogation centre at Dulag Luft, Oberusal. Out of interest I had a look at his interview notes – it did not surprise me to discover that he gave nothing away! I have to say that we respected this enemy enormously, both as a fighter pilot and a man.

Josef Niesmark, a member of JG26's groundcrew, tells an interesting Bader story:

The crate in which Wing Commander Bader's spare legs were dropped was taken as a souvenir by a soldier from Number 1 Army Group. Wherever he was posted throughout the war, the crate went with him, eventually arriving in Kloster Handrupp, Germany. In 1945 the soldier was posted elsewhere and was unable to take the crate, so I took possession of it. It was not possible, however, to keep it with me during the remainder of the war, so I hid it, together with some other souvenirs, in a Handrupp church. Of course we were retreating, moving from place to place, eventually surrendering at Flensburg. At the end of June 1945 I was released from a British prisoner-of-war camp but did not at first return to Germany. When I did, much later, I went to Handrupp to collect the crate and its contents. However, the church in which I had left it had been taken over by Polish soldiers and I was too frightened to enter the building and collect my belongings. So there ended the story of the crate and my unusual association with Douglas Bader.

It may surprise some to know that Douglas Bader was not the only legless fighter pilot. Following a mid-air collision during training on 12 May 1939, Midshipman Colin Hodgkinson also lost both legs. After his accident Hodgkinson became driven

Colin Hogdkinson, the other legless Spitfire pilot of the Second World War. By coincidence, he was also captured near St Omer.

by the desire to fly a Spitfire, inspired by Douglas Bader's success. He was transferred to the RAF and realised his ambition, with 131 Squadron, on 19 September 1942; coincidentally, the squadron was based at Westhampnett. Flying Officer Hodgkinson's autobiography, *Best Foot Forward*, was published in 1957. Although it was successful, his story was overshadowed by *Reach for the Sky*. In 1996 Colin Hodgkinson wrote to me:

Flying without real legs, as it were, caused no real problems in a Spitfire for their involvement was largely restricted to aileron control. This was also the case in respect of a number of other British aircraft of the period, such as the Hurricane, Fulmar, Master, Swordfish, and Anson, all of which I flew. All had airbrakes controlled by a lever on the control column. US and German military aircraft, however, all had pedal brakes, flexed by the toes, and to fly these types, e.g. a Mustang, for the likes of Douglas Bader and me was a very "hairy" operation!

I was with 131 Squadron at Westhampnett for just a few weeks only as we were soon posted to Castletown, in northern Scotland. However, during my period of operational flying I flew some 130 offensive sorties against the enemy, a statistic including fighter sweeps, and daylight bomber escort duties, Rhubarbs, low-level attacks on trains, shipping, motorised transport *et al*; other low-level missions included escorting Beaufighters over the North Sea to attack German shipping off the coasts of Holland and Belgium. I also flew many ASR operations.

On 23 November 1943 we were on a high-level reconnaissance flight over NE France, but I suffered an oxygen system failure. I remember breaking cloud cover; there was a lot of flak, my engine was dead, and I was looking for a place to land on what looked like, in my dazed state, a patchwork quilt. Two days later I woke up in a Luftwaffe hospital in St Omer, assuming, naturally, that the Germans had pulled me out of the wreckage. Certainly they led me to believe this, continually telling me how lucky I had been.

Imagine my surprise when, 40 years later, I received a telephone call from a school teacher in St Omer, a M Martinez, whose daughter, whilst staying with an English family near Solihull last summer, had told my story; the son of the house had tracked me down. I then found that in reality I owed my escape to the courage of two French farmers, Albert Desazures and Andre Mareville, who, at great personal risk, had pulled me out of my burning Spitfire – what they did not know was that the fuel tanks were virtually full.

I owe my life to these two gallant Frenchmen who not only risked theirs in saving me but could have been shot for their act of courage.

To return to the Tangmere Wing, 'Johnnie' Johnson attributes to Douglas Bader the gift of great leadership. Other pilots have criticised Bader's leadership at Tangmere, however, so perhaps only those of the 'inner sanctum' were exposed to their leader's true qualities. By 1945 many of his subordinates had aspired to senior rank. To name but two, Hugh Dundas was among the RAF's youngest Group Captains, remaining a true Baderphile until his death in 1995, and Gp Capt 'Johnnie' Johnson was officially the RAF's top-scoring fighter pilot. As Johnson has said, when his time to lead came, he modelled himself on Douglas Bader.

Although the first sweep after Bader's capture was led by Wg Cdr Don Finlay DFC, formerly CO of 41 Squadron, Bader's place as Wing Leader was actually taken by Paddy Woodhouse, who had commanded the Wing's 610 Squadron from April to June 1941. Woodhouse was undoubtedly a most capable, enthusiastic and motivated Wing Leader; throughout the remainder of August, following his appointment on the 14th, he led the Wing on nine sweeps. In fact, as Wg Cdr Bader had almost

Wing Commander Don Finlay, DFC, seen here as CO of 41 Squadron, led the Tangmere Wing on its first Sweep after Bader's capture.

exclusively based himself at Westhampnett, this change of leadership did not affect the Wing to the extent I had assumed. Ron Rayner recalls:

As I have said, we in 41 Squadron were based at Merston, and in the two weeks we were a part of the Tangmere Wing before Douglas Bader was shot down, I only saw him twice. To us, the most important thing was the squadron, and indeed squadron commander, not the Wing or its leader. Going on a stage further, possibly even our own particular flight may even have been more important than the squadron as a whole.

In any case, the identity of the Tangmere Wing had changed when 41 Squadron replaced Stan Turner's 145 Squadron on 28 July 1941. On 29 August Ken Holden's 610 Squadron withdrew to Leconfield, being replaced at Westhampnett by 129 'Mysore' Squadron. On 6 October 'Billy' Burton's 616 Squadron, the only squadron remaining from Bader days, flew north for rest at Kirton, its place in the Tangmere Sector being taken the following day by 65 Squadron. By October, therefore, the Wing was entirely new, albeit with a proud tradition to uphold.

In *Reach for the Sky* Paul Brickhill gives the distinct impression that Douglas Bader created what was known in the RAF as either the 'finger four' or 'cross-over four' formation. In reality, as already recounted, the first man to reconsider fighter tactics and apply them to the new, fast, monoplanes was Werner Mölders. 'Vatti' worked out the Schwärm in Spain during 1937. This tactical initiative was to prove an enormous advantage to the Germans during the first two years of war. 'Johnnie' Johnson explains:

The RAF version of the "finger four" was really Cocky Dundas' idea. We had all seen the Germans flying in these loose formations. In 1941 we could see these Schwärms of German fighters, lean and hungry looking with plenty of room between them. Our training, however, was quite disgusting. I remember flying on 15 September 1940, climbing up to the south when my section leader said: "You're too far out", and my wing was overlapping his at the time! The idea of the "vic", of course, was that we all manoeuvred as one, 24 machine-guns firing together. It was disgusting, and because of our antiquated tactics a terrible number of young chaps were to be slaughtered without even knowing what had hit them because they were concentrating intently upon tight formation flying. That was even towards the end of the Battle of Britain. Astonishing.

Prior to going to Tangmere, we of 616 Squadron were not flying "vics" but in pairs. I remember that in the autumn of 1940, Dundas and I were scrambled together from Kirton, just a pair of us flying out, covering each other like a pair of hunting dogs. When we got to Tangmere we were told that we were going to fly three fours in line astern. Sometimes they put a pair of weavers over the squadron but these were often never seen again, being the first to be picked off. Then Bader arrived and at first we flew in the three fours, the loose fours being in line astern, but then Dundas, who of course had already been shot down, suggested that we should fly the fours in line abreast. Consequently, after a little experimentation, we adopted this in May 1941. Prior to that, there was no tactical training, no-one ever taught me how to get on the tail of a 109. Bader was the first man who started to talk to us about tactics. He had the ability to dissect an air battle and learn from it.

I think that a lot of the trouble with our tactics was that the Air Marshals got promoted quickly and so they had little operational experience. Leigh-Mallory used to come down and see us in a Proctor flown by his PA; he probably had not flown himself since the First War. They said that Dowding was so hamfisted that you had to keep out of his way! There has been a lot of fuss made about Keith Park flying his Hurricane around, but he only flew from station to station, never operationally. It was therefore people like Bader and Malan who dictated the tactics, and this could have lost us the war.

Sir Archie Winskill adds:

By the time we joined Douglas Bader at Tangmere, fighter tactics were already changing; instead of the "vic" we were flying in a much looser formation, the "finger four". Three sections of four, each aircraft well spread out, made up a squadron. Thus 12 pairs of eyes could cover the squadron, lookout being in all directions. The same wide formation principle applied when Bader led the Wing, the three component squadrons being 400/500 yds apart and stepped up in high altitude.

Again, much has already been written regarding Bader's fascination with tactics; certainly Hugh Dundas and the Wing Leader can genuinely take credit for introducing the four-section, line-abreast formation into Fighter Command. However, as 'Johnnie' Johnson indicates, it is disgusting that it took so long for the RAF to imitate the Luftwaffe's tactics, which had been in use since 1937.

The question of German tactics raises another issue. *Reach for the Sky* again gives the false impression that Fighter Command was sweeping the enemy from the sky over France in 1941. In reality this was not so. Like the Spitfire, the Me 109 had been created as a defensive fighter; during the Battle of Britain both the Spitfire and Hurricane had been used in that role, for which they had been intended. In 1941 Fighter Command was trying to use the Spitfire in an offensive role for which it was not designed, just as the Germans had used the Me 109 in 1940. In 1941, however, the Germans were able to use the Me 109 in its intended defensive role, and therefore

Fighter Command's guns certainly were loaded in 1941, but did the Non-stop Offensive actually achieve anything of value?

had an immediate advantage. The German controller, alerted by radar to the Beehive's approach, scrambled his forces in good time and climbed them to great height, just like his RAF counterpart during the Battle of Britain. From on high the Me 109s rained down on the Spitfires in what Wg Cdr David Cox DFC has described as 'dirty darts'. The intention was that the RAF formation would be broken by this charge, during which it was hoped a couple of Spitfires would be destroyed or damaged, as Ron Rayner experienced to his discomfort during such an attack. The stragglers would then be picked off, often right back as far as the English coast. These tactics fully exploited the positive qualities of the Me 109, and the 'dirty dart' thus largely saved the Me 109 from dogfighting with the Spitfire, when it was inferior owing to its wider turning circle. These diving tactics also confused the RAF pilots, who were taught to fight in a horizontal plane.

By the spring of 1941 the survivors of the Battle of Britain were largely starting to be rested, such as the commanders of Tangmere's squadrons upon Wg Cdr Bader's arrival in March. Thus Fighter Command opened the Non-stop Offensive with many inexperienced replacement pilots. On the other hand the Luftwaffe, who did not so rest their pilots, was largely an experienced foe. Incredibly, the OTUs did not provide an acceptable level of air-to-air gunnery training until 1943. Many new pilots only had the opportunity during training to fire their guns into the River Severn, and their first shot in anger was actually to prove their first experience of air-to-air firing. The German pilots, however, were taught to shoot and, despite Adolf Galland's initial fears, the concentrated fire produced by grouping the Me 109F's armament in its nose produced devastating results.

Attacks on targets in France could not damage, much less cripple, the German war machine, and Germany's heavy industry in the Ruhr valley was beyond the range of escorting fighters at that time. On 12 August 1941 the RAF sent a force of Blenheims to Cologne during daylight. Spitfires escorted the bombers to the Dutch coast, where they had to turn back owing to lack of fuel. Although 50 Blenheims hit the target, 12 were shot down. Such losses were obviously unsustainable, so during daylight Bomber Command returned to using escorted, penny-packet forces in what amounted to little more than nuisance raids. Even so, the price was high. With little to defend, the German pilots were not necessarily obliged to engage, and were able to pick the right moment to attack.

Those who have read *Reach for the Sky* will no doubt be shocked to learn that, by the end of 1941, the statistics of the day-fighter war over France were an incredible two to one in the Luftwaffe's favour. However, Fighter Command's combat claims were astronomical. For example, during June 1941 the Command's pilots claimed a total of 176 enemy aircraft destroyed and 74 probables, whereas the Germans actually lost 44 aircraft, an overclaiming ratio of virtually five to one.

Possibly the two most relevant reasons for overclaiming in this context were that, firstly, with so many fighters in the sky, as in the Duxford Wing days, it was inevitable because the same aircraft were destroyed by a number of different pilots, each unaware that they were not attacking alone. Secondly, in contrast to the Spitfire, the Me 109's standard evasive tactics involved diving at high speed. The Messerschmitt's engine was fuel injected, and therefore did not cut like the Spitfire's Merlin, but, as the German pilot pushed his throttle forward, thick black smoke would issue from the exhaust. A Spitfire pilot's claim to have destroyed an enemy aircraft, having seen it suddenly pitch down, streaming black smoke, in a steep high-speed dive into the cloud below, is therefore understandable. In reality, however, the Me 109 pilot probably levelled out in the safety of the cloud and returned to base, albeit perhaps in a damaged aeroplane.

The claims of RAF pilots were frequently accepted with little or no supporting evidence. This is a demonstrable fact, although some might dispute it. The Germans, however, as already related, recorded both their losses and claims with characteristic Teutonic thoroughness. For example, on 17 June 1941 the Kanalgeschwadern claimed 20 RAF fighters destroyed, while Fighter Command actually lost 17 such aircraft destroyed or damaged. Conversely, during Circus 68 on 9 August 1941 the RAF claimed 22 Me 109s destroyed, 10 probables and 8 damaged, whereas the Luftwaffe lost only two Me 109s in the day's action. On the same date the RAF suffered five Spitfires destroyed and three damaged, and the Germans claimed seven destroyed. Repeatedly, the German claims are more accurate. Despite a perhaps understandable reluctance on the part of British researchers to accept their accuracy, the German records and statistics can be proven. Sir Archie Winskill recalls:

> I was shot down near Calais on 14 August 1941, which was, in fact, the first sweep on which the Tangmere Wing flew after Wing Commander Bader was lost. I baled out and was fortunate to receive help from the French which ultimately enabled me to escape over the Pyrenees and return home via Spain and Gibraltar. Whilst I was hiding on a farm in the Pas-de-Calais, I was visited by a British agent, Sidney Bowen, who was from an escape organisation based in Marseille. He asked me why more Spitfires were crashing in France than Me 109s; I had no answer for him.

Owing to the interceptions of German communiques by *ULTRA*, the actual German losses were well known at the highest level of command in England. However, had these been released to either the public or the squadrons there would have been a serious morale problem, to say the very least. The Non-stop Offensive was increasingly stepped up after the German invasion of Russia, to assure Stalin that the Allies were making every effort to alleviate pressure on the Soviet Union, but what did it achieve in real terms? June 1941 had seen JG2 and JG26 entrusted with the defence of the Kanalfront; at no time did any units have to withdraw from the east to reinforce them. Although there is no intention of denigrating the obvious courage, tenacity, and sacrifices of the RAF aircrews, it is easy to understand why the Luftwaffe dubbed Leigh-Mallory's 1941 policy the 'Non-sense Offensive'.

One thing the Allies did gain during 1941 was the experience necessary for the eventually successful daylight strategic bombing campaign waged by the Americans. The USA entered the war somewhat belatedly, on 7 December 1941, and even then only because of Japan's surprise attack on her fleet at Pearl Harbor. Although the 'Eagle' volunteer pilots had flown with the RAF during Britain's Finest Hour, American aircraft did not enter the European arena until 17 April 1942, when Gen Ira Eaker led a formation of Boeing B-17 four-engined heavy bombers to the Rouen-Sotteville railway marshalling yards. Soon the Flying Fortresses would be escorted to Berlin itself by purpose-built long-range escort fighters; North American Mustangs, Republic Thunderbolts and Lockheed Lightnings. With the might of the USA, which was able to build upon the RAF's experience of 1939–41, ultimate victory for the Allies was assured from the day Eaker went to Rouen.

An informed opinion of the aircraft involved in these early wartime battles is also essential. 'Johnnie' Johnson gives his views:

I thought that, until we got the Spitfire Mk IX, the Germans always had a slight edge

During the 1970s Gp Capt Sir Douglas Bader was the subject of a 'This is Your Life' television programme compered by the late Eamon Andrews. Seen here are, left to right: Sir Douglas Bader, 'Johnnie' Johnson (obscured), Jeff West, Sir Alan Smith, Sir Hugh Dundas and Eamon Andrews. Was it any surprise that afterwards the bar was drunk dry?

Sir Douglas Bader at Duxford during the making of 'The Battle of Britain' in 1968. Who could tell that he had artificial legs? Sir Douglas was particularly proud of this picture for that reason.

over us. The Me 109E was slightly superior to the Spitfire Mk IA because of its 20 mm cannon and fuel injection. By comparison we had a First World War-type weapon in the 0.303 in Browning. I also thought that the Me 109F was slightly superior to the Spitfire Mk V. Of course then the Fw 190 saw everybody off. It drove us back to the coast – our depth of penetration over France was far shorter in 1942, just because of that aeroplane. Of course at first, when we reported a new fighter with square wingtips and a radial engine, the Intelligence people told us that they were obsolete Curtiss Hawks captured in 1940. Incredible! It was not until we got the Spitfire Mk IX that the balance at last tipped firmly in our favour.

The phenomenon of the all-consuming Bader charisma, and his incredible natural magnetism for the media, has meant that he has always overshadowed those who also served. The intention of this book was to provide the first objective overview, by giving the 'unknowns' a chance to tell their stories. Clearly, from the foregoing chapters, many others made enormous contributions but received little or no recognition for their efforts. The great success of many of Bader's subordinates, such as Johnson, Dundas, and Crowley-Milling is well known, and has previously been touched upon, but what happened to the unknowns? To mention but three of this book's contributors, Frank Twitchett left the RAF in 1950 to start a career in sales; Bob Morton, who was captured in July 1941, eventually came home and became a teacher; and Ron Rayner, who flew Spitfires operationally virtually throughout the entire war and won a well-deserved DFC, left the Service in 1945 to become a jeweller. All now enjoy retirement but maintain a keen interest in that most exciting period of their lives: when they flew Spitfires.

In Germany, the Tangmere Wing's foes are similarly proud of their fighting days, and the German Fighter Pilots' Association remains a thriving organisation. At Wittmund air base the modern Luftwaffe's JG71 'Richthofen' flies McDonnell Douglas F-4 Phantoms, and Germany is now Britain's ally. The Kommodore at

Three former JG26 Kanaljäger photographed in 1989. Left to right: Adolf Glunz (65 victories), Gerhard Schöpfel (40 victories), and Otto Stammberger.

Wittmund, Oberst Fahl, maintains a museum dedicated both to the Red Baron and to the wartime JG2 'Richthofen'. His base often hosts wartime fighter pilots' reunions, sometimes organised by Ottomar Kruse, a former Fw 190 pilot with JG26. Although JG26 itself does not have an official reunion association, 1995 saw its biggest gathering of old Kameraden since 1945.

When Adolf Galland was captured in 1945, Douglas Bader met him briefly at Tangmere and presented the former General der Jagdflieger with a box of cigars. Although Galland felt that Bader had not reciprocated the hospitality which he had himself extended at Audembert, they later became friends. Old age and ill health prevented Generalleutnant Galland from contributing to this book; sadly he died, aged 83, in February 1996.

In 1942, when Galland left JG26 to succeed Werner Mölders as the General of Fighters, Gerhard Schöpfel became Kommodore of JG26. In January 1943 he became Jafu for southern Italy, then Norway. In June 1944 he commanded JG4, and in November he became Jafu Hungary. Command of JG6, in northern Czechoslovakia, was his final post, in which capacity he was captured by the Russians and held by them until 1949. Upon his return to Germany he eventually secured an executive position with Air Lloyd at Cologne Airport. Herr Schöpfel is now 84 and living in Germany.

Frank Kamp served with the German Labour Corps in France during 1940, then fought in Russia with Infantry Battalion 198. He survived the eastern ordeal but was later captured by the Americans during their liberation of Southern France. After the war he was released from captivity in the USA and volunteered to return to his German home, which was in the British Zone of Occupation. However, the repatriation voyage was intercepted by the British, who marched the Germans back into captivity in England, holding them for another two years. Consequently Frank remained in England and became a civil engineer.

Left: *Frank Kamp pictured while serving with an infantry unit in Russia.*

Right: *A poignant reminder. Mrs Jean Allom, widow of Wg Cdr H.F. 'Billy' Burton, DSO, DFC, displays her late first husband's Irvin flying jacket.*

Whilst some who served at Tangmere during what 'Johnnie' Johnson has described as those 'stirring times' survived, many others sadly perished before 1945. Among these was 616 Squadron's CO, the very promising 'Billy' Burton. Having received news of his well-earned DFC on 5 September 1941, he was posted on 1 October to 11 Group HQ as 'Squadron Leader Tactics'. Early in 1942, however, Burton was posted to the Middle East and promoted to Wing Commander, leading the Curtiss Kittyhawk-equipped 239 Wing on tank-busting sorties. On 23 February 1943 he received a Bar to his DFC, and a DSO, for 'brilliant leadership', and he concluded his tour on 6 April. He had also been awarded the French Croix de Guerre for a daring low-level attack on a desert fort where Gen Leclerc was surrounded by German forces, as a result of which the General was able to escape. In May 1943 Air Cdre Harry Broadhurst, the leader of the Desert Air Force, brought several of his senior commanders back to England on leave. Back home, Wg Cdr H.F. Burton DSO DFC* found that 'Johnnie' Johnson, his former subordinate, was leader of the Kenley Wing. In fact, Johnson had just been awarded his first DSO. The station commander was also one of the Few, whom 'Billy' had known in the desert, Gp Capt Harry Fenton. Before his death in 1995, Air Cdre Fenton recalled: 'At Kenley I was even able to entertain in style on occasions. When "Billy" Burton and "Pedro" Hanbury visited us from North Africa, our catering officer excelled himself.'

'Billy' Burton's widow, Mrs Jean Allom, remembers:

"Billy" was to return to North Africa in a Hudson flown by Group Captain Gordon

Yaxley, a much decorated officer and senior to my husband. In actual fact, there were two Group Captains aboard the aircraft as, before Billy returned to the desert, Broadhurst had told Billy that he had been promoted and to put up his fourth stripe.

In retrospect, there seems to have been doom hanging over this flight as the Hudson should never have been flying that day – it was due to return several days earlier. The delay was caused by those servicing the aircraft discovering some desert insects therein, and so it had to be fumigated. Of course the date on which the flight to Gibraltar was then scheduled to take place, 3 June 1943, was one on which maximum Luftwaffe activity took place over the Bay of Biscay as Churchill was expected to be flying back to the UK. Only the day before, in fact, a Liberator had been shot down over the Bay – all aboard were lost, including the actor Leslie Howard. Also, with regard to "Billy"'s flight, Harry Broadhurst had been summoned to a top-level conference in London and so was not returning with them. He told me later that he would never in a million years have agreed to the flight going by day. Although I understand that "Billy" did everything possible to dissuade him, Yaxley, the senior man, decided to fly by day – with disastrous consequences. It is impossible to imagine why such an experienced officer as Yaxley took such a foolhardy course.

At 10:5 hrs the 117 Squadron Hudson was intercepted over the Bay of Biscay by a Ju 88C flown by Lt Heinz Olbrecht of 15/KG40. For the RAF, the German's success was a disaster. The official version records that three crew, plus one Group Captain, four Wing Commanders (including Burton, whose promotion was not yet official) and two Squadron Leaders all perished. Between them these officers had three DSOs, three DFCs and an MC. All remain 'missing' to this day. Jean Allom continues: 'Even after 50 years I can hardly bear to think of them trapped in an unarmed aircraft with no means of defence, especially considering the many deeds of gallantry performed by each man lost. The loss was actually such a blow for the Desert Air Force that the news was kept a secret.'

When he was killed, Wg Cdr Howard Frizelle 'Billy' Burton DSO DFC was 27 years old. Like Air Marshal Sir Denis Crowley-Milling, Air Vice-Marshal 'Johnnie' Johnson and Gp Capt Sir Hugh Dundas, Burton, the Cranwell Sword of Honour man, was clearly destined for a distinguished career. Instead he became just another name in the casualty lists published in *The Aeroplane*, another little-known and unsung hero of the Second World War. At the going down of the sun, we will remember them. It is perhaps appropriate, therefore, to allow his widow the last word on the Tangmere Wing at war:

On 1 October 1941 "Billy" was at last taken off operations and posted to 11 Group HQ as 'Squadron Leader Tactics'. He hated leaving 616, but it was obvious to all that he was desperately tired; after the long summer of operational flying he badly needed a rest.

I piled our few worldly goods into his little Morris Minor and set off for Uxbridge to try and find us somewhere to live. Tangmere was now in the past, but that summer is one that remains amongst my most vivid memories, perhaps because it was the first and last that "Billy" and I were ever to spend together.

St Omer Spitfire

The interest in recovering the remains of crashed wartime aircraft, known as 'aviation archaeology', began in England during the 1960s, when the sites of the remains of numerous Battle of Britain aircraft from both sides were excavated in south-east England. Over the years the interest has grown, and many museums and associations have been founded, their activities being regulated to some extent from 1986 onwards by the Protection of Military Remains Act. This legislation stipulates that, before an excavation can occur, a licence must be obtained from the Ministry of Defence. The would-be archaeologist has to submit information regarding the aircraft concerned, such as the date of the crash and the squadron, pilot and serial number. The Air Historical Branch then cross-references this information with casualty records and, providing the aeroplane in question is not that of a missing pilot or likely to contain large-calibre ordnance, permission will be granted.

Today, however, the majority of crash sites in England have been discovered and excavated, the remains of the aircraft recovered being displayed at various locations

Inspirational Spitfire: Mk VA W3185, Lord Lloyd 1. *This aircraft first flew with the Tangmere Wing's 145 Squadron but was damaged in action while being flown by Sqn Ldr Stan Turner. Repaired, on 28 July 1941 the aircraft became the personal mount of Wg Cdr D.R.S. Bader DSO DFC, leader of the Tangmere Wing, who is seen here climbing out of the aircraft. Note the black pre-war flying suit, personalised 'DB' code letters and the Wing Commander's rank pennant.*

around the UK. A truly outstanding museum is the Kent Battle of Britain Museum at Hawkinge, where the wreckage of over 400 aircraft shot down in the Battle of Britain can be seen, alongside many other relevant exhibits and full-size replica aircraft. Many of the relics displayed at Hawkinge were recovered during the 1970s and early 1980s, when interest peaked.

Now, however, enthusiasts are increasingly looking towards France for further investigations. On the Continent, perhaps surprisingly, aviation archaeology remains in its infancy, the British clearly having led the way. As momentum gathers over the next few years, however, it is likely that many more crash sites will be investigated, and our knowledge and understanding of this aspect of military history will therefore increase. Some ask why it is important to recover this mangled wreckage. The answer, quite simply, is that it provides the basis for a poignant reminder of the many sacrifices made so long ago.

Nearly a decade ago the late Grp Capt Peter Townsend brought together a young Frenchman, Dr Bernard-Marie Dupont, and myself because we shared similar interests in wartime aviation. Bernard's grandfather had been a Gendarme, and was involved in guarding a fatal Hawker Typhoon crash near the village of Le Parcq on 20 January 1944. The pilot, Richard Curtis, was buried locally. Bernard became so fascinated by this story that he began his own research, during the course of which we traced the pilot's relatives in England and many of his comrades. Bernard's project eventually culminated in the publication, in 1994, of a book, *The Night Afterwards: A Posthumous Friendship*. Obviously Bernard's help was a prerequisite with regard to the Bader Spitfire. My friend's response was immediately enthusiastic, and his work in France commenced.

By May 1995 Bernard had traced the descendants of Madame Hiècque of St Omer, the lady in whose house Wg Cdr Bader had been hidden before he was recaptured. The old lady herself had long since died, but her nephew, Jacques Fournier, who by coincidence also has no legs, still lived in the house next door to that occupied by his aunt during the war. Monsieur Fournier was able to put Bernard in contact with Madame Petit, the widow of Gilbert, who had waited for Bader outside the Clinique Sterin in St Omer on the night of his escape. Owing to commitments in England, however, it was not until early October that Colin Terry and I were able to travel to France and meet these marvellous people ourselves.

Colin and I had originally intended to fly to Le Touquet, but the weather closed in and we travelled as pedestrian passengers on a Stena Sealink ferry bound from Dover to Calais. The crossing was rough, but our excitement mounted nonetheless as the white cliffs of Cap Gris Nez came into view, together with the tiny village of Wissant, once Osterkamp's headquarters, and the port of Calais itself. Having rendezvoused with Bernard, we sped off to St Omer, the very mention of which is still likely to give a former wartime fighter pilot the 'twitch' even today! St Omer was an aerial fortress, around which were clustered many German fighter units, at such places as Longuenesse and Clairmarais. The town is some 35 km south-east of Calais and easily accessible off the N43. It is the first French town within hailing distance of Calais, at the heart of which we found a broad, cobbled square, the Place Foch, surrounded by cafes and dominated by the imposing Hôtel de Ville, which hosts a vibrant market.

Although St Omer appears to epitomise all that is French, it has only been a part of France since 1678, later than any other part of Artois. Through the town runs a wide and straight canal, the Aa, and it was on the western bank that we found the Quai du Haut-Pont, a long row of terraced houses facing the canal. Ushered from the street directly into a living room dominated by a large table, we met Monsieur and Madame Fournier together with Madame Petit. These simple French people were

Quai du Haut-Pont in 1995. Bader was hidden in number 196, the premises with the white-painted arches.

The Clinique Sterin in St Omer, from which Wg Cdr Bader escaped, photographed in 1995.

intensely proud of their association with 'Le Colonel' Bader, to the extent that we found ourselves watching a tape of the Douglas Bader 'This is Your Life' programme, despite the fact that our French hosts could not speak a word of English.

From the Fourniers and the diminutive, 80-year-old Madame Petit we learned first-hand of Bader's escape from the Clinique Sterin. Unfortunately it proved fruitless to examine the rear of the property with regard to the chicken-run in which Bader had hidden from the Germans, as a large warehouse had since been built over the site. However, we were able to visit the Clinique Sterin with Madame Petit, who pointed out the very window from which 'Le Colonel' had escaped, this being confirmed by the well-known photograph published in certain editions of *Reach for the Sky* showing the knotted sheets still hanging out of the window later the following day.

But where did Bader's Spitfire crash? Bernard explained how difficult it is in France to obtain information, even for a native like himself. Often the older generation do not wish to be reminded of the Occupation, and many are suspicious of the motives of young men not even born at the time. Clearly, more work was required in the Pas-de-Calais. We knew that Bader had been brought down in the area of St Omer, but no more. Colin and I returned to England, leaving the future of the operation in Bernard's hands.

On New Year's Day 1996 Bernard telephoned me. He was excited because he had spoken to two men in the village of Blaringhem, some 10 km south-east of St Omer, who appeared to have witnessed Bader's crash. One, he said, was first on the scene when Bader landed by parachute, and both, as young boys in the village, had visited the crash site on the same day. On 9 August 1941 the Tangmere Spitfires flew as the Target Support Wing to Circus No. 68, a bombing raid against the power station at Gosnay, near Béthune, some 25 km south-east of St Omer. We knew that the Spitfires had been 'bounced' by a numerically superior force of JG26 Me 109s somewhere in the vicinity of St Omer. The location of Blaringhem was therefore good news indeed, and plans were immediately made for Dr Dennis Williams, my right-hand man and technical expert, and I to visit the location in mid-February.

During mid-January Central Broadcasting made a short programme about my rather busy life as a serving police officer, family man and author. The interviewer's final question was: 'You are now writing book number six, and hope to recover the remains of Douglas Bader's Spitfire?' My response was brief and guarded, but sufficient to provoke almost overwhelming interest from the world's media after the item was broadcast at the end of January. Obviously I was aware of the interest in all things Bader within the enthusiast culture, and indeed that there was a general interest, but I was totally unprepared for the media storm which brewed after our intentions became known. For three days my telephone rang almost continually, and there was no escape even at work. My family suffered accordingly, and I kicked myself for having let the news slip out before we were prepared to deal with such pressure.

What the press did not appear interested in was the fact that I had not actually been to the supposed crash site myself! The story was that Bader's Spitfire had been found, and that was that. As might have been expected, the newspapers were full of inaccuracies, some of them alarming. A Sunday newspaper asked me how Bader had been brought down, and I explained that it had never been conclusively established whether he had collided with another aircraft or been shot down, and if so by whom, although my research would offer new information upon publication of the book. I refused to discuss the matter further and our conversation ended. The reporter consequently wrote on the newspaper's front page that I believed Bader to have been brought down by anti-aircraft fire as 'there were no German aircraft flying in the vicinity at the time'. As I had interviewed the survivors of both sides from this

Monsieur Georges Goblet (left) explains to Dr Bernard-Marie Dupont where he believed Bader's Spitfire crashed. Looking on is Monsieur Arthur Dubreu, who claims to have seen Bader's parachute descent.

incredible mêlée, probably involving over 50 Me 109s, the reader can imagine my astonishment at reading this statement. Many other newspapers and magazines, even an aviation monthly, used this article as their reference without speaking to me first, so the inaccuracy spread like wildfire, much to my very great frustration.

One Saturday in mid-February, however, found Dennis Williams and I waiting for Bernard in St Omer town square. He arrived with the two eyewitnesses, Monsieurs Georges Goblet and Arthur Dubreu. The latter's memory appeared outstanding:

I was 13 years old at the time, living in Steenbecque, and I remember the incident vividly. I saw a lot of 'planes, it was around mid-morning on a sunny day. There was a big dogfight and many contrails in the sky. I saw an aircraft coming down very fast and then a parachute opened. The aircraft crashed in a field and a cloud of black smoke and debris rose over the site. Due to the wind the parachute drifted slightly; it was the first parachute I had ever seen in fact, so I remember it very well. I wanted to see the pilot, so I ran after the rapidly descending canopy. The parachute seemed to land very fast, but the pilot hit some trees in an orchard which took the shock. The pilot was just sitting there, the silk billowing around him. I was horrified to see that he only had one leg, which was twisted at an unnatural angle. There was no blood and, although he seemed to be stunned from the landing, he did not appear otherwise concerned about his legs. I could not understand it at all. I was the first on the scene, but, before I could help, a German officer ran into the field, took charge and told me to clear off, which I did as I was very frightened of the soldiers. The Germans then carried the pilot to their waiting car and I went straight away to see the aircraft's crash site, a crater in a field. It was only after the war, when *Reach for the Sky* was published in French, that I realised whom I had seen captured.

Monsieur Goblet, himself a local historian, remembered:

I was 11 years old, living in Blaringhem, and with other boys from our village I went to the Spitfire crash site in the afternoon. There was a large crater, smoke still rose through the soil and the ground was still warm. The wings had been detached and lay in another field. It was about 20 years after the war, whilst conducting my own research into local matters, that I too realised whose Spitfire this was.

From information provided by author and historian John Foreman, a team member, we knew that although Fighter Command had lost five Spitfires on the day in question, 9 August 1941, only Bader's was definitely known to have crashed in the vicinity of St Omer. Monsieur Dubreu's testimony certainly indicated that he had seen Bader land by parachute, and both he and Monsieur Goblet were adamant that the crash site they visited was that of the Spitfire flown by the legless pilot. Furthermore, Dubreu categorically stated that he had gone there on the same day that he saw Bader. Eyewitness evidence, however, can be notoriously unreliable, as I know not only from investigating the events of 50 years ago, but also from my work as a policeman. Nevertheless, the crash site was certainly in the right area. The description of a crater indicated that the fighter concerned had 'gone in', and W3185, minus all or most of its tail, would certainly have done so. All eyewitness and circumstantial evidence therefore indicated that this could be Bader's Spitfire.

From John's researches we also knew that, despite Fighter Command's exaggerated claims, only one Me 109 had actually crashed in the action concerned. According to German records, Uffz Albert Schlager had crashed and was killed at Aire-sur-la-Lys. Did Monsieurs Goblet and Dubreu know anything about that incident, we wondered? Dubreu then went on to explain how the German aeroplane had crashed through the roof of an occupied farmhouse seconds after the Spitfire impacted a short distance away. The pilot, apparently, had baled out 'too late' and was killed, falling several hundred metres away from his aircraft. Both Dubreu and Goblet claimed to know the exact locations concerned.

We then went on a short car journey through an extremely remote area, the countryside barely undulating, until we drove up a single-lane track between two fields. Parking in the corner of one, our new French friends immediately became animated, describing the dramatic scene of yesteryear. We walked across the ploughed field until Monsieur Dubreu proclaimed: 'Ici, Monsieur'. Sweeps were then made of the area using conventional metal detectors, but these proved of limited use. We were therefore limited to walking across the potential site looking for fragments, and it was with great relief that several were found; a small, distressed piece of skinning, a 4 in section of fuselage longeron and an oval, stainless steel bracket painted in a dull aluminium. Dennis immediately identified the longeron as coming from a Spitfire, and noticed that the bracket bore a '300' prefix. The significance of this numerical designation is that most early-mark Spitfire parts were so stamped. Bearing in mind the unreliability of human memory after half a century, we were relieved to confirm that the crash site was indeed that of a Spitfire. Furthermore, the bracket also bore a '6S' stamping, which indicated that the aircraft was built at Southampton and not in the Castle Bromwich Aircraft Factory near Birmingham. This, too, appeared significant circumstantial evidence, as W3185, a presentation Spitfire named *Lord Lloyd 1*, was known to have been built at Southampton. Things certainly looked promising, although we were disappointed at not having been able to locate the exact impact spot with our metal detectors. Bernard then arranged for us to be shown the Schlager crash site, although rough, uneven grass and water again thwarted the use of metal detectors.

Having spoken to the farmer and obtained his consent for an excavation, we returned to England with news of the eyewitness testimonies and our fragments of Spitfire. However, we continually pointed out to the media that, until such time as the Spitfire's serial number was determined, confirming its identity, we maintained an open mind regarding whose aircraft we had discovered. Clearly, however, plans had to be made, and quickly.

We had been contacted by a television producer, and negotiations were already in hand for the project to be funded as part of the budget for a documentary to be broadcast on a national channel. Consequently, details of our requirements were passed on to the company concerned while we sat back and ticked off the days until 'D-Day'. As that day fast approached, however, a logistics meeting with the television people revealed that no arrangements had been made, although all the details had been provided several months previously and the expedition was just three weeks away. Ultimately we lost confidence in the situation and withdrew from the arrangements, choosing instead to organise the project ourselves. The only problem this was that I had to raise a substantial budget in a matter of days.

To cut a long story short, at the end of a very stressful two days the project had gained the sponsorship of *The Times* newspaper. The deal did not depend upon whether the aircraft found was Douglas Bader's or not, but entirely upon an exclusive story. This posed problems, however, as we had planned to hold a press conference and photo-call at the site on Sunday 5 May. Lady Joan Bader herself had expressed an interest in attending, and this was especially appropriate as I was now working closely with Keith Delderfield, secretary of the Douglas Bader Foundation. The Foundation, of which Lady Bader is president, is a registered charity and exists to provide a facility for amputees at Roehampton, in addition to upholding the late Grp Capt Sir Douglas Bader as an inspiration to the disabled. The Foundation was keen to benefit from any publicity arising from our project, and we were only too pleased to help a worthy cause.

We had also explored the possibility of obtaining sponsorship to fly Lady Bader and several former Tangmere Wing pilots to the site by helicopter. The pilots included Air Vice-Marshal 'Johnnie' Johnson, who had enthusiastically supported our project and wrote to me on 29 February 1996: 'I would very much like to see the site of DB's crash'. Unfortunately the date set for our operation, dictated by the French landowner, clashed with the Spitfire 60th anniversary celebrations at Duxford, with which 'Johnnie' was already involved, and prevented him from joining us. The helicopter also became an impossibility because our potential sponsor had no aircraft available on the day in question. Instead a private pilot, Michael J. Sparshatt-Worley, kindly offered to fly Lady Bader in a fixed-wing aircraft to the nearest airfield. Her Ladyship was to be accompanied by her son-in-law, Mr David Bickers, chairman of the Douglas Bader Foundation, Sir Alan Smith, Bader's regular wingman except for the occasion on which he was shot down, and Sqn Ldr Peter Brown, one of the Few, who flew with the Bader Wing in 1940.

While plans were being made, I presented the 'Spitfire Symposium '96' at Worcester Guildhall on 24 March, thus celebrating the Spitfire's 60th anniversary. Air Vice-Marshal Johnson was our guest speaker, and at my home the previous day we had enthused together about the possibilities of recovering the Bader Spitfire. The great man was eager to examine the fragments already brought back from France. At the symposium, Dennis Williams, a materials scientist employed by the Defence Research Agency, staged a superb display of Spitfire artifacts from various UK crash sites which had been subjected to his conservation process. This unique expertise has been used to provide the ultimate example of aviation archaeology, a complete aeronautical engineering research and conservation process which perfectly complements my own work regarding the battles and personalities. The symposium was well received, my own account of our French project and aspirations providing an ideal lead-in to Air Vice-Marshal Johnson's presentation on his air-fighting experiences.

When selecting the team for the expedition, we had to find the right blend of personalities and experience not only to recover the aircraft, but also to have a memorable weekend away. Fellow Malvern Spitfire Team members Bob Morris (a former fitter with 66 Squadron in 1940), Andy Long and Antony Whitehead joined Dennis Williams and myself, and in addition we invited David Brocklehurst of the Kent Battle of Britain Museum, John Foreman in appreciation of his efforts in respect of combat losses and claims, and Larry McHale, an enthusiast turned aviation poet. Keith and Luke Delderfield of the Bader Foundation had become so swept up with the whole thing that they wanted to participate in the excavation itself, so we were happy to include them as well. Also joining us, as an observer, was former Tangmere Wing pilot Bob Morton of 616 Squadron, who had been shot down near St Omer in July 1941. My wife, Anita, was also very much a part of the team, although her responsibilities included caring for the two youngest members, our son, James, aged three, and Hannah Louise, just nine months old.

The exact location of the wreckage posed a problem because it appeared to lie deep, beyond the range of conventional metal detectors. However, to locate R6644 in Worcestershire we had used a proton magnetometer designed and manufactured by Aquascan of Newport in Gwent, and we used this same sophisticated equipment in 1994 while searching for an elusive Battle of Britain Spitfire in Dorset. Aquascan's Bob Williams immediately offered assistance and briefed Dennis Williams regarding the use of his latest model. The device is best described as having a graphic display panel, from whose supporting electronics a length of cable extends to a bright yellow, bomb-like sensor known as a 'Towfish'. This is carried by an operator, and is highly sensitive to any magnetic anomalies. These devices are mostly used for marine survey work, so the range of detection is more than adequate for landbased operations. In this instance the soil appeared to be softer than anything we had previously dug, so we believed that the wreckage might be as deep as 20 ft down.

Eventually our expedition, dubbed 'Operation Dogsbody' by the media, after Bader's radio callsign, rendezvoused on the 09:45 P&O Dover to Calais ferry on Friday 3 May 1996. Before we left home we received a much-appreciated card from Air Marshal Sir Denis Crowley-Milling, formerly one of Bader's flight commanders and until recently chairman of the Douglas Bader Foundation. It said: 'Good hunting in St Omer!'

Whilst Channel bound, the team was joined by Peter Nicholls and Richard Hall of *The Times*, and at the Hotel Ibis in St Omer we met both Richard Barnett and Graham Essinghigh of Central Broadcasting. So started an extremely exciting weekend, and we were hounded by the British press from the second we arrived at the hotel.

On that memorable Friday the weather was terrible, a bitter wind gusting across Flanders and driving torrential rain. There was to be no respite that day from this continual downpour, and we found the field awash with surface water. The mud was glutinous and made any movement extremely difficult. Another problem was a series of high-voltage cables on pylons running across the field, which Dennis feared might affect the magnetometer. Nevertheless we pressed on, Larry 'Towfish' McHale struggling up and down with the yellow 'bomb' while Dennis monitored the control panel and directed the survey. The rest of us could only watch, as the operation depended entirely upon the magnetometer's performance. This put Dennis under enormous pressure, but eventually the control panel graph went right off the scale in the area indicated by Monsieurs Goblet and Dubreu. The survey continued, however, but no further readings were obtained. With the exact spot duly marked we left the site, cold, wet, covered in mud from head to toe and still not altogether confident that the pylons, or possibly a compressed-air pipe which we knew was nearby, had not affected the equipment. Clearly it was to be a nail-biting finish.

A corner of a foreign field. The St Omer Spitfire excavation begins, and onlookers gather while the pile of wreckage grows rapidly. (Andrew Long)

Back at the hotel, British journalists had left numerous telephone messages, and we continued to fend off their enquiries throughout the rest of the evening. It was quite obvious that we had to move hotels if *The Times* was to retain exclusivity. We decided to remain at the Hotel Ibis that night, but arrangements were made to transfer our party to another hotel, near Hazebrouck, the following evening. To our great relief the following day dawned with a bright blue sky, so we made our way to the site with somewhat uplifted spirits. The Central Television crew, Richard and Graham,

Left: *Action!*

Right: *One of the first substantial items recovered was a single propeller blade, seen here being prised from the thick clay.*

Prize find; Andrew Long, David Brocklehurst and Antony Whitehead give the propeller its first glimpse of daylight in over half a century.

An indication of just how difficult conditions were. The digger continually disturbed wreckage, which was extracted by hand from the bottom of the water, oil and petrol filled hole. The hole was eventually 15 ft deep.

The 'hole masters' display the fuel tank armour, into which the blind-flying panel had impressed itself.

Technical expert and deputy expedition leader Dr Dennis Williams displays the Spitfire's radio.

remained at the hotel to see whether we were being tracked, and apparently British journalists arrived in St Omer five minutes after we had left, hot on our trail.

At the crash site we met the mechanical excavator and French driver, and started work immediately. The first items were recovered about three feet down, and it soon became apparent that we had found the substantial remains of a Spitfire. Every bucket brought up more of the smashed fighter. Both compressed air bottles, the oxygen bottle, the armour from the pilot's seat and headrest, parts of the gunsight, the radio, fuel tank armour and numerous other components were soon part of a rapidly growing pile of wreckage. In the hole, David Brocklehurst, Antony Whitehead and Andrew Long worked feverishly, while Larry McHale, John Foreman and Bob Morris sifted through the pile of displaced earth for any further items. Dennis, toothbrush ever in hand, examined various components, identifying even the most distressed parts. One of the first items recovered was a single metal propeller blade, torn from the boss. This still proved nothing, as W3185 could have been fitted with either a metal de Havilland airscrew or the later Dowty Rotol unit, the latter having wooden blades. Eventually, after wreckage had been emerging from the hole for several hours, we watched as a Merlin engine was hoisted from the petrol, oil and water filled crater, which was now some 15 ft deep. At this point Peter Nicholls received an enquiring telephone call from *The Times'* London office; fortunately he had good news.

Left: *In July 1941 Sgt Bob Morton was shot down and captured near St Omer; 55 years later he joined our expedition to the Pas-de-Calais, over which he once flew with Bader's Tangmere Wing. Looking on are Richard Hall of* The Times *and Dr Dennis Williams.*

Right: *About a third of the wreckage recovered. These battered fragments will eventually be painstakingly reconstructed by materials scientist and team technical expert Dr Dennis Williams. As Sir Alan Smith said: 'Memorabilia to be proud of'. (Andrew Long)*

Luke and Keith Delderfield, together with Larry Mchale, Bob Morris and John Foreman, examine the Merlin engine.

Andrew Long, an aviation archaeologist since childhood and, together with the author, co-founder of the Malvern Spitfire Team, poses with the recently recovered Merlin engine. (Andrew Long)

Later examination of the Merlin revealed it to be a 60 series engine with a two-stage blower, as opposed to the 40 series installed in W3185. (Andrew Long)

So far, however, a constructor's plate, possibly bearing the aircraft's serial number, had defied discovery. The exhaust arrangement on the Merlin engine would at least have indicated whether this could have been a Mk V or a later mark with more exhaust pipes, but the exhausts were so badly damaged that identification was impossible. Even with much of the aircraft recovered, it could still not be identified. The wreckage was loaded into a farm trailer and the hole filled just as we were visited by Sqn Ldr Colin Hodgkinson, the RAF's other, lesser known legless Spitfire pilot. Soon afterwards the wreckage left the site for the first time in over 50 years, being transported to a nearby farm.

Because of the threat of our being discovered by journalists, the entire operation was undertaken in great haste, and the atmosphere was tense. The site is extremely remote, so we were confident that it would take them some time to find us, although it was inevitable that they would eventually succeed. It transpired that, once again, we left just in time, the pursuing pack arriving minutes after our departure. At our new hotel near Hazebrouck we learned from Bernard that he had been ambushed and followed by two British cars while returning Sqn Ldr Hodgkinson to Calais, and we suspected that a certain villager had tipped off the press. However, as Bernard was not rejoining us that evening, the reporters could gain nothing further.

The next problem was the likelihood of journalists having the Pas-de-Calais airfields covered the following morning to intercept Lady Bader's arrival. They all wanted a photograph of her Ladyship at the crash site, and as the competition had already discovered the location, the chances were that they would be lying in wait there as well. As the airfields at Longuenesse and Merville were apparently

Sir Alan Smith gives Central Television an interview. In 1941, as plain Sgt Smith, Sir Alan was Bader's No. 2 on virtually every sortie except the one on which the Wing Leader was lost.

considered our most likely rendezvous, it was decided to land the aircraft at Calais, Keith Delderfield and Dennis Williams providing transport back to a predetermined location. That having been decided, the celebrations commenced at the end of an exhausting day. Suffice it to say that we all wined and dined in style.

The following morning Dennis and Keith headed off to Calais and we later returned to St Omer, awaiting our guests' arrival in a supermarket car park, of all places. Right on time the convoy appeared, and in these bizarre circumstances we welcomed Lady Joan Bader, Sir Alan Smith, Sqn Ldr Peter Brown and David Bickers, together with their pilot for the day, Michael J. Sparshatt-Worley. From there we continued on to the farm, where the wreckage was picked over and examined, nothing as yet positively identifying the aircraft. When asked by Richard Barnett what her late husband would have thought of the operation, Lady Bader replied:

> I honestly don't know. He would either have said "What a load of idiots", or he would have been down the hole with a spade helping them. He was ashamed of having been brought down and captured; he never talked about it at all, except to jokingly say that another of his pilots had shot him down because he wanted his job!

Sir Alan Smith had last seen Bob Morton in July 1941, when the latter was shot down and captured. Until we communicated, however, Sir Alan believed that Bob, at the time a fellow sergeant, had been killed. He was therefore delighted to be reunited with his old friend, who was actually a member of our team. When interviewed by Central Television, Sir Alan remarked: 'When Douglas Bader was in the air you felt completely safe, he was a great leader. I think that this is a tremendous operation and memorabilia like this is both important and something our country can be proud of.' Squadron Leader Peter Brown added: 'I think it's all great fun. These comparative youngsters have learned first-hand about the Battle of Britain period and have brought the subject to the attention of a new generation. Well done!'

The television crew and *The Times'* photographer completed their work and we then headed for the site. Upon arrival, however, the press could be seen lying in wait at the crash site itself, about half a mile from the road. We stopped and conferred while Bernard and Peter drove up for a reconnaissance. They returned to confirm our worst fears, so Lady Bader very graciously agreed that as she could see the crash site we had gone close enough. As our convoy sped away the press bounded down the single-lane track like a pack of hounds. What they had not reckoned with, however, was Larry's car 'breaking down' and blocking the road, facilitating our escape. While we had to honour our exclusive promise to *The Times*, this subterfuge was hardly what we had in mind, and was not the reason we were in France.

As the press had been unable to talk to anyone, it was not surprising that the subsequent stories in British newspapers were largely inaccurate, although Phil Derbyshire of the *Daily Express* tactfully stated that 'Lady Joan Bader was due to visit the crash site yesterday, but changed her mind at the last minute', which seemed a good way of putting it! *The Times* reported inaccurately in just one respect, claiming that a 20 mm shellcase had been found in the wreckage. In fact it was a flare cartridge.

What took me completely by surprise, however, was the information circulated by the Press Association, which included Air Vice-Marshal Johnson's reported opinion when asked what he thought of our operation: 'Leave the thing alone. They will never reassemble it. It will only be bits, like something out of a secondhand shop.' In view of the Air Vice-Marshal's involvement with the project this appeared an irrational response, and we were all astonished at this totally unexpected turn of events. It came as no surprise, however, when I heard from Johnnie, first hand, what

Back home; the St Omer Spitfire's pilot's seat, fuel tank and head armour, together with both compressed-air bottles, one complete with bullet hole, and the bulbous oxygen bottle. (Andrew Long)

had really happened: 'I am not in the habit of changing sides! At Duxford I said that if D.B.'s Spitfire was in 10,000 pieces then it would probably be impossible to recover it – as usual I was quoted out of context.' The media, having twisted around what had really been said, was therefore entirely responsible for the controversial headlines which appeared in just about every national and provincial newspaper, such as 'Spitfire Ace Attacks Spitfire Plans' and 'Bader's Spitfire Flies into Verbal Dogfight', all of which were patently untrue.

Sir Alan Smith, however, had certainly enjoyed his trip to France:

> I enjoyed Sunday immensely. First of all being able to renew acquaintance with Lady Bader, and to meet Peter Brown, "Butch" Morton and many others. To see what was left of what we all hope is Douglas Bader's Spitfire and to recall what a great chap he was.
>
> To fly across the Channel at 4,500 ft and once again recall how narrow it is and be reminded that the Germans came that close!

Because of the furious pace at which the recovery had been undertaken, and due to the media fall-out upon our return, the most important work, that of identifying the Spitfire, was virtually put on hold for several days as we all returned to reality and our 'day jobs'. We had been immediately concerned, however, that the propeller blade recovered appeared too broad, and the hub was not the same as that of the de Havilland duralumin airscrew with which W3185 was probably equipped. However, as no other evidence had come to light, we had no alternative but to shrug off our unease and let events take their course. The engine may have indicated what mark of Spitfire we had recovered, but it was so clay encrusted, and the exhausts so damaged, that no detail was immediately obvious.

Eventually we were able to confirm that the recovered Merlin had a two-stage blower and 12 exhaust stubs (rather than six), indicating it was a 60 series engine. Therefore the aircraft in question could not possibly be W3185, which had a Merlin 40 series engine. Coupling the 60 series Merlin with the questionable propeller blade, our automatic assumption was that the St Omer Spitfire was probably a Mk IX. A constructor's plate bearing the vital serial number still defied discovery. Which Spitfire had we found? Certainly there was no body in the wreck, so it was unlikely to be the aircraft of a missing pilot. It was more likely that its pilot had safely baled out, or that his body had been recovered for burial at the time. The matter was now in the hands of team member John Foreman, a world authority on the combat losses and claims of both sides. So began another intensive period of research, during which John had to cross-reference hundreds of Spitfire losses against German combat claims.

Throughout the media involvement I had taken the line that although eyewitness and circumstantial evidence certainly indicated that this was Bader's Spitfire, we could not be sure until confirmation was found in the wreckage. Anyone presented with the same evidence would have proceeded as we did, and even with hindsight we would undoubtedly take the same action if placed in a similar situation again. Recovering the aircraft was the only means of resolving which Spitfire had been found. Make no mistake, the eyewitness evidence was most convincing. I recall that at the site, Richard Barnett, Central Television's reporter, was most excited at having interviewed Monsieur Dubreu, concluding there was little doubt that 'this *is* Bader's 'plane'. As the *Independent* had quoted me in January 1996, however: 'It's like going fishing; until you've been you don't know what you're going to catch'. The only problem now was that, having cast our line we had, after all, caught the wrong fish. However, we had all acted entirely in good faith upon the available evidence, and all

A Spitfire Mk IX. This long awaited mark entered service in June 1942 and bettered the Fw 190, which had proved superior in virtually every respect to the Spitfire Mk V.

involved in the project had reviewed the same facts. The only explanation is that Monsieur Dubreu, whom I still have no doubt saw Douglas Bader's parachute descent, somehow managed to confuse the time of his visit to the crash site, which we now knew could not possibly have occurred on the same day as W3185's crash.

Obviously the team was very disappointed at not having found W3185, but we were determined that our historical integrity should remain intact by releasing the truth as soon as possible. We were also aware that, once this news was out, there would be a stampede across to the Pas-de-Calais as other enthusiasts took up the gauntlet.

On 12 May I telephoned Lady Bader and explained the situation. Her Ladyship was extremely understanding, mainly expressing concern for the team after the very great effort made by all involved. I responded by saying that, although we were understandably disappointed at first, it had since been mutually decided that we had come too far down the road to give in. Lady Bader and I both agreed that the late Sir Douglas would certainly have endorsed our tenacious attitude.

The following day our official statement was released to the press. In part, it read:

> Despite the negative identification of the St Omer Spitfire, the team is delighted to have had the opportunity to publicise the inspiring story of the late Sir Douglas Bader and his pilots to a new generation, and in so doing assist in some small way the Douglas Bader Foundation, a registered charity providing a facility for amputees at Roehampton.
>
> The majority of the St Omer Spitfire's remains are in French hands and are likely to be offered to an as yet undecided French museum for permanent display.

Perhaps surprisingly, the media generally made little of the fact that we had not, after all, found Bader's Spitfire. The *Worcester Evening News* carried it on the front page, however, and devoted its billboards to the story twice. Later that week the news of a local serviceman diving on a First World War naval vessel again prompted the editor's 'Opinion', under the appropriate headline 'Feelings for our rich and valued past':

> There are some people who will never understand the fascination with relics of the two World Wars, but, thank goodness, there are many more who know the value of keeping a feel for the past's rich treasures.
> After one false start, Malvern bobby Dilip Sarkar may still be searching for Sir Douglas Bader's famous Second World War Spitfire fighter. But our continued appreciation of the feats of the men who defended our nation warrant his determination to, eventually, dig up the right one.
> If such people were not prepared to dig and dive, the heritage we are leaving for the generations to come would be poorer by a long, long way.

Meanwhile, John Foreman had worked away at his computer and, from a shortlist of 67 possibles, had identified the most likely candidate for the St Omer Spitfire.

Fighter Command had a busy day on 17 June 1943. During the morning Norwegian Spitfires escorted bombers on a Circus operation to Flushing, subsequently and accurately claiming five Fw 190s of JG1 destroyed. The Fw 190s of II/JG26 intercepted another Circus, and Lt Walter Matoni claimed one Spitfire. During the afternoon the Kenley Wing, comprising three Canadian Spitfire squadrons led by none other than Wg Cdr J.E. 'Johnnie' Johnson DSO DFC*, took off on a sweep of southern Belgium. Over Ypres the Spitfires engaged Fw 190s of III/JG26, chasing them south to St Omer. The Wing Leader claimed an Fw 190

An Fw 190 of JG2. This particular example was the first captured by the RAF, and was photographed at RAF Fairwood Common.

destroyed in the area of 'Ypres-St Omer', possibly that of Uffz Gunther Frietag, who crashed and was killed at Steenvorde. Flight Sergeant G.M. Shouldice claimed another Focke-Wulf north of St Omer. Oberleutnant Horst Sternberg, Staffelkapitän of 5/JG26, destroyed one of the Kenley fighters at 15:45, 5 km south-west of Hazebrouck. This was probably the one flown by Fg Off J.E. McNamara of 421 Squadron, who damaged an Fw 190 but was later reported missing. Sternberg was then shot down himself and baled out at Cappel, west of Hazebrouck, his most likely victor being Sqn Ldr P.L.I. Archer DFC, Commanding Officer of 421 Squadron. Archer's triumph, witnessed by members of his squadron, was short-lived, however, as at 15:56 he was shot down and killed by Uffz Paul Schwarz of 6/JG26, 10 km south-east of St Omer.

John Foreman predicted that the most likely candidate for our aircraft was LZ996, that being Squadron Leader Archer's fighter. The Commonwealth War Graves Commission confirmed that he was buried at Longuenesse (St Omer) Cemetery (although when Bernard-Marie visited the cemetery he discovered that the Commission had made a mistake on the piot's headstone by recording him as an 'Air Gunner/Instructor', an error regarding which we now seek rectification). John supplied further evidence in that Unteroffizier Schwarz's claim for a Spitfire destroyed 10 km south-east of St Omer tallies exactly with the excavated crash site. An eye-witness who contacted us after the excavation, Monsieur Queurleu, stated that the victorious German pilot had visited the crash site, from which the pilot's body was removed along with a quantity of wreckage. It was to be Schwarz's only aerial victory, however, as he was killed in a flying accident just over a year later on 16 July 1944. Oberleutnant Sternberg was later to be killed by American fighters on 22 February 1944, his score concluding at 23 victories.

Fore the record, Squadron Leader Archer's aircraft, LZ996, was a part of the Air

Squadron Leader Archer's grave at Longuenesse (St Omer) cemetery. The War Graves Commission has now been notified of the error as he was a pilot, not an air gunner/instructor.

Ministry's eighth order for Spitfire Mk IXs, a total of 680 being built in that batch between March and June 1943. LZ996's service career lasted just a fraction over a month, being delivered to 416 Squadron on 12 May 1943, moving to 421 on 20 May before being destroyed on 17 June 1943. As the machine was built at Castle Bromwich, one can only assume, therefore, that the small bracket bearing the '6S' Southampton stamp, discovered at the crash site in February 1996, was a mass produced component manufactured at Southampton but distributed to other Spitfire assembly centres. A Red Herring indeed! Bernard-Marie has since discovered the engine numbers on the St Omer Merlin: 82021 and 82075. 'M61' thereon also confirms the powerplant to have been a Rolls-Royce Merlin 61 engine. The problem is that unless the aircraft concerned suffered a flying accident prior to its demise, the engine numbers were not usually recorded anywhere which would also provide the RAF serial number. LZ996 did not suffer any such mishap prior to being destroyed, and so it is impossible to confirm identify of this aircraft via the engine number alone. A constructor's plate was also discovered after the recovery, and Spitfire expert Peter Arnold confirmed our belief that it came from an assembly such as the flap mechanism. However that serial number, AB6S170782, again fails to help us confirm the aircraft's individual RAF serial number. The inclusion of '6S' again suggests that although this Spitfire was actually built at Castle Bromwich, the component concerned may again have been built at Southampton. Confusing, isn't it?

After the discovery of LZ996 and not W3185 was circulated by the French media, we hoped that someone would come forward who had information concerning the true crash site. However, this has never happened, despite the efforts of the 'Voix du Nord'. The only noteworthy development was two French amateur aviation archaeologists, Laurent d'Hondt and Jean Pierre Duriez, claiming to have found the site at Basse-Rue, Racquinghem. The site was only three miles away from Blaringhem, and so was within the required radius of where Bader landed by parachute near Boesinghem. An eye-witness also spoke of a tail-less Spitfire. Laurent also produced other evidence: at the time of the crash the farmer was six years-old, dating it 1941, and a newspaper article in the *L'Echo de la Lys* dated 19 January 1945, referred to a British aircraft crashing at Basse-Rue, the pilot of which landed by parachute at Boesinghem. Although the Frenchmen were convinced on that basis alone, there was no mention of Bader specifically, and so the evidence suggesting this site as a contender was actually weaker than that which we had considered in respect of LZ996. Obviously, however, largely in view of the site's location, it at least had to be investigated if only for elimination purposes. Consequently Squadron Leader Peter Brown, Dr Dennis Williams and I joined Laurent d'Hondt and Jean Pierre Duriez at Basse-Rue on 3 August 1996, but no evidence whatsoever of a crashed aircraft could be found.

Even if W3185 had not 'gone in', considering the height at which its downward descent commenced and therefore likely speed upon impact, the front of the aircraft would almost certainly have made some impression in the French soil, similar I daresay to R6644 which we recovered at Madresfield, Worcestershire in 1987 (see *The Invisible Thread: A Spitfire's Tale* also by this author). In that case, although large components were not found, enough wreckage remained to make the excavation of interest and confirm identify of the Spitfire. Therefore as nothing could be found at Basse-Rue, I personally doubt the location as being the crash site of W3185.

During the spring of 1993, the Malvern Spitfire Team co-operated with the MOD and RAF to recover the Spitfire of a missing pilot from the Severn Estuary. Substantial aircraft remains were recovered, including parts of the aircraft's wings. On the mainspar was a plate indicating the modifications undertaken to the wing assembly, and other, instructional, plates were found relating to the cannon armament. All of these plates bore the RAF serial number, P8208, thus conclusively confirming the aircraft's identity. Unfortunately, our experience indicates that such plates are rarely found in land crash sites, due to the wings becoming detached and therefore being recovered at the time, together with any other surface wreckage. The point is that it is very difficult indeed to conclusively identify any Spitfire wreckage discovered in France due not only to this reason, but also the general lack of any French contemporary documentary evidence, and the confusion amongst eye-witnesses over half a century later. The latter is hardly surprising, though: between 1940 and 1944, French schoolboys saw *hundreds* of aircraft crash!

In view of the foregoing, I can only therefore conclude that unless there remains a French eye-witness with significant information who has yet to step forward, which I think is unlikely now, W3185 will never be found by design. Even if Bader's Spitfire was recovered by accident, due to the problems with serial numbers it may never be conclusively identified. As I have already said, it is as if the mystery intends to remain patently unsolved – forever!

Appendix

Published here for the first time are the statistics of the Tangmere Wing's operations during the time Wg Cdr D.R.S. Bader DSO DFC was Wing Leader; between 18 March and 9 August 1941. The appendix largely comprises details concerning the Wing's combat losses and claims, and has been largely contributed by John Foreman.

145 Squadron

Operational Record, 18 March–9 August 1941

20.03.41.
Flying accident: Spitfire P7603 forced-landed at Shoreham, Sgt Weber safe.

05.05.41.
Fg Off J.H.M. Offenberg: one He 60 destroyed, one Me 109 probable, Pointe de Barfleur.

13.05.41.
Flying accident: Spitfire P8071 forced-landed at Manston, Fg Off J.H.M. Offenberg safe.

21.05.41.
Spitfires P7493 and P7737 both Cat. E, collided over Tangmere during return from evening Circus. Flt Lt Stevens and Fg Off Owen killed.

04.06.41.
Fg Off Clarke: Ju 87 destroyed, Le Havre.

Flying accident: Spitfire P8323 Cat. E, abandoned near Worthing, Pt Off Sabourin safe.

11.06.41.
Flying accident: Spitfire P8230 damaged while landing at Manston, Sgt Robillard safe.

18.06.41.
12 Spitfires. 17:35–19:45 hrs. Circus No. 15 to Bois de Licques.
Spitfire P8254 Cat. E: shot down by Me 109, Sgt Palmer missing.
Spitfire P8328 Cat. E: shot down by Me 109, Sgt Turnbull missing.

21.06.41.
12 Spitfires. 11:33–13:10 hrs. Circus No. 16 to Longuenesse aerodrome.
Fg Off J. Macachek and Sqn Ldr H.F. Burton (latter CO 616) shared Me 109 destroyed, Bridge, Kent.
Spitfire P8341: Cat. B, damaged by Me 109 off Ramsgate, Sgt F.J. Twitchett slightly wounded.

10 Spitfires. 15:50–17:35 hrs. Circus No. 17 to Desvres aerodrome.
Sgt Grant: Me 109 destroyed, Le Touquet.
Spitfire P8339: Cat. B, damaged by Me 109, Flt Lt M.A. Newling unhurt.

22.06.41.
10 Spitfires. 15:07–16:50 hrs. Circus No. 18 to Hazebrouck.
Sgt J. Robillard: Me 109 destroyed, Port Phillipe.

25.06.41.
12 Spitfires. 15:47–17:40 hrs. Circus No. 23 to Longuenesse.
Flt Lt Arthur: Me 109 destroyed, Le Touquet.
Sgt Grant: Me 109 destroyed, Le Touquet.

26.06.41.
12 Spitfires. 10:45–12:25 hrs. Sweep (Circus No. 24 aborted).
Sgt W.J. Johnson: Me 109 destroyed, Gravelines.
Spitfire P8314 Cat. E: shot down by Me 109, Gravelines, Sgt Macbeth missing.

27.06.41.
12 Spitfires. 20:50–22:30 hrs. Circus No. 25 to Lille.
Flt Lt M.A. Newling: Me 109 probable, Lille.

28.06.41.
12 Spitfires. 07:44–10:00 hrs. Circus No. 26 to Commines.
Fg Off J. Macachek: Me 109 probable, near Cassel.

02.07.41.
12 Spitfires. 11:49–13:30 hrs, Circus Lille.
Spitfire P8536 Cat. E: Sgt J.G.L. Robillard reported missing, but evaded and later returned
   home safely.

05.07.41.
12 Spitfires. 12:19–15:00 hrs. Circus.
Fg Off J. Macachek: Me 109 destroyed, one damaged, Lille.

06.07.41.
12 Spitfires. 13:52–15:20 hrs. Circus.
Spitfire W3366: Flt Lt M.A. Newling lost in action.

07.07.41.
8 Spitfires. 14:36–16:35 hrs. Circus.
Spitfire X4667: Cat. E, shot down by Me 109. Sgt Silvester forced-landed wounded.

08.07.41.
10 Spitfires. 14:40–16:35 hrs. Circus.
Spitfire R7263: Pt Off Pine lost.
Spitfire R7218: Fg Off J. Macachek lost.

09.07.41.
8 Spitfires. 13:05–14:45 hrs. Circus Mazingarbe.
Spitfire P8070: Sgt McFarlane killed during solo head-on attack against four Me 109s.

14.07.41.
8 Spitfires. 09:35–11:25 hrs. Circus.
Sqn Ldr P.S. Turner: Me 109F destroyed, NE France.
Spitfire W3185: Cat. A, Sqn Ldr P.S. Turner unhurt.

23.07.41.
10 Spitfires. 13:31–21:24 hrs. Roadstead, Hague.
Sqn Ldr P.S. Turner: Me 109E destroyed, Ostend.
Sgt R.J.C. Grant: Me 109E destroyed, Ostend.

10 Spitfires. 19:38–21:24 hrs. Circus Mazingarbe.
Sgt F.J. Twitchett: Me 109 destroyed, Mazingarbe.
Spitfire P8712: Fg Off D.N. Forde missing in action.
Spitfire – : Cat. B, forced-landed Beachy Head. Pt Off Breeze unhurt.

610 Squadron

Operational Record, 18 March 18–9 August 1941

19.03.41.
12 Spitfires. 16:20 hrs. Defensive patrol.
Sgt Payne: Me 109 destroyed, S of Dungeness.
One Spitfire, serial number unknown, Cat. B to Me 109, forced-landed Hailsham, Sgt Hale
   wounded.

23.03.41.
Spitfire P7685: Cat. E, hit hill near West Dean, fate of pilot unknown.

03.04.41.
Flt Lt Morris and Sgt Ballard: Ju 88 destroyed (shared) S of Beachy Head.

15.04.41
4 Spitfires. 18:10–19:30 hrs. Defensive patrol.
Pt Off Ross and Sgt Richardson: Ju 88 destroyed (shared) off St Catherine's Point.
Spitfire P7684: Pt Off Ross missing in action.
Spitfire DW-R: Damaged by Ju 88, Sgt Richardson safe.
Spitfire P7613: Flying accident, forced-landed at Westhampnett, Sqn Ldr Woodhouse safe.

22.04.41.
1 Spitfire. 08:40 hrs.
Sgt Payne: Ju 88 destroyed, E of Bognor Regis.

25.04.41.
2 Spitfires. 07:25 hrs.
Sqn Ldr Woodhouse and Pt Off Stoop: Ju 88 destroyed, S of Brighton.

08.05.41.
Two Spitfires. 12:00 hrs. Patrol.
Sgt Mains: Me 109 destroyed, one Me 109 probable, Dover Straits.
Spitfire, serial number unknown, damaged by Me 109 in above action, Sgt Mains unhurt.

10.05.41.
Spitfire P7777: Flying accident, crash-landed at Westhampnett, Sgt Davis safe.

11.05.41.
2 Spitfires. 00:21–01:43 hrs. Night interception.
Sgt Warden: Ju 88 destroyed, Guildford.
WO Pegge: He 111 destroyed, Guildford.

12.05.41.
1 Spitfire. 22:30–22:51 hrs. Night interception.
Sgt Payne: Ju 88 destroyed, S of Brighton.

06.06.41.
Spitfire P8660: Flying accident, crash-landed at Westhampnett, Sgt Davis safe.

17.06.41.
12 Spitfires. 18:5–20:45 hrs. Circus No. 14 to Choques.
Flt Lt R.A. Lee-Knight: Me 109 destroyed, near Gris Nez.
Spitfire P8526: Cat. A, crash-landed at Merston, Sgt Mains unhurt.

18.06.41.
12 Spitfires. 17:38–20:20 hrs. Circus No. 15 to Bois de Licques.
Sgt Merriman: Me 109 destroyed, 20 miles S of Dungeness.

21.06.41.
12 Spitfires. 11:30–13:10 hrs. Circus No. 16 to Longuenesse aerodrome.
Flt Lt R.A. Lee-Knight: Me 109 destroyed, another damaged, both off Gravelines.

12 Spitfires. 15:00–17:33 hrs. Circus No. 17 to Desvres aerodrome.
Pt Off Scott: Me 109 destroyed, Le Touquet.

22.06.41.
12 Spitfires. 15:05–16:55 hrs. Circus No. 18 to Hazebrouck.
Sqn Ldr K. Holden: Me 109 destroyed, Hazebrouck.
Pt Off Horner: Me 109 destroyed, Hazebrouck.
Sgt Raine: Me 109 destroyed, Hazebrouck.

25.06.41.
12 Spitfires. 11:57–14:14 hrs. Circus No. 22 to Hazebrouck.
Pt Off Scott: Me 109 destroyed, Gravelines.
Flt Lt Crowley-Milling: Me 109 probable, Gravelines.
Spitfire, serial unknown: Cat. A, damaged by Me 109, Sgt Davies wounded.

11 Spitfires. 15:47–17:32 hrs. Circus No. 23 to Longuenesse.
Wg Cdr Aitken*: Me 109 destroyed, near St Omer.
Pt Off Horner: Me 109 destroyed, near St Omer.
Sqn Ldr Holden: Me 109 damaged, near St Omer.
Sgt Raine: Me 109 probable, near St Omer, and one damaged on airfield.
Spitfire P8399: Cat. E, failed to return, Pt Off Scott missing.
Spitfire, serial unknown: Cat. A, damaged by Me 109, Sgt Raine unhurt.
*This was The Hon. J.W.M. Aitken, CO of 68 Squadron, the son of Lord Beaverbrook, the
    Minister for Aircraft Production.

26.06.41.
10 Spitfires. 10:45–12:30 hrs. Sweep (Circus No. 24 aborted).
Pt Off F.A.O. Gaze: Me 109 destroyed, Gravelines.
Sqn Ldr Holden: Me 109 damaged, Gravelines.
Flt Lt Lee-Knight: Me 109 damaged, Gravelines.
Spitfire, serial unknown: Cat. A, crash-landed, Pt Off Gaze unhurt.

02.07.41.
12 Spitfires. 11:46–13:50 hrs. Circus to Lille.
Sgt Mains: Me 109 destroyed, N France.
Pt Off F.A.O. Gaze: Me 109 damaged, N France.

03.07.41.
12 Spitfires. 10:40–12:18 hrs. Circus to St Omer.
Flt Lt Lee-Knight and Pt Off J.R. Stoop: Me 109 destroyed, shared, Hazebrouck.
Flt Lt Lee-Knight: Me 109 damaged, Hazebrouck.
Sgt Merriman and Sgt R.D. Bowen (latter of 616): Hs 126 probable, Hazebrouck.

05.07.41.
12 Spitfires. 12:15–13:36 hrs. Circus.
Sgt Mains: Me 109 destroyed, Lille.
Spitfire, serial unknown: Cat. B, crash-landed near Telscombe Station, Pt Off Wilcox unhurt.
Spitfire P8521: Cat. A, Overshot at Hawkinge, Sgt Mains safe.

06.07.41.
12 Spitfires. 13:31–15:20 hrs. Circus.
Sqn Ldr Holden: Me 109 destroyed, NE France.
Sqn Ldr Holden and Pt Of F.A.O. Gaze: Me 109 destroyed, shared, NE France.

08.07.41.
2 Spitfires. 11:55–12:35 hrs. Interception.
Sgt Merriman: Me 109 destroyed and one probable, S of Portsmouth.

12 Spitfires. 14:40–17:10 hrs. Circus.
Flt Lt Lee-Knight. Me 109 destroyed, NE France.
Spitfire P8504: Pt Off F.G. Horner missing (captured).
Spitfire DW-H: Pt Off J.R. Stoop missing (rescued, wounded).

10.07.41.
12 Spitfires. 11:36–13:55 hrs. Circus.
Sqn Ldr Holden: Me 109 destroyed, NE France.
Spitfire P8520: Pt Off P. Ward-Smith missing (captured).
Spitfire P8523: Sgt Blackman lost, killed at Maizieres, St Pol.
Spitfire P8374: Sgt L.H. Anderson lost.

11.07.41.
8 Spitfires. 11:08–12:18 hrs. Sweep.
Sgt Merriman: Me 109 probable, NE France.
Sgt Grey: Me 109 damaged, NE France.

14.07.41.
Spitfire P8656: Cat. E, crash-landed and overturned, three miles E of Heathfield. Sgt R.W.
   Richardson injured.

17.07.41.
8 Spitfires. 19:00–20:25 hrs. Sweep.
Pt Off F.A.O. Gaze: Me 109 destroyed, Hardelot.

19.07.41.
8 Spitfires. 13:10–15:28 hrs. Circus.
Sgt W. Raine: Me 109 probable, Dunkirk.

21.07.41.
12 Spitfires. 07:40–09:40 hrs. Circus to Lille.
Sgt Merriman: Two Me 109Fs destroyed, N France.

23.07.41.
8 Spitfires. 19:38–21:45 hrs. Circus to Mazingarbe.
Wg Cdr D.R.S. Bader and Sgt W. Raine: Me 109 destroyed, shared, Mazingarbe.
Pt Off J.E.I. Grey: Me 109 probable, Mazingarbe.
Spitfire DW-S: Cat. B, Sgt Philpotts wounded.

07.08.41.
12 Spitfires. 17:11–18:50 hrs. Circus to Lille.
Spitfire DW-A: Cat. B, crash-landed at Friston. Sgt McWatt wounded.

616 Squadron

Operational Record, 18 March – 9 August 1941

27.03.41.
2 Spitfires. 14:00 hrs. Scramble.
Flt Lt C.H. Macfie: Me 110 damaged, Littlehampton.
Spitfire P7732: Flying accident, forced-landed at Durrington, Sgt Sellars safe.

21.04.41.
12 Spitfires. 09:00–09:15 hrs. Channel Patrol.
Spitfire P7812: Missing after action St Catherine's Point, Sgt Sellars lost.

24.04.41.
2 Spitfires. 14:35–15:41 hrs. Rhubarb.
Flt Lt C.H. Macfie: Me 109 destroyed on ground, Maupertus airfield.
Spitfire P7736: Shot down by flak, Maupertus airfield, Sgt McDevette killed.
Spitfire P7771: Flying accident, bellylanded at Tangmere, Sgt Mabbett safe.

05.05.41.
2 Spitfires. 07:24–08:00 hrs. Interception.
Fg Off L.H. Casson and Fg Off R. Marples: Ju 88 damaged, shared, S of Tangmere.
Spitfire P7753: Cat. E to return fire from Ju 88, Fg Off Casson baled out near Littlehampton.

08.05.41.
2 Spitfires. 12:00 hrs. Patrol.
Wg Cdr D.R.S. Bader: Me 109 probable, Dover Straits.
Spitfire P7827, QJ-A: Cat. B to Me 109 during above action, Fg Off H.S.L. Dundas crash-
    landed at Hawkinge.

09.05.41.
Spitfire P7829: Flying accident, bellylanded at Westhampnett, pilot believed safe.

17.05.41.
2 Spitfires. 16:35 hrs. Interception.
Fg Off H.S.L. Dundas: Me 109 destroyed off Shoreham.

18.06.41.
12 Spitfires. 17:35–19:45 hrs. Circus No. 15 to Bois de Licques.
Spitfire, serial number unknown: Cat. B, overshot, Tangmere, Pt Off Leckie injured.

19.06.41.
12 Spitfires. 16:57–18:25 hrs. Operation *Derby* to Le Havre.
Flt Lt C.H. Macfie: Me 109 damaged near Le Havre.

21.06.41.
12 Spitfires. 11:39–13:24 hrs. Circus No. 16 to Longuenesse aerodrome.
Sqn Ldr H.F. Burton and Fg Off Macachek (latter of 145 Sqn): Me 109 destroyed, shared,
    Bridge, Kent.

12 Spitfires. 15:52–17:33. Circus No. 17 to Desvres aerodrome.
Wg Cdr D.R.S. Bader: Me 109 destroyed North of Boulogne.
Spitfire P7730: Cat. E, shot down near Boulogne by Me 109, Pt Off Brown missing.

22.06.41.
12 Spitfires. 15:09–16:56 hrs. Circus No. 18 to Hazebrouck.
Fg Off R. Marples: Me 109 destroyed off Gravelines.
Fg Off L.H. Casson and Sgt Beedham: Me 109 destroyed, shared, off Gravelines.

23.06.41.
12 Spitfires. 19:53–21:40 hrs. Circus No. 20 to Desvres aerodrome.
Spitfire P7435: Cat. E, damaged by Me 109 and abandoned over Channel, Sgt Beedham
   rescued.

25.06.41.
10 Spitfires. 11:58–13:55 hrs. Circus No. 22 to Hazebrouck.
Wg Cdr D.R.S. Bader: Me 109 destroyed, Gravelines.
Wg Cdr D.R.S. Bader and Sgt J. West: Me 109 destroyed, shared, Gravelines.
Fg Off H.S.L. Dundas: Me 109 damaged, Gravelines.
Fg Off R. Marples: Me 109 damaged, Gravelines.
Spitfire, serial number unknown: Cat. B, damaged by Me 109, Sgt McCairns unhurt.
Spitfire, serial number unknown: Cat. B, damaged by Me 109, crash-landed at Hawkinge,
   Sgt R.A. Morton unhurt.

12 Spitfires. Circus No. 23 to Longuenesse.
Wg Cdr D.R.S. Bader: Me 109 destroyed, St Omer.
Spitfire P8272: Cat. E, shot down by Me 109 near St Omer, Sgt Jenks missing.
Spitfire P7327: Cat. E, shot down by Me 109 near St Omer, Sgt Brewer missing.

26.06.41.
12 Spitfires. 10:45–12:10 hrs. Sweep (Circus No. 24 aborted).
Pt Off J.E. Johnson: Me 109 destroyed over Gravelines.
Fg Off L.H. Casson: Me 109 damaged over Gravelines.
Spitfire P7815, YQ-N: Cat. E, crashed during forced landing at Bacton, Norfolk,
   Sgt R.A. Morton unhurt.

02.07.41.
12 Spitfires. 11:50–13:43 hrs. Circus to Lille.
Pt Off P.W.E. Hepple: Me 109 destroyed, N France.
Sgt A. Smith: Me 109 destroyed and one damaged, both N France.

03.07.41.
12 Spitfires. 10:40–12:18 hrs. Circus to St Omer.
Sgt R.D. Bowen and Sgt E.W. Merriman (latter of 610 Sqn): Hs 126 probable, shared.
Spitfire P7980: Missing in action, Sgt Crabtree captured, later escaped and returned home.

10 Spitfires. 15:00–16:25 hrs. Circus to Hazebrouck.
Sgt D.W. Beedham: Me 109 probable, Hazebrouck.

04.07.41.
9 Spitfires. 14:16–16:50 hrs. Circus to Choques.
Pt Off J.E. Johnson: Me 109 damaged, five miles south of Gravelines.
Sgt R.A. Morton: Me 109 damaged.

05.07.41.
12 Spitfires. 12:17–15:00 hrs. Circus.
Spitfire P8651: Missing over Lille, Flt Lt C.H. Macfie lost, captured.

06.07.41.
12 Spitfires. 13:33–15:20 hrs. Circus.
Wg Cdr D.R.S. Bader: Me 109 destroyed, N France.
Pt Off J.E. Johnson: Me 109 destroyed, S of Dunkirk.
Sgt A. Smith: Me 109 probable, NE France.
Sgt D.W. Beedham: Me 109 damaged, NE France.
Spitfire P8500: Missing in action, Sgt J.A. McCairns evaded and returned home.

07.07.41.
10 Spitfires. 14:43–16:23 hrs. Circus.
Spitfire, serial number unknown: Cat. E to Me 109, Sgt Bowen crash-landed at Hawkinge,
   unhurt.
Spitfire, serial not known: Flying accident, Cat. A, damaged during landing at Friston, Sgt
   J.G. West safe.

08.07.41.
12 Spitfires. 05:35–07:30 hrs. Circus.
Spitfire P7837: Cat. A, damaged while landing at Westhampnett, Pt Off Johnson safe.
Spitfire P7856: Cat. A, hit sea during sweep, landed at Hawkinge, Fg Off Marples safe.

09.07.41.
8 Spitfires. 13:03–15:15 hrs. Circus to Mazingarbe.
Sqn Ldr E.P. Gibbs: Me 109 destroyed and one probable, NE France.
Sgt A. Smith: Me 109 damaged, NE France.
Spitfire P8070: Missing in action, Sqn Ldr E.P. Gibbs lost but evaded and safely returned.
Spitfire P8386: Shot down by Me 109 near St Omer, Sgt R.A. Morton captured.

10.07.41.
8 Spitfires. 11:38–13:50 hrs. Circus.
Flt Lt H.S.L. Dundas: Me 109F destroyed, NE France.
Sgt J.G. West: Me 109F destroyed, NE France.
Pt Off P.W.E. Hepple: Me 109F damaged, NE France.

11.07.41.
8 Spitfires. 14:56–16:59 hrs. Rhubarb.
Sgt A. Smith: Two Ju 87s destroyed on ground, Norrent-Fontes.

12.07.41.
7 Spitfires. 09:29–11:19 hrs. Circus.
Sgt A. Smith: Me 109F probable, NE France.
Pt Off P.W.E. Hepple: Me 109F damaged, NE France.

14.07.41.
12 Spitfires. 09:35–11:25 hrs. Circus.
Pt Off J.E. Johnson: Me 109F destroyed over Fanquembergues.
Sgt A. Smith: Me 109E damaged, NE France.

19.07.41.
9 Spitfires. 13:11–15:26 hrs. Circus.
Wg Cdr D.R.S. Bader and Fg Off H.S.L. Dundas: Me 109F destroyed, shared, Dunkirk.
Wg Cdr D.R.S. Bader: A further Me 109F destroyed, and a probable, Dunkirk.
Flt Lt L.H. Casson: Me 109 probable, Dunkirk.

21.07.41.
11 Spitfires. 07:43–09:44 hrs. Circus to Lille.
Wg Cdr D.R.S. Bader: Me 109 destroyed, N France.
Pt Off P.W.E. Hepple: Me 109 probable, N France.
Sgt D.W. Beedham: Me 109 damaged, N France.

11 Spitfires. 19:52–22:00 hrs. Circus to Mazingarbe.
Wg Cdr D.R.S. Bader: Me 109F damaged, N France.
Pt Off P.W.E. Hepple and Pt Off J.E. Johnson: Me 109 probable, shared, N France.
Flt Lt H.S.L. Dundas: Me 109 damaged, N France.
Spitfire W3376: Shot down by Me 109 near St Omer, Sgt S.W.R. Mabbett killed.

23.07.41.
10 Spitfires. 19:41–21:46 hrs. Circus to Mazingarbe.
Flt Lt L.H. Casson: Me 109 destroyed, and one damaged, Mazingarbe.
Pt Off J.E. Johnson: Me 109 damaged, Mazingarbe.
Sqn Ldr H.F. Burton: Me 109 damaged, Mazingarbe.

07.08.41.
12 Spitfires. 17:14–18:45 hrs. Circus to Lille.
Sgt D.W. Beedham: Me 109F damaged.
Sgt J.G. West: Me 109F damaged.

09.08.41.
14 Spitfires. 10:42–12:53. Circus to Gosnay.
Pt Off J.E. Johnson: Two Me 109Fs destroyed, NE France.
Pt Off P.W.E. Hepple: Me 109F destroyed, NE France.
Sgt J.G. West: Me 109F destroyed, NE France.
Wg Cdr D.R.S. Bader and Sgt J.G. West: Me 109 destroyed, shared, NE France.
Wg Cdr D.R.S. Bader: Me 109F destroyed, NE France.
Fg Off R. Marples: Me 109F probable, NE France.
Spitfire W3185, D-B: Missing, Wg Cdr D.R.S. Bader DSO* DFC captured near St Omer.
Spitfire W3458: Missing, Flt Lt L.H. Casson shot down and captured near Marquise.

41 Squadron

Operational Record, 28 July–9 August 1941

28.07.41.
Arrived at Merston and relieved 145 Squadron.

07.08.41.
12 Spitfires. 17:10–18:50. Circus to Lille.
Sgt Mitchell: Me 109F probable, Béthune.
Spitfire, serial unknown: Flt Lt Draper missing, later reported as having been captured.

Bibliography

During the research for this book many published references and contemporary records were consulted, the latter being available to all at the Public Record Office. In addition, I have quoted from my own private correspondence and tape-recorded interviews, and from extracts from the log books and various other personal papers of survivors. The titles listed below offer further background reading and are recommended.

Bader, Douglas, *Fight for the Sky* (Sidgwick & Jackson,1973)
Bekker, Cajus, *The Luftwaffe War Diaries* (MacDonald, 1966)
Brickhill, Paul, *Reach for the Sky* (William Collins, 1954)
Burns, Michael, *Bader: The Man and His Men* (Arms & Armour Press, 1990)
Caldwell, Don, *JG26: Top Guns of the Luftwaffe* (Orion Books, 1990)
Dundas, Gp Capt Sir Hugh, *Flying Start* (Stanley Paul, 1988)
Foreman, John, *Battle of Britain: The Forgotten Months* (Air Research Publications, 1988)
Foreman, John, *1941: Part 1*, and *1941: Part 2* (Air Research Publications, 1993 & 1994 respectively)
Franks, Norman, *RAF Fighter Command* (Patrick Stephens, 1992)
Galland, Adolf, *The First and the Last* (Methuen, 1955)
Jefford, Wg Cdr C.G. *RAF Squadrons* (Airlife, 1988)
Johnson, AVM J.E., *Wing Leader* (Chatto & Windus, 1956)
Lucas, 'Laddie', *Flying Colours: the Epic Story of Douglas Bader* (Stanley Paul, 1981)
Morgan, Eric, and Shacklady, Edward, *Spitfire: the History* (Key Publishing, 1987)
Motorbooks International, *JG26: Photographic History of the Luftwaffe's Top Guns* (Motorbooks International, 1994)
Musciano, Walter, *Messerschmitt Aces* (Tab/Aero Books, 1989)
Obermaier, Ernst, *Der Ritterkreuz Träger Der Luftwaffe 1939-45, Vol 1 – Jagdflieger* (Verlag Dieter, 1966)
Philpott, Brian, *German Fighters over England* (Patrick Stephens, 1979)
Price, Dr Alfred, *Battle of Britain Day* (Sidgwick & Jackson, 1990)
Ramsey, W.G. (Ed), *The Battle of Britain Then and Now Mk V* (After the Battle, 1989)
Ramsey, W.G. (Ed), *The Blitz Then and Now*, Vols I & II (After the Battle, 1989 & 1990 respectively)
Sarkar, Dilip, *Spitfire Squadron* (Air Research Publications, 1990)
Sarkar, Dilip, *The Invisible Thread: A Spitfire's Tale* (Ramrod Publications, 1992)
Sarkar, Dilip, *Through Peril to the Stars* (Ramrod Publications, 1993)
Sarkar, Dilip, *Angriff Westland* (Ramrod Publications, 1994)
Sarkar, Dilip, *A Few of the Many* (Ramrod Publications, 1995)
Scutts, Jerry, *Fighter Operations* (Patrick Stephens, 1992)
Shores, Chris, and Williams, Clive, *Aces High* (Grub Street, 1994)
Turner, John Frayn, *The Bader Wing* (Midas Books, 1981)
Wynn, Ken, *Men of the Battle of Britain* (Gliddon Books, 1989)

Index

The
Douglas Bader Foundation

Sir Douglas Bader was a legend in his own lifetime. His bravery in overcoming the trauma of losing both legs to become a hero as a WW2 fighter pilot has been well chronicled and portrayed on the screen; most of us will have seen *REACH FOR THE SKY*.

Bader, however, achieved far more than this. Once hostilities had ceased, he became very successful in his professional life, developed considerable golfing skills and devoted much of his time in helping others with similar disabilities to his own, encouraging them by example to *FIGHT BACK*.

Following his untimely death, the Douglas Bader Foundation was established, not just as a memorial to this great man, but also to promote and further develop his philosophies in helping disabled people in whatever way he could.

In 1993 the Foundation opened *THE DOUGLAS BADER CENTRE* which was built, equipped and fully funded for the first two years of operation, by the Foundation.

The Centre provides the latest equipment, modern facilities, programmes and opportunities for those with disabilities to enjoy sport, leisure and recreation, to improve their fitness, extend their social rehabilitation, and aid re-integration whilst supporting their clinical rehabilitation. Furthermore, the world-famous Roehampton Walking School now has a new permanent home within the Douglas Bader Centre

The Foundation has now embarked on the establishment of
THE DOUGLAS BADER GRANT SCHEME:
This unique and innovative project enables those with disabilities to continue their social rehabilitation and re-integration once the clinical processes have ceased.

How you can help:
The cost of each Grant varies between £5,000 and £10,000. The more we raise, the more disabled people we can help.

- **Corporate Sponsorship** – for companies and organisations wishing to associate their name with this worthwhile scheme.
- **Covenants** – one of the most useful ways of helping. With income tax at 25%, £33 can be recovered by us on every £100 covenanted by a tax-payer.
- **Regular Donations** – a welcome and straightforward way of contributing over any period of time, monthly, quarterly or annually. Donations can be made by bankers order.
- **Single Gifts** – of course these are always very welcome. If you prefer to make a single gift on which we can reclaim your income tax forms for Deposited Covenants (under £250) or Gift Aid (£250 and over) are available on request.
- **Straightforward donations** – an easy and direct way of making your contribution.

To make a donation or for further information please contact:
Keith Delderfield, Operations Director,
THE DOUGLAS BADER FOUNDATION
The Douglas Bader Centre, Roehampton Lane, London SW15 5DZ
Tel: 0181 788 1551   Fax: 0181 789 5622
Charity Registration No.: 800435